Perspectives on Southern Africa

Black Power in South Africa

Mkho Sampalo

Irvine June 83

Black Power in South Africa

The Evolution of an Ideology

Gail M. Gerhart

UNIVERSITY OF CALIFORNIA PRESS
BERKELEY · LOS ANGELES · LONDON

University of California Press
Berkeley and Los Angeles, California

University of California Press, Ltd.
London, England

Copyright © 1978 by
The Regents of the University of California

First Paperback Printing 1979
ISBN 0-520-03933-5
Library of Congress Catalog Card Number: 75-13149
Printed in the United States of America

1 2 3 4 5 6 7 8 9

Contents

Preface

THIS BOOK EXAMINES THE DEVELOPMENT OF AFRICAN nationalism in South Africa over the three decades since the Second World War. While it necessarily recounts events of historical importance, its primary emphasis is on the intellectual dimension of black political history, and in particular on the interplay of ideologies which has marked the postwar era and which has brought many present-day African intellectuals to their current Black Power perspective.

Because the orthodox nationalist or Black Power school of African politics in South Africa—in contrast to the multiracialist or more liberal school—has in the past been given rather less consideration than it deserves by historians and political scientists, the central purpose of this study will be to trace and analyze the evolution of this increasingly significant strain of African political thought. In so doing, we shall have occasion to look at the role of the African urban intelligentsia, out of whose frustrations, ambitions, and shifting world view the most important formulations of African ideology have taken shape, and, more specifically, at the role of four individual nationalist thinkers whose contributions to the evolution of orthodox African nationalism have been particularly influential. One, Robert Sobukwe, is a major figure with an international reputation. The other three—Anton Lembede, Ashby Peter Mda, and Steve Biko—are more obscure personalities whose places in history are still far from fixed.

Much of the information and interpretation in this book is drawn from interviews with South Africans, carried out between the years 1968 and 1973. In addition to my own interviewing, I have made use of transcribed interviews conducted by Gwendolen Carter, Thomas Karis, and Sheridan Johns on their visits to South Africa in 1963 and 1964. Documentary materials have also been a major source, and here again I have benefited greatly from the work of other researchers, most notably Professors Carter and Karis, and Benjamin Pogrund of the Johannesburg *Rand Daily Mail,* through whose efforts much valuable historical material on South Africa has been preserved.

Political pamphleteering, once the nearly exclusive preserve of white groups in South Africa, became in the period after the Second World War a widespread means of political communication among blacks as well. Thanks to the timely work of researchers, and to the equally industrious efforts of the South African police looking for evidence to incriminate government opponents, much ephemeral material of this kind has been preserved in accessible form, either in libraries or in public trial records. For example, in the case of South Africa's famous Treason Trial of 1956–61, the documents presented in evidence now fill twenty-eight reels of microfilm, available to scholars through the Cooperative Africana Microform Project of the Center for Research Libraries in Chicago. In addition to pamphlets, flyers and circulars issued by African political movements and their non-African support groups, other materials thus preserved include private correspondence, speeches, and organization reports and minutes. Ironically, access to these invaluable primary sources is today much easier for foreigners than for South Africans, for whom possession of such banned documents is a criminal offense.

Newspapers and periodicals published in South Africa and by South Africans living in exile have provided a rich source of information and insight, as have memoirs and monographs by South Africans personally involved in the struggle for black liberation. We can only hope that in the future still more of those who have participated in the making of South African history will be moved to record their experiences and observations so that posterity can better understand the complex legacy of the past. The best histories of the struggle for freedom in South Africa will someday by written by African historians. When that time comes, if present resources are any indication, there should be no lack of records—documentary, oral, and personal—from which they can work.

During my research and writing many people both in Africa and the United States generously gave me their time and assistance. I am especially grateful to the late Robert Sobukwe, who cheerfully defied his banning orders to answer my many questions. My thanks also go to Z. B. Molete, Peter 'Molotsi, Peter Raboroko, Charles Lakaje, Elliot Magwentshu, P. K. Leballo, T. T. Letlaka, Nana Mahomo, Ellen Molapo, Joe Molefi, A. B. Ngcobo, J. D. Nyaose, Matthew Nkoana, P. L. Gqobose, Elliot Mfaxa, and R. A. Tsehlana, who did their best to explain to me the history of the Pan Africanist Congress. A. P. Mda, Joe Matthews, Jordan Ngubane, Oliver Tambo, Duma Nokwe, and Helen Joseph offered me many insights into the history of the ANC in the 1940s and 1950s, and Steve Biko, Harry Nengwekhulu, Saths Cooper, Temba Sono, and David Thebehali contributed greatly to my understanding of the Black Consciousness movement. The national offices of the South African Students' Organisation and the National Union of South African Students gave me valuable help with documentation, as did the libraries of the South African Institute of Race Relations and the University of the Witwatersrand. My debt is also great to others who must remain anonymous.

Fellowship funds from Columbia University and a grant from the National Institute of Mental Health made my research possible, and Professors Marcia Wright and James Mittelman of Columbia gave me much useful advice during the original preparation of this manuscript as a doctoral dissertation. Mary Benson and Peter Walshe subsequently offered helpful criticisms. At an earlier stage, Richard Suzman and Professors Kenneth B. Clark, Edward Tiryakian, and Sheridan Johns did much to inspire my initial interest in the study of South Africa and race relations generally. Moral and logistic support from my husband, John Gerhart, and my mother, Dorothy Gillam, have helped sustain me throughout the preparation of this study. To Benjamin Pogrund and Gwendolen Carter I owe a special debt for their great encouragement and generosity, but most of all I would like to thank Thomas Karis, without whose constant help and interest this study would never have been either undertaken or completed.

Abbreviations

AAC	All African Convention
ANC	African National Congress
ARM	African Resistance Movement
ASSECA	Association for the Educational and Cultural Advancement of African People of South Africa
BPC	Black People's Convention
COD	South African Congress of Democrats
CPSA	Communist Party of South Africa
ICU	Industrial and Commercial Workers' Union
NEUM	Non-European Unity Movement
NIC	Natal Indian Congress
NRC	Natives' Representative Council
NUSAS	National Union of South African Students
PAC	Pan Africanist Congress
SACPO	South African Coloured Peoples' Organisation
SACTU	South African Congress of Trade Unions
SAIC	South African Indian Congress
SAIRR	South African Institute of Race Relations
SASO	South African Students' Organisation
SPRO-CAS	Study Project on Christianity in Apartheid Society
SRC	Students' Representative Council
UBC	Urban Bantu Council

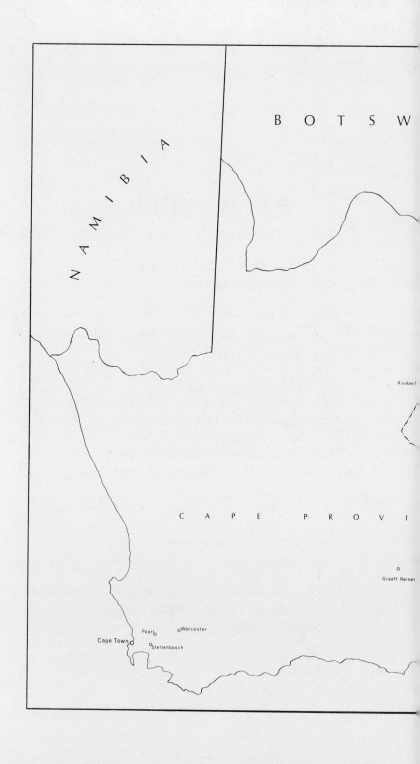

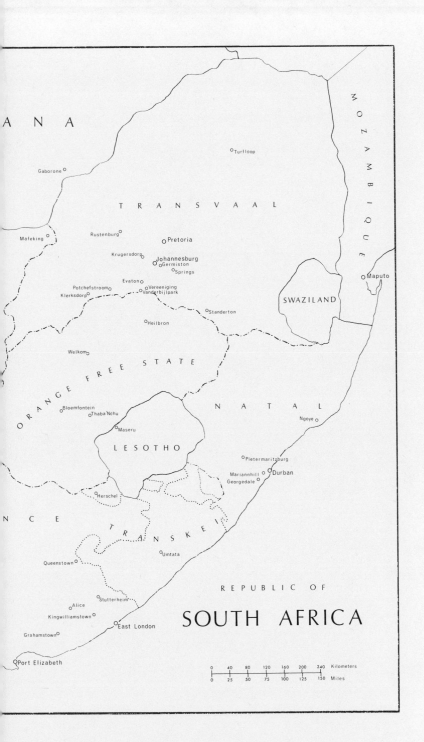

 A N A

Gaborone ○

T R A N S V A A L

Turfloop ○

Mafeking ○

Rustenburg ○

Pretoria ○

Krugersdorp ○

Johannesburg ○
Germiston ○
Springs ○

Potchefstroom ○

Evaton ○

Vereeniging ○
Vanderbijlpark ○

Klerksdorp ○

Standerton ○

Heilbron ○

Welkom ○

O R A N G E   F R E E   S T A T E

Bloemfontein ○

Thaba'Nchu ○

Maseru ○

L E S O T H O

Herschel ○

N C E

T R A N S K E I

Queenstown ○

Umtata ○

Alice ○

Stutterheim ○

Kingwilliamstown ○

Grahamstown ○

East London ○

Port Elizabeth ○

M
O
Z
A
M
B
I
Q
U
E

Maputo ○

SWAZILAND

N A T A L

Ngoye ○

Pietermaritzburg ○

Mariannhill ○
Durban ○
Georgedale ○

REPUBLIC OF

SOUTH AFRICA

| 0 | 40 | 80 | 120 | 160 | 200 | 240 | Kilometers |
| 0 | 25 | 50 | 75 | 100 | 125 | 150 | Miles |

1

Ideological Responses to Inequality

BETWEEN JUNE AND DECEMBER 1976, A WAVE OF
urban unrest rocked the Republic of South Africa and dramat-
ically focused the world's attention on the festering problem of
apartheid. In the African township of Soweto outside Johannesburg early on the morning of June 16, a policeman fired on
a group of student demonstrators, killing a 13-year-old boy. A
melee ensued, government buildings and vehicles were set on
fire, and bands of school children defied bullets and teargas to
pelt police with stones and bottles. In spite of official assur-
ances that the situation was under control by the night of the
16th, violence and arson continued the following day and
began to spread to other black townships across the country.
By August the death toll had mounted into the hundreds,
creating a political embarrassment for Prime Minister John
Vorster in the midst of his strategic negotiations with the
United States over the fate of Rhodesia and Namibia. The
thwarting of South Africa's military aims in Angola earlier in
1976 had revealed some of the strength of external forces
arrayed against the apartheid status quo. The urban riots provided a glimpse of the forces for change gradually gathering
strength within South African society itself.

The immediate grievance which touched off the June unrest
was a government decision to force African school children to
study half of all subjects above the elementary school level

through the medium of Afrikaans. Underlying the resentment of this decision was a deeper frustration with the government-imposed "Bantu Education" system, which subjects African children to a financially starved and ethnically segregated type of schooling designed to prepare them for an inferior status as adults. Taken alone, the grievances of Africans over inferior education, as well as over poor wages, jobs, and housing, might not have provided sufficient fuel to sustain the conflagration begun by demonstrations over the language issue. But added to these long-standing grounds of dissatisfaction were a host of new factors in the political equation of 1976: the demonstration effect of Portugal's collapse in Mozambique and Angola; spiralling inflation and unemployment; the determination of the Vorster government to force urban Africans to accept paper citizenship in tribal "homelands"; and lastly, the widespread dissemination, particularly among students, of an aggressive ideology of "Black Consciousness."

Of all the causes leading up to the June confrontation, this last was the most important in accounting for the determination and resilience of the youthful militants who spearheaded the anti-government demonstrations. Awakening late to the connection between the defiant mood of the townships and the so-called Black Consciousness movement which had become entrenched in black schools and universities over the preceding few years, the Vorster regime began a concerted drive in late July to detain known leaders of Black Consciousness organizations. The time when their ideology might successfully have been suppressed, however, had long passed, and no amount of retaliation by the state against individuals could undo the fact that Black Consciousness had already brought about a mental revolution among black youth.

The Black Consciousness movement belongs to a long intellectual tradition in South Africa and the primary purpose of this book is to explore that tradition in order to enhance our understanding both of contemporary events and of the dynamics of black politics in South Africa in the past. The focus will be on the three decades since the Second World War, the period which has seen the most marked acceleration of tension between the races. No single book has ever done justice to the full scope and complexity of South Africa's political history, and this book will be no exception. Those who are searching for a grand synthesis of themes and theories now or in the future, however, may find their task eased by detailed studies focusing on specific ideologies or movements which have contributed to the total historical fabric. The aim of this study is to trace and analyze one such strand: the school of African nationalist thought in South Africa—long a minor school but one now becoming major—which has emphasized racially exclusive strategies for the overthrow of white domination.[1]

The South African Ideological Spectrum

In the chapters which follow, the reader will frequently be referred to points on the spectrum of political ideology in South Africa, and it may therefore be useful at the outset to outline briefly the range of competing political viewpoints which have arisen out of South Africa's unique historical circumstances.

1. Readers wishing to begin from a broader overview of black politics in South Africa should refer to Edward Roux, *Time Longer Than Rope* (Madison,1966); H. J. and R. E. Simons, *Class and Colour in South Africa 1850–1950* (Harmondsworth, Middlesex, 1969); Mary Benson, *The African Patriots* (London, 1963); Peter Walshe, *The Rise of African Nationalism in South Africa* (Berkeley and Los Angeles, 1971); Thomas Karis and Gwendolen Carter, eds., *From Protest to Challenge*, 4 vols. (Stanford, 1972 to 1977); and Leo Kuper, "African Nationalism in South Africa, 1910–1964," in Monica Wilson and Leonard Thompson, eds., *The Oxford History of South Africa*, vol. 2 (Oxford, 1971).
    Works detailing the highly oppressive nature of the South African system as a whole include Gwendolen Carter, *The Politics of Inequality* (New York, 1959); Heribert Adam, *Modernizing Racial Domination* (Berkeley and Los Angeles, 1971); Pierre Van den Berghe, *South Africa, A Study in Conflict* (Berkeley and Los Angeles, 1967); Leonard Thompson and Jeffrey Butler, eds., *Change in Contemporary South Africa* (Berkeley and Los Angeles, 1975); and Wilson and Thompson.

Political ideologies in any time and place can be grouped into those which tend to reinforce the existing order and those which aim, to one degree or another, at its alteration or destruction. In South Africa, the former category includes the ideologies of apartheid and trusteeship, while the latter encompasses such outlooks as liberalism, Marxism, African nationalism, and what for want of a neater term might be called the ideology of a Fanonesque apocalypse. In order to put the rise of Black Power thinking into preliminary perspective, let us start from a brief look at these six ideologies.

Apartheid, or the doctrine of racial segregation, is the philosophy of the National party which has ruled South Africa since 1948.[2] The earliest roots of race discrimination can be found in the seventeenth century when whites first colonized the Cape of Good Hope, but apartheid as a full-fledged political ideology developed much later, following the transition to an industrial economy in the late nineteenth and early twentieth centuries. Pressed both by white employers and white workers, who shared an interest in the tight control of black labor, successive governments enacted a structure of laws and regulations designed to guarantee the superior economic status of whites and to perpetuate a master-servant relationship between the races in all spheres. Gradually gaining ground against the entrenched vestiges of integrationism built into the political system inherited from Britain at the time of Union in 1910, segregationists achieved a major breakthrough in 1936 with the removal of the last Africans from the common voters' roll of the Cape Province—a political turning point to which we shall refer again in due course.

The present ascendance of apartheid as an ideology began with the 1948 election victory of Daniel F. Malan and the National party, which at that time drew its support almost entirely from rural and working-class Afrikaners. The crudeness of apartheid during its earliest years of triumph has often been

2. Confusion regarding the term "Nationalist" can be avoided if it is noted that the ruling whites of the National party are always referred to with a capital "N".

documented. Set alongside the public pronouncements of Malan, Strijdom and Verwoerd on the subject of race, the views of "Pitchfork Ben" Tillman, Theodore Bilbo, or Orval Faubus do not appear extreme.

By the 1960s, under the pressure of growing political consciousness among Africans and a chorus of criticism at home and abroad, it became strategically necessary for the apartheid ideologists to try to make a virtue out of what had previously seemed merely a matter of economic and political necessity. Officially, therefore, the old ideal of *baasskap* or white "bossship" has in the last two decades given way to the new ideal of "separate development," a policy by which inequality between the races is redefined as mere difference, and the basis for segregation is redefined as one of "national identity" rather than skin color. Although a minority hard-line or *verkrampte* element has opposed this updating of apartheid, the majority or *verligte* wing of the National party, which supports it, has prevailed.

Moving to take advantage of the rest of the world's approbation for decolonization, the *verligte* ideologists have declared the population of South Africa's impoverished and fragmented black rural reserves to be separate tribal "nations" evolving toward eventual "independence." Within the remaining 87 percent of the country, defined as "white" even though its population is overwhelmingly black, apartheid now accords Africans only the status of immigrants, and justifies their regulated and rightless condition on the grounds that the proper areas for their self-fulfillment are the tribal bantustans or "homelands," where they are free to "develop along their own lines." Beneath this new facade, the exploitation of blacks as cheap migratory laborers continues apace. To the majority of the white electorate the occasional updating of apartheid theory and terminology poses no problems; small changes are an easy price to pay for the maintenance of the basic structure of power and privilege.

White *trusteeship*, the ideology associated for many years with the United party and English-speaking conservatives, is similar to apartheid in its concern for the preservation of white supremacy, but varies from the ultra-racism of apartheid in that it accepts, in theory, the possibility that nonwhite races may eventually fully assimilate "white" civilization. This potentiality is generally regarded as realizable only in the distant future, and until such time as it can be realized, trusteeship holds that the proper relationship between white and black is analogous to that of guardian and ward.

Trusteeship has the advantage for whites of combining a conscience-salving benevolence with a practical policy aimed at indefinite maintenance of white privileges. Africans for many years believed in its promise of eventual equality, and restrained their demands accordingly. Had blacks been willing to keep the faith longer, trusteeship might have continued to meet the ideological requirements of many whites indefinitely. But like colonized people elsewhere, South African blacks eventually grew impatient with the unfulfilled promises of their rulers and began to call for more than token political rights. As the "wards" became more restive, the white electorate saw increasingly more virtue in *baasskap* and less in the paternal benevolence of "guardianship." The result, over the years after 1948, was a gradual narrowing of the gap between apartheid and trusteeship on the political spectrum, until as election campaign formulas they became nearly indistinguishable.

While the great majority of whites have rejected the assimilationist ideal of trusteeship as contrary to their self-interest, a much smaller number of whites has long continued to believe sincerely in the goal of an eventual common, nonracial society. Depending on the nature of their opposition to the status quo, these whites can be roughly grouped as liberals and radicals. The latter, looking at South Africa from Marxist perspectives, have stood for the destruction not just of racial inequality but also of the entire capitalist economic system in South Africa. Liberals, while standing for sweeping changes in race relations and for the elimination of the worst forms of racial exploitation, have in general not directed their attacks against the basic structure of the South African system.

Like the proponents of trusteeship, *liberals* have often proceeded from a paternalistic view of race relations, but they have also been moved by religious or humanitarian biases to feel that the black wards of the white man deserve a free and fair chance to "grow up" and become the white man's equal. Whites, in fact, according to the usual liberal view, have a duty to promote the black man's assimilation, through education and through the extension of political rights appropriate to his level of acculturation. Unlike apartheid, which calls for blacks to "develop along their own lines" and in pursuit of their own separate variants of culture, liberalism has always recognized one common human standard of measurement: the adoption of "civilized" or modern, western ways. Until 1936, the qualified but nonracial Cape franchise with its premise of gradual democratization was an embodiment of the liberal ideal. "Equal rights for all civilized men," ran the classic liberal credo, echoed at the time of the founding of the Liberal party in 1953, "and equal opportunity for all men to become civilized."

Whereas apartheid and trusteeship are indigenous ideological products of South African conditions, South African liberalism has its philosophical taproot in Europe and in Christian and democratic traditions. Besides recognizing the principle of human equality, it has sought to protect the other pillars of democracy: civil liberties, the rule of law, a free press and an independent judiciary. In addition, true to western tradition, South African liberalism has tended to look to parliamentary democracy as the best and only legitimate vehicle for the achievement of political change—a sound outlook in many democracies, but a self-defeating one in South Africa where political power is the monopoly of a privileged minority which has no interest in sharing power with the disenfranchised majority.

Perhaps the most distinctive trait of South African liberalism until recent years has been its optimism in the face of all evidence that white racism was becoming invulnerable to change through ordinary political means. Many liberals no doubt looked uncritically to the historical precedent of Britain, where universal franchise was successfully achieved in evolutionary stages.[3] Others, being of a religious or moralistic turn of mind, simply refused to believe that Christian goodwill would not eventually outweigh or modify selfish class interests. Had this illusion been confined at an early stage only to the relatively few sincere white liberals—intellectuals, educators and clergymen for the most part—the longterm political effects might not have been particularly noteworthy. But as we shall see, it was liberals who set the tone for much of African political thought in the years before 1936, and who must therefore share some of the responsibility for the anemic state of African political organization during the first thirty years after Union.

The precise political manifestations of liberal ideology have varied considerably over time, changing with the particular outlooks and electoral fortunes (or more often misfortunes) of liberal politicians. Pierre van den Berghe has rightly pointed out that the so-called "Cape liberalism" of the late nineteenth and early twentieth centuries was in fact really conservative paternalism or trusteeship, not liberalism at all, truly liberal views in these years being confined to a relatively small minority of whites, even in the Cape.[4] Had national politics in the 1930s and 1940s favored the flowering of a humanitarian spirit, liberalism would have produced a powerful champion in the brilliant Jan H. Hofmeyr. But historical trends all pointed the other way, and Hofmeyr's liberal instincts were smothered by the exigencies of United party politics. Under the impetus of the Defiance Campaign, a passive resistance campaign waged by the African National Congress and the South African Indian Congress in 1952, liberals in the United party split away to form the Liberal party, which survived in spite of government harassment—and heavy voter rejection of its "one man one vote" platform—until 1968. Today, many liberals take refuge in the Progressive Reform party, represented since May 1976 by twelve MPs, which stands for a policy of qualified franchise and the eventual creation of a federal system.

3. Janet Robertson, *Liberalism in South Africa 1948–1963* (Oxford, 1971), p. 113.
4. Van den Berghe, *South Africa.*

White *Marxists* in South Africa, like white liberals, have turned their backs on the ideologies of race dominance and have adopted a world view which puts them in sympathy with the black majority. Like the true liberals, they have always been a small minority within the white population, but because of their ties to blacks, their importance has, like that of the liberals, been far greater than their scant numbers might suggest. Through joint political efforts and the exchange of ideas across the color line over many years, white radicals have contributed a great deal to the assimilation of socialist ideas by black militants.

In contrast to liberals, South African Marxists have not stopped at defining racial equality as their goal. Full equality, in their view, requires the dismantling of the entire capitalist economic order from which South Africa's gross forms of inequality and exploitation have sprung. Moral cynicism has pervaded their analysis of society, and they have scorned the liberals' optimistic faith in the triumph of generous impulses over the forces of economic determinism. With Marxists everywhere, they have held that the natural laws of society and history favor the eventual triumph of socialism, and they have seen class conflict as the fundamental mechanism of change. Theories of class struggle, however, have never been easy to reconcile with South African reality, given the racial nature of the conflict and the non-working-class character of most black leadership. Most Marxists have resolved this disparity between theory and reality by adopting a two-stage concept of change: first the democratic revolution (to be brought about by political organization, economic action, and in more recent theory, by armed revolt), then the transition to socialism (preferably by democratic means, once the black majority has become enfranchised). Since the foundations of socialist consciousness among blacks would have to be laid in the first stage of the struggle, most white Marxists have regarded as axiomatic their own involvement and even leadership in the fight for black political rights. Acting primarily through the legal Communist party in the 1920s, '30s and '40s, and later through the underground Communist party and legal organizations allied with it,

white Marxists have done much to identify themselves with the
African cause and to lend it many kinds of support.

Given that Africans have long seen around them disparities
of wealth, privilege and power as great or greater than any
described by Marx in nineteenth-century Europe, it is important to note some of the reasons why socialist ideology has not
enjoyed greater popularity in South Africa. Government persecution of members of the Communist party and of "statutory
communists"—those alleged to be "furthering the aims of
communism"—has done much to discourage African interest.
Equally important have been the anti-communist views of
white missionaries, teachers, liberals, and politicians generally,
expressed over many years, which have done much to foster
similar attitudes among blacks. Many Africans, moreover, lacking education or knowledge of the workings of their own society, have lacked the intellectual sophistication to grasp the
more analytical points of Marxist ideology. The working class
African who does gain any degree of political consciousness
notices immediately that in South Africa, race and not class is
the real determinant of status. Class-based interpretations do
not tally with his observation of reality. For the typical educated middle class African in recent decades, socialist ideas
have usually had even less appeal. His background has conditioned him to regard communism as atheistic and materialistic, as well as politically dangerous; his own personal aspirations are bourgeois; and he often bridles at the suggestion that
blacks might have anything to learn from the white socialist,
whose manner is often that of the intellectual know-it-all—the
paternalistic "guardian" in a new guise.

These obstacles to the growth of a socialist consciousness
notwithstanding, a certain number of black workers and intellectuals have always been attracted to the doctrines of the
Communist party and its successor organizations. Less orthodox variants of Marxism have also attracted followings.
The Non-European Unity Movement, an organization which
has enlisted the loyalty of a significant number of African and
Coloured intellectuals over the last thirty years, is a Marxist
group which has been anti-Soviet and anti-white in the sense of

rejecting all white leadership, including that of white socialists, on the grounds that blacks must find their own feet politically before making alliances. Somewhat similar positions have been taken by the Pan Africanist Congress and the South African Students' Organisation, movements which will be described much more fully in subsequent chapters. These two organizations have pledged themselves to "African socialism," an ideology which neither has precisely defined.

Moving along the ideological spectrum to *African nationalism,* it is important to seek some precision of definition since this is the "ism" which will be center-stage in the rest of this book. The vast literature on nationalism makes it clear that no single definition is adequate for all cases. Confronted with the problem of defining "nation," most historians and political scientists are forced to conclude, rather tautologically, that people comprise a nation if they think of themselves as comprising a nation, and that no single factor of common language, culture or historical experience weighs as heavily as the self-conscious will to nationhood per se. But whatever the basis for nationalist feeling may be, nationalism inevitably seeks expression through the creation or maintenance of a nation-state, that is, a polity based on the self-willing "nation" and dedicated to the protection of its identity and interests. Neither nationalist sentiment nor mere statehood alone can make a nation in the fullest sense; both conditions must exist. Thus, for example, the Jewish people were not fully a nation until the creation of the state of Israel, and the state of Kenya will not fully be a nation until Kenyans put away their local ethnic loyalties in favor of a wider Kenyan identity.

Do Africans in South Africa comprise, or potentially comprise, a nation? "Separate development" proposes to create a collection of African states based on tribal identity, and it is the hope of the apartheid strategists that these states will foster the growth of parochial nationalist sentiments which will work against any wider black unity. Seen in historical perspective, this plan seeks to reverse a long process of social and political integration which has already gone far toward destroying parochial ethnicity among Africans. Beginning as early as the mid-nineteenth-century wars of white conquest, perceptive African leaders like Moshesh of the Basuto realized that the failure of African ethnic groups to unite would mean victory for the invaders. Once the 1909 Act of Union had sealed into law the inferior status of Africans in the new South African state, the arguments for African unity became even more compelling. Coming together at Bloemfontein in 1912, a distinguished group of African chiefs and educated leaders founded the African National Congress (originally known as the South African Native National Congress), an inter-ethnic association pledged to defend the rights and represent the interests of Africans as a whole to the Union government. It was their intention, the ANC's founders said, to build a "nation." We cannot know with certainty what each of them understood by this, but we do know that ethnic parochialism was rejected, and that Africans were urged to develop a solidarity based on their wider identity as a racial group subject to common conditions of discrimination.

The founding of the African National Congress is generally regarded as the earliest major manifestation of African nationalism in South Africa, yet the type of nationhood to which the ANC founders aspired did not make them nationalists in the full sense since they did not seek to create a state based on their prospective nation. They sought instead to win rights for Africans within the white state, along the lines promised—but forever left unfulfilled—by the proponents of trusteeship and liberalism. Given this integrationist goal, African solidarity became less an end in itself than a means for exerting pressure on reluctant whites. Long after the ANC had become thoroughly disillusioned with both trusteeship and liberalism, it was to retain this basic belief in the primarily functional role of African solidarity. Until the end of its legal existence in South Africa in 1960, and on into its period of exile, the ANC was to continue to stand for African rights within the framework of a pluralistic democracy, the "nation" being ultimately defined not as the community of black Africans only, but as the multiracial community of all people born in South Africa. Thus the ANC has been less an African nationalist movement in the strict sense of the term than a

oppressor, "them," the colonizers who have stolen his land and crushed his manhood. "The native," said Fanon, "is in fact ready at a moment's notice to exchange the role of the quarry for that of the hunter. The native is an oppressed person whose permanent dream is to become the persecutor."[7] For him there is no solution other than to kill or drive out the colonizers, to turn the tables on his rulers until the last are first and first are last. As his political sophistication grows he comes to realize that intellectual and bourgeois members of his own race are seeking ways to depolarize the struggle; but he still finds it difficult to consider any middle ground of compromise in the present or reconciliation in the future.

To date in South Africa, only the short-lived terrorist movement of the early 1960s known as Poqo has given full expression to this type of thinking. Nevertheless there can be no doubt that attitudes of the type described by Fanon have long existed to one degree or another. African leaders with a liberal bent have spoken of these attitudes as a menace to rational, principled politics, and whites have bought pistols, tanks and helicopters in anticipation of the moment when the palpable hostility of Africans might spill over into bloody revolution. Hoping to harness the powerful undercurrent of mass anger, the Pan Africanist Congress made a premature attempt to initiate revolutionary action in 1960. Poqo, the PAC's successor movement, went much further in trying to draw out violent sentiments, but likewise failed to back its effort with adequate organization. Renewing the trend away from liberal principles of reconciliation and nonviolence in the 1970s, the South African Students' Organisation has advocated polarization of the struggle along Fanoneque lines, and has rejected all white-conceived evolutionary solutions.

Ideology and the Black Struggle

The ideologies summarized here have been deliberately over-drawn in order that the distinctions between them could be

7. *Ibid.*, p. 53.

made clear. Every South African who has crossed the minimum threshold of political consciousness has views which would fall somewhere along the spectrum described. For every person who holds a stereotyped view, however, there is another whose outlook is a hybrid of more than one ideological type. Thus today, for example, leaders of the white Progressive Reform party combine elements of apartheid and liberalism in their ideology, while the Black Consciousness movement borrows ideas from both Fanon and orthodox African nationalism, at the same time utilizing insights from Marxist analysis.

Of all the ideologies on the spectrum, the one most likely to appear in hybrid form is African nationalism, and we have seen that a distinction must be drawn between orthodox African nationalism and nonracial nationalism, which is a blend of orthodox nationalism and liberalism. The tension between these rival schools of nationalism has been a major theme of African intellectual history over the past thirty years, much as black American history in the same period has seen a tension and cross-fertilization of ideas between the schools of racial integration and separatism. In South Africa, the lines of conflict have seldom been clear-cut, and the range of overlap between competing ideologies has sometimes been great. Nevertheless, at the risk of making premature historical judgments, it is possible to trace certain patterns and trends in African politics and to project these trends forward in the form of some tentative predictions about the future.

We shall find, for example, that although some of the premises of liberal thinking still survive among highly politicized Africans, the history of postwar African political thought is one of a protracted process of tearing loose from liberalism as a world view. This erosion of liberalism and the rise of increasingly radical forms of nationalism in its stead clearly constitute a trend and a portent for South Africa's future. In surveying the last thirty years we shall also see that while the great mass of Africans has regarded the struggle as one against apartheid and the starker forms of racial domination, nationalist intellectuals have at times defined the immediate enemy as the nonconformist white allies of the African—the liberal and radical drop-outs from the ideological ranks of white supremacy. We shall see that in spite of the appeal of Marxist analysis in one form or another to many Africans, the racial basis of the conflict has often made it difficult for African nationalists and white Marxists to work out a mutually supportive relationship. None of the predicaments which have faced nonconformist whites in the past are likely to become any less acute in the future. Trends in black South African political thinking are steadily in the direction of polarization and erosion of the ideological middle ground between whites and blacks, in spite of the continued existence of some whites who are pro-black, and in spite of the government's success in deflecting much African attention toward the political and psychological "solution" of the bantustans. At this stage one can only speculate about whether South Africans will find a way to resolve their conflicts through a process of reform that minimizes violence, or whether white intransigence will eventually bring the country to the point of a full revolutionary confrontation.

All things considered, the possibility of violent upheaval appears very strong. Black aspirations continue to rise, fed by observations of black progress elsewhere in the world, and even encouraged to an extent by the rhetorical promises of "separate development." Year by year, blacks with rising levels of skill become more indispensable to South Africa's industrial economy. Meanwhile, National party goals remain unchanged, apartheid's illusory "decolonization" of the bantustans proceeds, and all signs point toward indefinite Nationalist power and popularity with the white electorate. Whites sit comfortably in control of the massive administrative and police forces of the state. No one can be certain, however, how effective these forces would ultimately prove if blacks could unite in applying the leverage of their numbers, their economic strength, and their potentially superior morale.

While some necessary attention will be given in the chapters which follow to the economic factors affecting the collective political strength of Africans, the primary focus will be on the last, more intangible, factor of African morale, and in particular on the efforts of African political elites to direct and manipulate African mass attitudes through the agency of political ideology. African morale, as the most discerning African leaders have perceived, is at any given time a composite product of many separate social and psychological forces, all of which taken together have the potential to create the confidence and hope necessary to inspire mass action. Of all the forces which enter into the collective factor of morale, the most important is political consciousness, or an understanding by individuals of their relationship to their society and, to one degree or another, an understanding of how the parts of that society function in relation to one another. As we shall see, the ideologically-oriented leaders of African movements have disagreed on what basic "definitions of the situation" should be inculcated in the masses at large, and they have also differed regarding what self-images or definitions of identity Africans should be urged to adopt. Elite-formulated ideologies have therefore been mixed in their impact on mass political consciousness.

Another component of African collective morale is solidarity, actual or potential, or the sense among Africans that they share a common position in society and therefore have common interests. One of ideology's functions, for the purposes of African leaders, has been its usefulness in defining the line between oppressed and oppressors, the united "us" from the enemy, "them." Once again, however, African ideologues have disagreed among themselves on the precise parameters of solidarity: does the "us" of the oppressed include all Africans, all nonwhites, or all who oppose apartheid?[8]

8. The South African population was estimated in 1975 as

African	18,136,000
Coloured	2,368,000
Asian	727,000
White	4,240,000
	25,471,000

M. Horrell et al., comps., *A Survey of Race Relations in South Africa* [1976] (Johannesburg, 1977), p. 31.

In addition to their efforts to exploit these basic properties of ideology—its ability to help create consciousness, identity, and solidarity—some African ideologues have gone a step further and attempted to use ideology to reorient African ethical perspectives so as to more easily reconcile popular concepts of moral rectitude with increasingly radical African political goals. This use of ideology as a device to affect African normative values has been, and will undoubtedly in the future continue to be, one of the most fundamental forces of change in African politics.

Throughout this exploration of African attempts to use ideology as a weapon in the South African race conflict, we shall consider the genesis of black South African political thought from two contrasting but interrelated viewpoints. On the one hand, African ideological formulations will be considered as the abstract conceptualizations which they in part have always been, sincerely or cynically held, but usually deliberately devised by African intellectuals searching for an effective strategy of psychological warfare. On the other hand, we shall also consider the ways in which the ideological world views of African leaders have been a product of the social and psychological situation of the elites or individuals who put them forward for mass consumption. Writers on ideology and on the sociology of knowledge have debated the precise role of ideology in political life, and in particular the question of whether ideas themselves or economic and social forces are the prime movers in human history. It will not be an objective of this book to debate this question per se, although some of the insights of theoretical writers will enter the analysis which follows. Rather, it will be an aim of this study to look at ideology in the South African case both as causal and caused, both as an independent variable largely created through the individual intellectual efforts of a few key thinkers, and in a broader sense as the product of African political culture and tradition.

This is a study of history-in-progress, and as such it faces certain problems which do not occur in studies dealing with long-bygone events. In the case of history in the making, E. H. Carr once remarked, one not only learns about the present and future in the light of the past, but also learns about the past in the light of the present and future.[9] When the outcome of a conflict is not yet known, as in South Africa, it becomes difficult to draw full conclusions about the significance of past events and trends, for how we evaluate them must depend on their relevance to things which have not yet happened. It becomes necessary, therefore, in establishing criteria of judgment and selectivity of historical facts, to resort to some degree of speculation, implicit or explicit, about the most likely future course of South African politics. If South Africans succeed in achieving an egalitarian society without racial polarization and violence—however dim that prospect at present—then a re-evaluation of past political developments will be necessary. If, on the other hand, South Africa is indeed heading for massive racial confrontation, then the background to polarization becomes a subject deserving the historian's closest attention.

9. E. H. Carr, *What Is History?* (Harmondsworth, Middlesex: Penguin Books, 1968), pp. 68, 123.

2

The Social Foundations of Black South African Politics

A World Made by Whites

The study of black politics in South Africa in the postwar era must begin from a general consideration of the social history of the South African industrial revolution, that period roughly from the discovery of minerals in the 1860s and 1870s until the first major boom of manufacturing in the early 1940s. It was in this period, a time of sweeping change for blacks and whites alike, that the fundamental social and economic relationships of subsequent years were laid down, and with them the attitudes, values and expectations that became the foundation of later race relations.

In the second half of the nineteenth century South Africa's African population was still heavily rural and strongly traditional in culture, with the exception of pockets of mission activity, particularly in the Cape and Natal, where small communities of African Christians were undergoing the transition to a more Western lifestyle. Whites, meanwhile, although by no means constituting a homogeneous or united racial community, had by the same period arrived at a more or less common set of attitudes towards what was known as "the Native problem." Final military conquest of the remaining autonomous

African chiefdoms was regarded as essential for white security, and this objective was systematically achieved by the defeat of the Zulus under Cetshwayo in 1879 and the last mopping-up operations against the tribes of the northern Transvaal in the 1890s. Once white administrative hegemony was secure, an even more powerful and long-standing common concern became paramount: the desire of virtually all whites, rural and urban, to acquire maximum service, at minimum cost, from African labor. As the demand for black workers mounted in the mining industry, so too did the requirements for African farm labor as the country's growing urban economy stimulated the expansion of agriculture.

The result was a long series of legislative acts directed at pushing Africans off the land and into the employment of whites, a pattern of white policy which persists to the present day and has profoundly affected the character of both urban and rural African society. At first, taxation of rural Africans was relied on to force men into wage labor, and the natural forces of over-population and crop failure were accepted as healthy catalysts in the recruitment of workers. When these stimulants eventually proved inadequate to meet white demands, the sweeping Natives Land Act of 1913 was enacted to eliminate once and for all the possibility that large numbers of rural Africans would be able to maintain a self-sufficient peasant existence. The Act, besides abolishing the right of Africans to buy land outside limited and already crowded reserve areas, stripped many Africans outside the reserves of their right to own livestock, and abolished the various systems of share-cropping which had enabled large numbers of African squatters on white-owned farms to live a relatively independent and prosperous life.[1] The result over time was a large-scale movement of Africans off the land, either into a state of permanent

1. Background on land policies can be found in Sol T. Plaatje, *Native Life in South Africa* (New York, c. 1920); Francis Wilson, "Farming, 1866–1966," in Wilson and Thompson; T. R. H. Davenport and K. S. Hunt, eds., *The Right to the Land* (Cape Town, 1974); and Colin Bundy, "The Emergence and Decline of a South African Peasantry," *African Affairs* 71, no. 285 (October 1972): 369–88.

urbanization, or into a migrant pattern of repeated shifts between rural reserves and contract employment in "white" towns.

Although whites generally opposed the idea of the African as an independent peasant producer, this did not mean that they accepted him as a townsman free to make his way into employment through the operation of an open labor market. Just as the independent African on the land threatened to undercut the livelihood of white farmers by depriving them of labor, the independent African in town threatened to compete for jobs with unskilled whites, mostly rural-bred Afrikaners, who were also being rapidly drawn into the urban labor market. In order to protect the status and prosperity of whites, therefore, it was necessary that the whole townward movement of Africans be closely controlled.

In the view of white urban-dwellers, and it was a view that coincided well with the interests of the mining industry, the ideal African laborer was a migrant who worked on short contracts for whites and left his family behind in a rural reserve. Not only could the migrant be paid less, on the grounds that part of his family's support was derived from his plot of land, he could also be accommodated — in compounds or hostels — in such a way that he put down no firm roots in the white man's city. The alternative seemed to be "white" cities overrun with "surplus" Africans whose place ought properly to be in the countryside, in the labor reservoirs of the reserves, or in the employ of white farmers. "It should be understood," declared the Native Affairs Commission in 1921, "that the town is a European area in which there is no place for the redundant Native, who neither works nor serves his or her people but forms the class from which the professional agitators, the slum landlords, the liquor sellers, the prostitutes and other undesirable classes spring."[2] Long after the number of permanently urbanized Africans had passed the million mark in the 1940s, it

2. *Report of the Native Affairs Commission for 1921*, pp. 25–27, quoted in D. Welsh, "The Growth of Towns," in Wilson and Thompson, p. 187.

remained official policy to regard all African town-dwellers as temporary sojourners in the white man's domain.

The transition to city life would not under any circumstances have been easy for rural Africans, but as Welsh has shown, "the tensions, upheavals, and dislocation accompanying the urbanization of any people were exacerbated for Africans by official policies directed against the stabilization of urban African communities."[3] The poverty of city Africans was, and to this day remains, extreme, in part because of the persistence of wage scales geared to migrant conditions. The determination of whites to restrict African urban influx and to exclude all "surplus" individuals, including women and children, was, and is, the root cause of severe family disruption, a social evil giving rise to a host of other ills including widespread illegitimacy and crime. By the late 1930s, for Africans who did manage to take up urban residence as family units, shanty dwellings were often the only form of shelter available mainly because white reluctance to consider Africans as anything but temporary townsmen had over time produced a housing shortage of massive proportions. Meanwhile, prohibitions on African urban freehold tenure had worked strongly to limit incentives and to prevent the creation of a stable urban class at the higher end of the African social scale. Finally, pervading the lives of all urban Africans and all Africans aspiring to become urban, there was the welter of pass and permit laws designed to insure white control over all aspects of African movement and employment. Besides making it difficult for Africans to change employers in search of higher wages, these laws were the principal instrument in white efforts to apprehend and expel all "surplus" urban residents. After 1948, the pass acquired an added function in response to the persistent demand of white farmers for a guaranteed labor supply: Africans found with their pass books out of order were given the "option" of prison or a stint of farm labor on the white *platteland*.[4] From cradle to grave, in

3. Welsh, "Growth of Towns," p. 219.
4. See F. Wilson in Wilson and Thompson for a discussion of the prison labor system. Before pass laws were made uniform throughout South Africa in 1952, somewhat different laws applied in each of the

town and country, the African was enmeshed in a web of laws and policies masterfully designed to maximize the benefit to his white overlords while minimizing any sacrifice or inconvenience on their part.

Peasants and Proletarians

On the eve of World War II, although the townward movement of Africans was well underway, some 80 to 85 per cent of South Africa's 6.6 million Africans still lived on the land. Of these, about 2.2 million lived as laborers on white farms. The rest, who were the majority of rural Africans or some 3.2 million, eked out a living in the increasingly impoverished reserves, supplementing their resources with the wages earned by migrant relatives.[5] By any kind of political reckoning, the

---

four provinces, with restrictions on African movement being the least stringent in the Cape. African men were required to obtain official permission to enter or leave the Transvaal, the Orange Free State, Natal, and the Transkei. No African adult could remain without permission for more than 72 hours in any urban area unless he or she had resided there continuously since birth, or had been employed there continuously for ten years, or had been there continuously and lawfully for fifteen years without being employed for any period outside the area. Numerous regulations covering work-seekers, self-employed Africans, and Africans deemed "idle or undesirable" could be enforced by requiring that Africans at all times carry documents detailing their employment status. Some Africans of high occupational status were until 1952 exempt from many of these regulations, but were required to carry documents proving they were exempt. From 1954 onward, pass laws were extended to cover African women. By 1957, the number of convictions under these laws had reached an annual total of 365,911, or just over 1000 convictions per day. Details of these and other aspects of the pass laws up to 1960 are given in M. Horrell, comp., The "Pass Laws" (Johannesburg, 1960).
5. Census of 1936, cited in L. Marquard, The Native in South Africa (Johannesburg, 1948), pp. 4–5. Population distribution at that time was:

	Africans		Whites
Reserves	3,226,033	Towns	1,307,285
Towns	1,149,228	Farms	696,227
Farms	2,221,980		
	6,597,241		2,003,512

typical South African peasant of the late 1930s was still parochial in his orientation and quite thoroughly uninterested in
the social and political causes which were increasingly capturing the attention of urban Africans. Rarely did his world view
encompass any geographical area outside his own district or
tribal region. Making his grievances known meant complain-
ing to the local chief or perhaps to the white commissioner, but
beyond that his awareness of the political dimensions of his
environment was limited. Yet if any stratum of black South
African society could have been described as proto-nation-
alistic in outlook, it was the peasantry, for it was the peasant
who, more than any other African, felt most deeply and
immediately the sting of dispossession and the injustice of
conquest. Land occupied by his parents and grandparents
within living memory was now in the possession of whites;
where African herds had once wandered freely, fences now
barred the way. Aspects of material culture brought by the
Europeans—cooking pots and bicycles, medicines and even
white religion—could be accepted and appreciated, but the
white man himself was forever a conqueror, an invader whose
presence was tolerated only because Africans lacked the power
to expel him. Organized and sustained revolt was an impossi-
bility, but clues to the peasant mind could be read in the prolif-
eration of rural independent churches, led by Africans in rebellion against white authority, and in the popularity of cult
leaders like Wellington Butelezi, a Zulu who travelled around
the Transkei in the late 1920s prophesying that American
Negroes would soon descend in airplanes to drive whites into
the sea.[6]

6. Bengt Sundkler, whose *Bantu Prophets in South Africa* (2nd ed.,
London, 1961) is the definitive work on African independent
churches, concluded that the insecurity of African land tenure following the Land Act was a critical factor in the separatist movement.
"From 1913, the burning desire of the African for land and security
produced the apocalyptic patterns of the Zionist or Messianic myths,
whose warp and woof are provided by native land policy and Christian, or at least Old Testament material," p. 330. Scholars dispute
whether African independent churches should be considered manifestations of proto-nationalism or of an escapist tendency among

In between the peasant and the townsman proper, there were Africans in many stages of semi-urbanization, from the tradition-bound migrants to men, perhaps with some formal education and perhaps accompanied in town by their wives and families, who aspired to become permanent townsmen but who still had ties to the countryside and expected to return there in their old age. Well into the 1930s and '40s migrants and semi-migrants tended to predominate, but the number making the permanent transition to city life also rose steadily. Women, who in 1912 made up only 19 percent of all Africans in towns, by 1936 comprised 36 percent of the urban African population, an indication that large numbers of families had shifted their principal homes from country to town.[7] The specific pattern of urbanization varied from city to city as did the major types of work available to Africans—mining on the Reef, factory work in Port Elizabeth, East London and Johannesburg, stevedoring in Cape Town and Durban, service and domestic jobs everywhere—but whatever the particular pattern, the transition from old existence to new was an arduous one, calling for many social adjustments and much endurance of hardship. In Johannesburg on the eve of World War II, for example, according to de Ridder, one City Council house existed "for every estimated twenty-eight Africans living in the city. The rest . . . were living in shacks and squatter camps, without water or sanitation."[8]

Not surprisingly, the primary focus of African energies during this process of transition was on the problems of sheer survival. When the basic necessities of life, food and shelter, could rarely be taken for granted from one week to the next, a materialistic orientation was inevitable. Lack of education and

---

Africans. The Wellington movement is discussed in Hunter, *Reaction to Conquest* (2nd ed., London, 1961) pp. 570–72, and by Roux, *Time Longer Than Rope*, pp. 139–41.

7. E. Hellmann, "Social Change Among Urban Africans," in H. Adam, ed., *South Africa, Sociological Perspectives* (London, 1971), p. 160.

8. J. C. de Ridder, *The Personality of the Urban African in South Africa* (London, 1961), p. 28.

the inappropriateness of many rural traditions would in any case have made most Africans ill-equipped to master the urban environment, but in addition to these initial handicaps, there was always the added element of the white public's indifference to black hardship. Not only were African wages almost invariably below subsistence level, but a vast array of barriers greeted the African in all his striving for self-improvement. "One feels that the urban African is a little bewildered," one African intellectual observed.

> He makes every effort to adjust himself to urban living and to accept a western way of life; but he finds that there is a strong authoritative pressure to obstruct such a change. For instance, in a property-owning society he cannot own property, — in a society which has grown and prospered by workers organizing themselves his own organizations are restricted. In fact it seems that authority is not anxious to assist him in making adjustments from rural to urban living. He is thus uncertain and not sure of his goals.[9]

The double-rootedness of so many workers slowed the consolidation of a full-blown proletarian class, conscious of its own identity as a social group and united around a set of common goals. Political consciousness among the most exploited section of African workers, the goldminers on the Reef, was still further limited by the mine compound system, which provided basic shelter and food for the worker but isolated him from the influence of political and trade union organizers. Many African mineworkers, moreover, were not even South African-born but were recruited on contracts from Portuguese East Africa, the High Commission Territories and other British colonies in east, central, and southern Africa. Under these circumstances, in spite of the extensive intermingling of African ethnic groups on the Reef and in other urban areas, no sense of a racially-based "nationhood" arose spontaneously to replace the continuing interethnic rivalries carried over from an earlier era. "The writer can discover few signs of the de-

9. D. G. S. M'timkulu, *African Adjustment of Urbanization* (n.d.), p. 4, quoted by Welsh in Wilson and Thompson, p. 219.

velopment as yet of a race consciousness among urban Africans," wrote Johannesburg's best-known white social worker in the late 1930s.

> Among church members and readers of the Bantu newspapers, there is undoubtedly a sensing of the common bonds that should unite the different tribes. But this feeling lacks maturity, and is counteracted by new antipathies between Africans due to friction in urban location [township] life. There is no general feeling of racial solidarity which leaders can appeal to. Attempts at economic and political organization are spasmodic and ineffective. Social and recreational organizations require constant persistence and patience on the part of workers to keep them functioning. The African's emergence from the dominance of the tribe has given him a sense of freedom. The urge is upon him to progress. But the obvious ways are blocked and barred against him and the result is bewilderment, frustration. Appeals to him to unite and fight his way out, do not arouse him. The White man is too strong.[10]

Most rural-born workers, having little or no formal education, found the workings of a modern economic system far beyond comprehension. The fatalism characteristic of the peasant's world view, or what one African intellectual called "a certain disinclination or disdain to inquire into causes and effects," left most with little perspective on their own existence, obliged to take life as it came, without reflection or analysis.[11] How laws were made or who made them, complex issues of political morality such as who should vote and why, the choice between fascism and democracy, capitalism and socialism, these were questions which the average worker could begin to fathom only after long and patient explanation from someone with a much higher level of political consciousness. "It is regrettable to note that the African people as a whole do not understand the laws that contain the principles of Colour Bar," wrote David Bopape in Johannesburg in 1947, expressing the constant challenge to the would-be political organizer. "These

10. Ray Phillips, *The Bantu in the City* (Alice, Cape, 1938), p. 381.
11. S. M. Molema, *The Bantu—Past and Present* (Edinburgh, 1920), p. 313.

laws must be explained clearly."[12] As late as 1961 it was estimated that only one in eight Africans in Johannesburg read a
newspaper, and in the prewar years the proportion was undoubtedly much lower.[13] In the eastern Cape, where there is
both a long tradition of mission education and a high degree of
ethnic and linguistic homogeneity, the level of political awareness tended to exceed that of the Transvaal, yet even in the
Cape the worker's first concern was always with bread-and-
butter issues and not with the "abstractions" of politics.

Whereas the peasant in his home surroundings often had a
chief to whom he could turn for an informed opinion on public
matters, the urban worker could look to no such leader of
comparable natural authority. Those urban notables who did
emerge, usually as a result of exceptional educational or professional achievement, were generally too cautious in their own
views and activities to provide much stimulation for those
below themselves on the scale of political awareness. Where the
ethnic identity of such a notable was strong, workers from his
own language group might form ties of loyalty and trust, but as
workers gradually became more conscious of class differences
among individuals of their own race, there was a tendency for
the more politically sophisticated to reject middle class
Africans as "tea drinkers"—men who dissociated themselves
from the lower classes and preferred the polite society of
European tea parties.

Unable to generate more than a sprinkling of talented leaders from its own ranks, the prewar African proletariat-in-the-
making at no time posed any credible threat to the total political and economic hegemony of whites. Here and there over the
early part of the century were dotted instances of brief or spon-

12. *African National Congress (Transvaal), Secretarial Report Submitted at
the Annual Provincial Conference Held at Krugersdorp on Saturday 25th and
Sunday 26th October, 1947,* signed by D. W. Bopape, Secretary, p. 1
(Carter-Karis collection). Naboth Mokgatle, *The Autobiography of an
Unknown South African* (Berkeley and Los Angeles, 1971), provides a
detailed account of one worker's gradual political awakening during
the late 1930s and early 1940s.
13. De Ridder, *The Personality of the Urban African,* p. 47.

taneous protest—a strike by African sanitation workers in 1918 and a pass-burning movement in 1919—but only for a few years, with the meteoric rise of the Industrial and Commercial Workers Union (ICU) of Clements Kadalie in the mid-1920s, did Africans show signs of grasping their potential as an organized working class. The Communist Party of South Africa, shifting its emphasis from white to black workers within a few years of its founding in 1921, made advances in the organization of African trade unions and the provision of night schools for workers, but measured against the enormity of the task, even these achievements seemed barely more than brave beginnings.

Overbearing white attitudes of contempt and condescension toward nonwhites inevitably took a heavy psychological toll in the personality development of urban Africans, shaping habits of fear and subservience.[14] Long before the rigid legal application of apartheid, Africans were not allowed to walk on the sidewalks of downtown Pretoria and the black man who failed to drop to the back of a shop queue was liable to have his ears boxed by indignant white customers. For many Africans, the only way to cope with the brutality of race relations and with the cultural disorientation of the urban adjustment was to internalize the role and personality which white stereotyped expectations imposed, that of the stupid but good-natured child, dependent on superior white "parents" for constant guidance. For the unschooled peasant, however secure and self-confident he might be within his identity as a tribesman, experience in the city brought a sense of awe and respect for the superiority of the white man's skills. For the man with school-

14. There have been many studies of African attitudes and psychology. See, for example, de Ridder, *The Personality of the Urban African;* I. D. MacCrone, *Race Attitudes in South Africa* (Johannesburg, 1965); A. G. J. Crijns, *Race Relations and Race Attitudes in South Africa* (Netherlands, 1959); E. A. Brett, *African Attitudes* (Johannesburg, 1963); W. O. Brown, *Race Relations in the American South and in South Africa* (Boston, 1959); and M. L. Edelstein, *What Do Young Africans Think?* (Johannesburg, 1972). Fiction by Africans is also a rich source of information on attitudes.

ing, this impression of white superiority was reinforced by contact with white missionaries intent on having the African reject his own culture in favor of a white-approved way of life.

Culture contact, in short, despite the material satisfactions which it brought to many Africans, was not in general a psychologically rewarding experience. Synthesizing elements of old and new, a distinctive African urban subculture did gradually come into being, but underneath its often vibrant and gay exterior lingered a continuing crisis of the spirit. Unable to focus frustrations on their true source, Africans tended to turn aggressive impulses on one another and inward onto themselves, engaging in fights and violent crimes against other Africans or escaping into the consciousness-numbing world of drink and drugs. Except for the conventional wisdom that one should adopt a groveling meekness in the presence of employers and policemen, no clear consensus existed on how best to deal with whites. The white man's power could not be challenged; the African's dependence on white favor was all-pervading. Contrary to Frantz Fanon's stereotype of the colonized mind, no conscious and angry determination that "the last shall be first and the first last" as yet, at the time of World War II, seemed to mark the thinking of African workers. Such an attitude could arise only after a long process of political awakening had begun to give Africans a new sense of their place in the world and a new set of expectations regarding the future.

Black Bourgeoisie

White officialdom rejected the would-be African townsman, for all his indispensability as a laborer, on the grounds that he was a nuisance, a threat, and a drain on the public coffers. The self-sufficient African peasant was likewise frowned upon, since his very existence was inconsistent with white interests. The strongest white disapproval, however, was reserved for the educated African who imitated European ways and aspired to some form of work above manual labor. "The raw, untutored, unclad Kafirs, fresh from their 'kraals' [homes] up the mountains are by far the best and the most trustworthy workmen," one Kimberley diamond-digger of the late nineteenth century declared. "Above all things, mistrust a Kafir who speaks English and wears trousers."[15]

Fortunately for later generations, white opposition to African education failed to deter European and American missionaries from founding educational institutions for the "civilizing" (and Christianizing) of blacks. At mission secondary schools such as Lovedale and Healdtown in the Cape, Adams College in Natal, and later such institutions as St. Peter's and Kilnerton in the Transvaal, and eventually at the University College of Fort Hare, founded in 1916, an African middle class was fostered and imbued with knowledge of the wider world.[16] Able to enter more rewarding occupations than their illiterate and semi-literate fellows, members of this elite were relieved of some of the pressure for survival which kept the urban masses on a perpetual treadmill of material con-

15. Quoted by Welsh in Wilson and Thompson, p. 181.
16. Fort Hare was known originally as the South African Native College. Its first B.A. was granted (to Z. K. Matthews) in 1923. By 1941, it was producing about 30 nonwhite B.A.'s and B.Sc.'s a year, the great majority of whom were Africans. By 1959 it had awarded 29 postgraduate degrees, 687 B.A.'s, 507 B.Sc.'s, 452 Union Education Diplomas (postgraduate teaching degrees), and 193 advanced diplomas or certificates in Agriculture or Theology. Eighty-five graduates had gone on to qualify as medical doctors. *A Short Pictorial History of the University College of Fort Hare, 1916–1959* (Alice, Cape, 1961), pp. 48–51. By 1961, 2200 Africans held university degrees, including those who who had studied at Witwatersrand, Cape Town, and Natal Universities, and by correspondence with the University of South Africa. L. Kuper, *An African Bourgeoisie* (New Haven, 1965), p. 149. University graduates form the elite of the African middle class, but many Africans without degrees occupy high-status jobs. A survey in 1946 listed the following numbers of Africans in middle class occupations: 13,953 teachers (mostly primary level), 8 university professors or lecturers, 43 medical doctors, 3,125 general nurses, 78 maternity nurses, 2,697 clergymen, 23 lawyers and law clerks, 10 journalists and writers, 69 social workers, 289 interpreters and translators, and an unknown number engaged in business. M. Horrell, *South Africa's Non-White Workers* (Johannesburg, 1956), pp. 80–81.

cerns. More articulate and more conversant in European languages, and better equipped to understand the political and economic forces at work around them, they formed a natural leading sector of African society, standing between the conquered, unassimilated mass and the white conquerors, on whose culture and achievements they sought to model their own fast-changing lives.

Though not cut off from contact with traditional society, this African elite was in many ways alienated from traditional customs and norms. A belief in the superiority of European culture was basic to its world view, and its goals were unabashedly assimilationist. Having come through the experience of missionary boarding schools, it was well steeped in the liberal and Christian presumptions which prevailed in these institutions, including the optimistic liberal faith in the inevitability of progress. For those who had travelled and studied abroad—and there was an impressive number of Africans who managed to do so in the years before university education became available in South Africa—experience in Europe and America had reinforced a fundamental belief in a Protestant ethic of hard work and patience, and a faith in the white man's basic instinct for fair play.[17]

From the time of Union in 1910 on through the removal of Cape African voters from the common roll in 1936, there was abundant evidence of the anti-African trend in white politics, and for many politically aware members of the African middle class the result was disillusionment, discouragement, and a growing skepticism about the high-sounding promises of Christianity and white trusteeship.[18] Beneath these pessimistic

17. See, for example, R. D. Ralston, "American Episodes in the Making of an African Leader: A Case Study of Alfred B. Xuma (1893–1962)," *International Journal of African Historical Studies* 6, no. 1 (1973): 72–93.

18. The Cape franchise enabled qualified Africans to vote for members of Parliament and the Cape Provincial Council. Educated and propertied Africans in other provinces hoped for an eventual extension of this system countrywide. In 1936, after a ten-year political effort, and in an atmosphere of crisis among middle class Africans, Prime Minister Hertzog and his predominantly Afrikaner supporters from the northern provinces succeeded in eliminating the Cape

sentiments, however, the currents of liberal faith still continued to run strong, producing an uncomfortable ambivalence in all African political efforts. Occasionally an African intellectual would exhibit an unusual absence of illusion, as did Solomon T. Plaatje when he published his perceptive book, *Native Life in South Africa,* as a protest against the 1913 Land Act; but more often, the political pronouncements of leading Africans revealed a predisposition towards wishful thinking and a tendency to substitute moralistic analyses for hard political calculation. There are "straws that show which way the wind is blowing, indicating that the younger generation is gradually working away from the antediluvian notions of a segregation founded on mutual ignorance and suspicion," wrote D. D. T. Jabavu in 1928, expressing sentiments typical of African optimists at the time.

> It is our belief that with the spread of better understanding in Church and college circles the future of South Africa is one we can contemplate with a fair degree of optimism in the hope that Christian influences will dispel illusions, transcend the mistaken political expedients of pseudo-segregationists and usher in a South Africa of racial peace and goodwill.[19]

African vote and replacing it with a watered-down system under which qualified Africans, voting on a separate roll, elected four Senators and three MPs to be "Native Representatives" in Parliament. To placate Africans and their sympathizers, the African reserves were expanded (to approximately their present size), and an elected Natives Representative Council (NRC) was created to serve as an advisory body to the government. Coloureds were removed from the common voting roll, again in an atmosphere of political crisis, in 1956. All provision for nonwhite representation in Parliament was abolished in 1959.

19. D. D. T. Jabavu, *The Segregation Fallacy and Other Papers* (Alice, 1928), p. 24. Jabavu later became a professor at Fort Hare. S. M. Molema in his book, *The Bantu—Past and Present,* published in 1920, observed that Africans were divided in their views of the future between "pessimists" and "optimists," with the latter, in his view, being in the "slight majority," p. 348. Molema's own views, and the views of other prominent political spokesmen of this period, including John Dube, Pixley Seme, R. V. Selope Thema, Rev. Z. R. Mahabane, Rev. James Calata, Dr. A. B. Xuma, and even Jabavu, are marked by a high degree of contradiction and ambiguity, suggesting that, at least in the case of African political leaders, an "either/or" description is not entirely accurate.

Moral awakening, the dissipation of white "ignorance" through better education, and confidence in the ability of white liberals eventually to popularize their creed with the rest of white South Africa: these were the prescriptions for progress on which the majority of first-generation educated Africans rested their hopes. Given the processes of education and acculturation through which they themselves had passed, it is difficult to see how they could have perceived their world in any other terms. Raised in Christian environments where the level of tolerance, sympathy and general moral rectitude was very much higher than in South African society at large, most—apart from a few exceptional men like Plaatje, who was largely self-educated—were ill-prepared to come to grips with the realities of power politics and the selfish drive of organized white interests.

Even if most middle class Africans had not already absorbed a liberal world view during their formative years, the hostility which they experienced from white society at large would have caused them to turn for support to those few whites who were prepared to lend them a sympathetic ear. If they tended to overvalue the opinions and political judgments of these sympathizers over most of the prewar years, the miscalculation was an understandable one; when whites as a whole rejected educated Africans, this link with a few individual members of white society took on a compensatory emotional value. Invariably, the well-intentioned advice offered by white liberals stressed patience, hope, and the necessity for African self-improvement; all forms of radicalism or "extreme" action were decried on the grounds that they would arouse white fears and thereby set back the African cause. The best hope of the African, wrote the influential Reverend Ray Phillips in 1938, lay in "the patient extirpation of the fallacious conclusions of the White man." What was needed was for Africans

to convince the White that the thing they want is far removed from personal societal relationships, or insatiable economic and political power. They must convince him that their great desire is the attainment of the right to live an unobstructed existence with the normal privileges of decent citizens in a civilized state.

He recommended to Africans the approach of conservative American Negro leaders, who he said,

> feel that by creating in the White man a confidence in the Negro as a normal human being, capable of culture, and with understandable human desires, the way to advance will be gradually opened. . . . He is quietly keeping at it, with here and there an advance, a modification of his lot, an easing of restrictions and bars as the result of the increase of confidence and understanding which he is creating. This is the attitude commended for the African.[20]

By the time Phillips published this particular piece of advice, however, relations between the African elite and its white sympathizers had already become somewhat frayed in the course of the political crisis of 1935–36, during which liberal politicians had done conspicuously little to defend African voters threatened with removal from the Cape common roll. One of many successive waves of disillusionment had swept through African middle class society, edging African opinion as a whole one small but perceptible step away from the liberal norm. White liberals lost some of their earlier aura of respect, and African leaders increasingly tended to bridle when counselled to be patient and passive. Irritation with the conservatism of the liberal establishment shows through, for example, in a letter from Dr. A. B. Xuma, President General of the ANC, to a white friend in 1943. Speaking of the South African Institute of Race Relations, a liberal stronghold, Xuma wrote,

> I honestly feel that the Institute . . . stands in the way of African organizations and democratically thinking Europeans especially as it is taken in official quarters as a body that represents African opinion. The position is most embarrassing to some of us who are personal friends of its officials, but do not have the same outlook in Race Relations. We hate to appear to be fighting others personally, when, in fact, we are acting in self-preservation and have to be saved even from our friends if necessary.[21]

During the war years, this process of estrangement between

20. Phillips, *The Bantu in the City,* pp. 386–87.
21. Letter from A. B. Xuma to D. M. Buchanan, 5 January 1943 (Xuma papers).

white liberals and African leadership was to accelerate, until
the explicit rejection of white liberal guidance became one of
the rallying cries of younger African intellectuals in the mid-
and late 1940s.

Yet in spite of growing African dissatisfaction with liberal
counsels of patience and even an increasing cynicism about
liberal motives, it is important to note that the great majority of
educated Africans, through the 1940s and beyond, continued
to adhere to a basically liberal conception of social and political
goals as well as to an evolutionary view of change. What most
westernized Africans wanted—and what all whites except for a
small minority have at all times preferred to deny them—was
the fulfillment of the paternalistic promises of trusteeship: un-
fettered opportunity to assimilate European culture and learn
modern skills, opportunity to demonstrate African compe-
tence and to be accepted, however gradually, as equals in a
common, competitive society. The right of whites to lead the
way was generally assumed; what the African sought was simply the right to be included as a "junior partner" in the white
man's ruling councils, until such time as he was ready to play
his full part as an equal.

Alternative conceptions of change or of goals did not com-
mend themselves to the majority of educated Africans. The
Communist party, which called for change through the organization and politicization of the lower classes, was usually
rejected outright by mission-trained Africans who had been
taught that communism stood for violence and for a "crass,
materialistic . . . outlook on life which rejects all religious and
moral idealism."[22] Nationalism of the Wellington Butelezi
variety likewise went against the grain. To most men and wom-
en who were already incorporated into the white-built system
at a fairly sophisticated level—as clerks, teachers, traders,
nurses, interpreters, lawyers and the like—it seemed obvious
that the white man was in South Africa to stay, and that assimilation into his culture and political system ought logically to be

22. R. Phillips, "Communism or Christianity, the Present Day Question for Native Youth," *South African Outlook*, 1 August 1929, p. 148.

the objective of all Africans. The higher the barriers to real integration, the more desirable it seemed.

Realists and Rebels

Because the African middle class has provided most of the national leadership for Africans, middle class attitudes, which, as we have seen, arose originally out of mission training and the desire for integration, have tended to provide an ideological norm for organized African politics. Individual leaders drawn from the educated middle class have sometimes displayed distinctive styles and have often held varying views on how Africans ought best to direct their energies at any given time; but running through every major organized African effort, both in the prewar period and later, is the common thread of the Christian liberal tradition, shaping all political language, goals, strategies, and concepts of change.

Every movement for social and political change has its own inner dynamics, however, and every norm has its deviants. In South Africa over the last thirty years, deviants from the Christian liberal frame of reference have been essential catalysts of change in black politics. Like more typical African leaders, these deviants have also exhibited a wide variety of individual styles and opinions. But for the sake of exploring their collective role in African politics it will be useful here to draw a stereotyped picture of their attitudes and values so as to bring out the nature and extent of their deviance from the norm. Rather than referring to these two stereotypes—the liberal norm or the anti-liberal deviant—under the familiar rubric of moderates-and-militants or conservatives-and-radicals, we shall call them "realists" and "rebels," labels that more nearly capture the flavor of black South African political life.

From the time of Union until the electoral victory of the Afrikaner Nationalists in 1948, the paternalistic doctrine of trusteeship formed the basis of official government policy toward Africans, notwithstanding that in practical terms it was a doctrine honored more in the breach than in the observance. To most educated Africans the principle of trusteeship seemed sound. They considered it realistic to think of Africans as a whole progressing gradually and in step-by-step evolutionary stages, and they saw no reason to question the right of the white "trustees" to define the criteria of merit by which African progress was to be measured. To accept this conception of change was simply to accept "reality"; to wish for the rapid Europeanization of all Africans or for the instant acceptance of racial equality by whites was simply to wish for the impossible. Politics too, for the African realist, was the art of the possible. Africans might object to many specific points of government policy, but their power to challenge white authority was very limited. Their best hope lay, in the realist's view, in taking whatever oportunities the situation afforded for the expression of African opinion and using these opportunities to impress whites with the seriousness of African claims. In the 1920s, the liberal-initiated Joint Councils of Africans and whites—private interracial discussion groups formed in many South African towns—seemed to provide such an opportunity for African leverage. After 1936, the Natives' Representative Council, established as compensation for the loss of the Cape franchise, was regarded by realists as a forum in which critics of the government could make their voices heard. Even if the NRC was not as influential as Africans initially had hoped, the realist's position was always that half a loaf was better than none, and that the African's best strategy was to take whatever he was given and use it to get what he wanted.

What the realist often took for granted as good or useful, the African rebel rejected as an illusion, a sop, or a malicious fraud perpetrated by whites to uphold white interests. To the rebel, the most important aspects of reality were not the backwardness of the Africans or their powerlessness; seeing reality meant primarily seeing through the deceit and artificial standards of the white man. Where the realist was a skeptic at most, the rebel was an out-and-out cynic. All white politics, including liberal politics, "are grounded in the doctrine of the hegemony of the economic and political interests of the white people," remarked an African school teacher of the rebel school in 1953. "This reality is often symbolically represented as belief in the values of Western culture or in the standards of white civilization. We are not impressed."[23] Missionaries of a liberal-assimilationist bent had taught Africans to look forward to the achievement of an ideal society where rewards would be based on merit rather than race. Where the realist tended to accept this promise and to earnestly press for its fulfillment, the rebel rejected the whole premise of an integration based on the acceptance of nonwhites by whites. Reflecting the orientation of the aspiring middle class, the realist saw change in terms of blacks entering a white system. In the rebel, an element of the peasant's perspective was present: South Africa was the black man's land in which the white was an unwelcome intruder. Unable to envision a return to the pre-European past, the rebel was rarely certain of precisely what type of ideal society he wanted to put in place of white domination; but he was nevertheless sure of one thing: no future ideal society, no ultimate cultural identity for the African, and no means for attaining a better future could ever be defined *for* blacks *by* whites. If Africans were to achieve freedom and fulfillment, they would have to do it themselves in the face of opposition, overt or covert, from every section of the white population. To succeed, in the rebel's view, Africans had to learn to "think African," to define their own goals in terms of their own interests and priorities as an oppressed people.

Where the realist was inclined to see white politics as the real arena of power, the rebel looked more to the strength of the African masses as the vital determinant of change. The realist, looking at the disorganized and demoralized state of most urban Africans in the prewar years, was reinforced in his natural tendency to see black progress in terms of a measured extension of rights and liberties from the top down. If middle class African leaders spoke out about the people's angry mood or their rising suspectibility to "agitators," it was not because they welcomed mass militance but rather because they found the threat of mass upheaval to be a handy stick with which to beat fearful but well-intentioned whites. In keeping with the

23. Peter Raboroko, letter to *The Bantu World*, 23 May 1953.

outlook of white liberals, they placed great faith in the power of enlightened self-interest, and they firmly believed that all whites would eventually wake up to the supposed fact that their own progress and security depended on the progress of Africans.

To the rebel's way of thinking, the realist was a conscious or unconscious elitist who feared the might of the people and therefore sought to ignore or underestimate it. Elevating the supposed revolutionary fervor of the masses to grandiose heights in his own imagination, the rebel tended to think of the potential power of an organized African proletariat and to conclude that latent power and actual power were one and the same. Africans had not already risen up to break their chains, the rebel felt, not because of any shortcoming on the part of the masses but only because African leadership was too cautious and conservative. What Africans needed was heroic leaders, men of a more rebellious type, who would renounce the comfortable politics of the realists and would instead be the embodiment of the masses' burning desire for freedom and for action.

One principle deeply ingrained in the Christian-liberal realist was the rejection of violence as a technique of conflict resolution. Not only was violence associated with primitivism and lack of "civilization," but it was seen as invariably destructive and never, as in Fanon's philosophy, for example, as a therapeutic or constructive force. For older Africans who had grown up in the nineteenth century and had personally lived through the final stages of African military defeat, there could be nothing romantic about the prospect of a future black-white clash of arms. To the rebel, however, violence between South Africa's races was never a possibility that could be ruled out on either moral or practical grounds. To some, whose impatience for change overrode all rational calculations of strategy, violence seemed an inevitable and even desirable prospect. It was perceived as the natural reaction of the mentally healthy African whose self-confidence had never been undermined by white "training." "Uneducated people wherever they are in this country know very well that the oppressor is a white man," one African militant declared at a political rally at Alexandra township in Johannesburg in 1955. "If you could give the Pedis firearms and tell them to use them, they will come to shoot the Europeans without having been told. But give a revolver to an educated African here in Alexandra, he will say 'thank you, now I am safe from *tsotsis* [criminals],' because we were taught at school that a European is superior and that our fathers were thieves."[24]

Where the realist regarded the possibility of violent revolution with apprehension, the rebel lived for the day of confrontation. The difference in their outlooks was, most fundamentally, a temperamental one. Where the realist looked primarily to past experience as a guide for action, the rebel's inclinations were more intellectual and theoretical. Where politics was the art of the possible for the realist, the rebel saw politics as a matter of bed-rock principles, as something linked to his own personal search for integrity and identity. Not surprisingly, most rebels—from the time the type first begins to appear on the South African political scene about the time of World War II—have been drawn from the youngest adult generation, while realists have been older. Not infrequently, the realist is the rebel of an earlier decade whose world view has mellowed with the passing of time. To the realist, the rebel is an immature and emotional fellow with little practical insight into the mass mind which he claims to represent. To the rebel, the realist is a hopeless coward and opportunist, out of touch with popular feelings, and pathetic in his search for compromise and accommodation with whites.

In tracing the evolution of Black Power politics in the chapters which follow, it will be possible to observe the extent to which these contrasting "realist" and "rebel" stereotypes approximate the political outlooks of contending leaders and parties. Beyond any doubt, the factor of individual personalities has been a major variable in determining the course

24. Robert Resha, 15 May 1955, as quoted by a state witness in the Treason Trial *(Crown vs. F. Adams and twenty-nine others)*, trial transcript, p. 9954. The Pedis are a relatively traditionalist group in the northern Transvaal.

of black politics. More difficult to assess, however, are the ways in which personality itself, or the salience of certain personality traits among leaders, is determined in turn by political conditions. But this is to anticipate a line of inquiry best deferred for later consideration. First a journey into history is essential.

3

Lembede and the ANC Youth League, 1943–1949

Lembede Comes to Johannesburg

Sometime in 1943 a young Zulu schoolmaster gave up his teaching post in the rustic Heilbron district of the Orange Free State and moved to Johannesburg to begin a period of apprenticeship for the legal profession. The population of Johannesburg was swelling in the wartime industrial boom. Africans driven off the land by poverty and lured by the expanding demand for labor flooded into the slums of the Witwatersrand, throwing up new rough and tumble shantytowns as their numbers multiplied. Anton Muziwakhe Lembede became part of this massive townward migration, but the ambitions and desires that drove him set him far apart from the masses of illiterate and semi-literate rural folk around him. At twenty-nine he had raised himself from peasant origins into the ranks of the small African middle class by obtaining a bachelor of arts degree through correspondence courses with the University of South Africa. Determination and innate brilliance had seen him through a rigorous program of self-education which had now, in 1943, led him to qualify, again by correspondence, for the additional degree of bachelor of laws. Pixley Seme, the aging lawyer who had agreed to article him as a clerk, was a prestigious figure in African middle class circles. Educated in America and Britain and socially well-connected, Seme combined the best elite credentials with a long-standing reputation as a pillar of the community, dating from his youthful days, when he had been a principal figure in the founding of the African National Congress. Had Lembede desired nothing more than professional success and status in urban African society, he might have been satisfied with his achievements in 1943, but his imagination and ambitions ranged wider.

A gulf of years and experience separated Lembede's generation from Seme's. Though revered as a nationalist patriarch, Seme represented a variety of nationalism belonging to earlier decades of the century, when educated Africans had clung to the promises of trusteeship and placed great faith in the benign influence of Christianity. Traditions of cultural assimilation in the Cape had provided some basis for this optimism, even during the years after Union when all other omens for African political progress were decidedly negative. Faced with limited options, the small African elite of Seme's day had accepted counsels of patience and waited for enlightenment to take its anticipated course. In the meantime, there was scope for able and aspiring individuals to earn positions of prestige and power in the African community. This Seme had done, and under his autocratic leadership the ANC had declined in the 1930s into an annual conclave of his own sycophantic personal followers. In the years when white prejudice was supposed to have withered, African resolve withered instead; as white prejudice battened itself on the drive for money and power, Africans sustained themselves on the illusion that politics was a matter of patient persuasion, polite formalities and moral indignation. By the late 1930s, frustrated but unable to alter his basically conservative conception of the political process, Seme had retired from active participation in the ANC and had reluctantly watched its leadership pass to younger men.

The world of social and political ferment that Anton Lembede entered in 1943 was very different from the one in which Seme's outlook had been framed. It was a harsher world, one in which younger Africans with access to education were growing up with fewer illusions about the nature of white rule. Where the thinking of Seme's elderly generation had been largely a response to British and American models, and the middle-aged generation of African leaders had oriented themselves towards what they believed were the good intentions of Jan Smuts and his liberal protegé, J. H. Hofmeyr, intellectuals of Lembede's age group had been most affected by observations of the Afrikaner nationalists, who by the war years had set themselves with ruthless determination on the road to political dominance. The assimilationist traditions of the Cape had been hopelessly compromised with the adoption of the Hertzog Bills in 1936, and would-be African reformers with a more up-to-date sense of political possibilities had begun to turn their eyes from the quiet Cape to the Transvaal, where industrial development was beginning to create an urban working class of vast potential strength. Educated Africans conscious of the workings of politics in the white world were still relatively few in number, but they were significantly more numerous than in Seme's day, and the possibility that an energetic intelligentsia might awaken an African proletariat to action was no longer quite the impractical notion it had been thirty years earlier.[1]

More important than the increasingly real possibilities for mass organization were the changes in political attitudes that were accompanying the coming of age of Lembede's generation. To the middle class leaders of earlier decades, whose outlook was firmly anchored in the "realist" tradition, the idea of trying to organize sustained protests by African workers was not only ruled out by the dictates of practicality, but also by a sensitivity to canons of "civilized" and respectable behavior.

1. The number of Africans employed in manufacturing more than doubled from 151,889 in 1939/40 to 369,055 in 1949/50. While 18.9% of the African population was recorded as urbanized in 1936, this percentage had risen to 27.1 by 1951. Over the same period the number of Africans employed in private industry rose by 111% in the Southern Transvaal, 190% in the Durban area, 242% in the Western Cape, and 287% in the Port Elizabeth area. See H. J. Van Eck, *Some Aspects of the South African Industrial Revolution*, 2nd ed. (Johannesburg, 1951), p. 16; South African Institute of Race Relations, *South Africa's Changing Economy* (Johannesburg, 1955), p. 40; M. Horrell, *South Africa's Non-White Workers* (Johannesburg, 1956), pp. 69–70; and Walshe, *The Rise of African Nationalism*, pp. 300–303.

Africans aspiring to acceptance in the white world found the prospect of rabble-rousing among illiterate workers uncongenial. Intellectually, culturally, and emotionally, the gap separating educated, westernized Africans from their lower class brethren was too wide to be easily breached. Even had this not been the case, whites of all persuasions—except for a handful of politically marginal communists—were so united in holding up an unflattering picture of the African "agitator" that any black man self-conscious about his image in the eyes of whites was likely to be strongly deterred from thinking in terms of mass organization. The public statements of early African leaders frequently cast the "agitator" in an unfavorable light, portraying him as a man who appealed to emotion rather than reason, and who stirred up dangerous racial sentiments. "Let me say, with all earnestness," wrote the Reverend John L. Dube, the first President of the ANC, in 1926,

> . . . that unless there is a radical change soon [regarding the grievances of the Africans] herein lies a fertile breeding ground for hot-headed agitators amongst us Natives, who might prove to be a bigger menace to this country than is generally realized today. Let us all labor to forestall them: that is my purpose in life, even if I have to labor single-handed. . . . We are all of us here to stay, and there is plenty of room for us. . . . Race cooperation must be the watchword.[2]

By 1943, however, a profound skepticism regarding white motives and the promises of "trusteeship" had set in; faith in the inevitability of enlightenment was dead, and a new mood of defiance and self-assertion was taking its place in setting standards of thought and behavior among younger Africans. Looking at events in the world beyond South Africa, many Africans had experienced a sharpening of race-consciousness during the Italian invasion of Ethiopia in 1935–36, when the

---

2. J. L. Dube, *The Clash of Colour* (Durban?, 1926), p. 11 (Gubbins Library). The brief but spectacular rise of the ICU indicates that mass organization might not have been as impractical as most middle class leaders assumed. ICU leadership was principally working class and lower middle class.

white world had stood aside as one of Africa's two independent black states fell to conquest.

The coming of World War II initially aroused fresh hopes among Africans, and many could not help sensing that the entire world was about to turn over a new leaf. The war inspired new thinking about old problems. Thousands of Africans recruited into the South African forces as noncombatants were witnessing the war against Hitler at first hand and would come back with a new sense of the realities of racism and nascent fascism at home. It was a period in which full scope and inspiration were offered to schemers and planners, and Anton Lembede was one such thinker who had instinctively begun to rise to the challenge of the times. In Johannesburg he was to find himself drawn into a remarkable group of young men, members of the ANC, who were, like himself, questioning the world view of their elders and groping towards a new analysis of the African predicament.

Under the leadership of Dr. Alfred B. Xuma, the ANC had revived somewhat from its moribund condition under Seme. Xuma, a man in his late forties at the time he assumed the ANC presidency in 1940, was, like Seme, educated in the United States and Europe, and belonged to the most prestigious stratum of African urban society. Though he personally lacked a common touch, he appreciated the importance of drawing far greater numbers of ordinary Africans into the ANC, and he had taken steps to strengthen and unify the organization's structure and procedures and to put it on a sounder basis financially through the regular collection of dues. By 1943 plans were afoot for the leasing of the organization's first official headquarters, a small office in Rosenberg Arcade off Market Street in downtown Johannesburg, adjacent to Seme's law office. There was talk of employing paid secretaries and organizers.[3]

3. For a detailed account of organizational developments in the ANC during Xuma's presidency (1940–49), see Walshe, *The Rise of African Nationalism,* pp. 379–411.

These sound measures had earned Xuma wide respect in the Congress, but among some of the more impatient younger members such steps forward had only encouraged a frustrated desire for even more sweeping reforms. In the view of these younger stalwarts, "the people" were ready to march but African leadership was hanging back, still mentally ensnared in a "dying order of pseudo-liberalism and conservatism, of appeasement and compromises."[4] Just as ten years later when members of the Africanist movement were to consider and reject as impractical the setting up of a rival movement, the young dissidents of 1943 judged that their best hope lay in trying to redirect and reform the ANC from within. A resolution at the ANC's annual conference in Kimberley in December 1943 had urged the establishment of a Congress Youth League. Just about the time Lembede arrived in Johannesburg, assorted sets of politically-minded friends were already meeting and planning for the formation of such a body. A core of organizers coalesced in early 1944, and with Dr. Xuma's cautious approval, the League was formally launched at a meeting held Easter Sunday, 1944, at the Bantu Men's Social Centre in Johannesburg.[5]

It is not clear at exactly what point Lembede began to take part in planning for the League, but we know that he was drawn in at an intermediate stage by two close friends from earlier years, Ashby Peter Mda and Jordan Ngubane. Mda, then twenty-seven, was a fellow teacher aspiring to enter law, and Ngubane, then twenty-six and a former schoolmate of Lembede's at Adams College in Natal, was a journalist working on the staff of *The Bantu World*, the country's largest newspaper

4. Letter from A. P. Mda to G. M. Pitje, 24 August 1948, reproduced in Karis and Carter, vol. 2, pp. 319–21.
5. Information on the formation of the Youth League is drawn both from published sources and from interviews with A. P. Mda, Congress Mbata, and Oliver Tambo, and from interviews of Gwendolen Carter and Thomas Karis with Mbata, William Nkomo, Jordan Ngubane and Joe Matthews. Documentary sources include Ngubane's unpublished autobiography and Matthews' note, "Chronology of the Formation of the ANC Youth League" (both in Carter-Karis collection).

for Africans. Both men had already lived in Johannesburg for a number of years, and both were astute observers of the ANC. With the help of these two politically experienced friends, Lembede gradually began to find his feet in the Youth League circle, and in a matter of months he had emerged as the most striking personality and daring thinker in a group that included an impressive number of outstanding future leaders, including Oliver Tambo, Nelson Mandela, and Walter Sisulu. In September 1944 the League gave recognition to Lembede's unusual talents by electing him its first president.

Lembede's Early Life

Anton Lembede was the principal architect of South Africa's first full-fledged ideology of African nationalism, and since his ideas were in certain ways so clearly rooted in the circumstances of his youth, some of the scanty facts which are known about his early life must be noted.[6] He was born in the rural Georgedale district of Natal, not far from Durban, in 1914, eight years after the suppression of Bambata's Rebellion, and two years after Seme, the Msimang brothers and a handful of others representing the young Zulu intelligentsia of the day had travelled to Bloemfontein to participate in the founding of the African National Congress. Lembede's parents were tenant sharecroppers on a white-owned farm at the time of his birth, but sometime in the late 1920s they moved to the small nearby town of Isabelo so that their children could attend school. Accounts of Lembede's childhood stress the poverty of his family, and his schoolmates later recalled the extreme deprivation of his three years at Adams College, when his shabby clothing marked him out as the "living symbol of African misery."[7]

From what external or inner sources Lembede drew his unusual zeal for knowledge must remain a matter for speculation.

6. Information on Lembede's life has been drawn in part from interviews with Congress Mbata, Peter 'Molotsi, A. P. Mda, P. K. Leballo, J. B. Marks, Charles Lakaje, Jordan Ngubane and Oliver Tambo.
7. Ngubane, unpublished autobiography (Carter-Karis collection).

His mother had received some elementary schooling, and had worked for a number of years as a teacher before her marriage to Lembede's father. She appears to have taught her children the equivalent of several years of school at home before the family's move brought them access to a Catholic mission primary school. African farm workers, then as now, led a grueling life, and children were required to work long days in the fields alongside their elders. The concern of his parents for their children's education brought Lembede an escape from this life of near-slavery at about the age of twelve or thirteen, and a voracious appetite for study and academic disputation marked the rest of his days. A practising Roman Catholic to his death, Lembede may also have been inspired by his early exposure to Catholicism to hone the edge of his sharp intelligence on the cosmic questions of divine will and human destiny. It is interesting to note that Mda and Ngubane, Lembede's closest intellectual colleagues in the formulation of the Youth League's ideology, were both also raised as Catholics.

On completing elementary school, Lembede was awarded a bursary to train as a teacher at Adams College near Durban. Life at Adams, a liberal institution founded by American Congregational missionaries, was far removed from both the harshness of rural helotry and the realities of urban dehumanization and exploitation. Thinking back in later life, Albert Lutuli recalled that in his days on the Adams faculty in the early 1930s

> the world seemed to be opening out for Africans. It seemed mainly a matter of proving our ability and worth as citizens, and that did not seem impossible. We were, of course, aware of the existence of color prejudice, but we did not dream that it would endure and intensify as it has. There seemed point . . . in striving after the values of the western world. It seemed to be a striving after wholeness and fulfillment.[8]

Lembede too must have felt on his arrival at Adams in 1933 that the world was "opening out," and that ability and diligence would reap their just reward. To what extent at this stage of his

8. Albert Luthuli [Lutuli], *Let My People Go* (London, 1963), p. 42.

life he subscribed to the liberal premises of cultural assimilation and evolutionary change, we do not know. From his avid pursuit of education at Adams and thereafter we can perhaps assume that, at least initially, he too thought in terms of "proving his ability and worth" by European standards of merit.

Whatever the deepest sources or immediate stimuli of his ambitions were, Lembede by the end of adolescence seems to have set his sights high. His bursary had put him through the three-year normal school, but he had used his spare time to do the academic high school course at Adams on his own, and in 1937 he passed the matriculation exams with a distinction in Latin. Over the next six years, while holding a series of teaching posts in Natal and the Orange Free State, he studied privately to qualify for the bachelor's and LL.B. degrees.

It was probably in the Orange Free State that Lembede first confronted the full unpleasantness of race rule. The Free State is to this day the heartland of the most reactionary elements of rural Afrikanerdom, and these were the years when white nationalism was being fanned into frenzy by the example of Nazism and the contentious decision of the Smuts government to enter the war in defense of Britain. Lembede had purposely gone to work in the Free State in order to perfect his knowledge of Sesotho and Afrikaans.[9] According to Mda, who first befriended him in 1938, Lembede in his eagerness to learn Afrikaans found himself drawn to the ideas issuing at the time from *Die Transvaler,* whose editor, Dr. H. F. Verwoerd, daily put forth South Africa's own local variant of Hitlerian master race ideology in his column *Die Sake van die Dag* [The Affairs of the Day]. On renewing their acquaintance in Johannesburg in 1943, Mda found Lembede rather uncritically fascinated with the spirit of determination embodied in fascist ideology, to the point where he saw nothing wrong with quoting certain ideas of Hitler and Mussolini with approval. Mda set himself the task of disabusing Lembede of some of his more dangerous

---

9. By the time of his death, Lembede was proficient in at least seven languages: Zulu, Sesotho, English, Afrikaans, High Dutch, German and Latin.

fancies and turning his intellectual powers toward a deeper consideration of South Africa's problems. Lembede by this time had decided to study for a master's degree in philosophy, an almost unprecedented undertaking for an African, and his friendship with Mda rapidly developed into an intellectual sparring partnership in which the two read, argued, and reasoned their way together, with some participation by Ngubane, toward a new philosophy that could serve the interests of African emancipation. By the time the Youth League was launched in April 1944, this new conception—which Lembede called "Africanism"—had taken shape in their minds and had begun to make an impression on the thinking of their colleagues in the Youth League circle. While Mda and Ngubane stayed relatively in the background, concentrating on problems of organization, strategy and propaganda, Lembede emerged as the chief spokesman for the new philosophy, the more abstract components of which were his own intellectual creations.

The Philosophy of Africanism

Lembede's "Africanism" offered prescriptions for change based on a new analysis of the South African situation and fresh insights into the motivations of the groups in conflict. As an ideology it eventually fell short of the vaunted expectations of Lembede himself, who envisioned it becoming a fighting creed for all Africans. Nevertheless, as a stage in the evolution of African political thinking it is of great historical interest because it represented a break with unproductive earlier approaches, showed a willingness to experiment with new perspectives on the race problem, and was an honest attempt to confront rather than avoid some of the African's most difficult dilemmas. As a first attempt to formulate a creed of orthodox nationalism for black South Africa, it initiated a tradition on which later nationalists were to build, and supplied that tradition with its foremost intellectual hero—Lembede himself.

From his wide reading in history and philosophy, and from an observation of the strength which ideological fanaticism had lent to the Afrikaners, Lembede arrived at the conclusion quite early in his contact with the ANC that an ideology as such was essential for Africans if they were to maximize their resources in the unequal struggle against white dominance. Others in the Youth League, observing the contrast between the disciplined determination of the Afrikaners and the indecisive, drifting character of most African leadership, had reached a similar conclusion, and a few had already developed an interest in Marxism as a possible ideological answer to African needs. Marxism did not attract Lembede, although he condemned capitalist exploitation and prescribed a vaguely defined socialism as the most suitable economic system for a free Africa; his religious training and convictions had set him against philosophies which appeared to deny man's spiritual nature, but more importantly, he associated Marxism in South Africa with the "white" South African Communist Party—a political force which, in his view, was as capable as any other, reactionary or liberal, in perpetuating what he perceived to be the stultifying evil of white paternalism.

Ideology seemed to Lembede to be the most potent medium through which African leadership could address itself to the fundamental psychological handicaps of the African masses. He was sensitive, as few in the older generation of Congress leaders appeared to be, to the crippling complexes of inferiority and dependence imposed on Africans by their treatment at the hands of whites, and he believed, perhaps too optimistically, that an ideology of bold African assertion would succeed in correcting the African's debasing self-image. Lembede's rural background gave him a certain detachment from the urban scene, and what he saw around him on arriving in Johannesburg seems to have filled him with a sense of dismay and urgency regarding the conditions of African urban life. The austerity of his own childhood, and the ascetic and disciplined life style he had adopted during his pursuit of higher education set him apart from the fast and free life of sophisticated Johannesburg Africans. What most aspiring young men took for the attractions and excitement of city life—flashy clothes, cinemas, jazz and jive, liquor and the scramble for money, even big money if one was willing to cross the thin line

Newcomers to the city prepare a meal in the traditional manner, Johannesburg 1947. The farm wagon which brought the family and its possessions to town now stands idle. *Pat English/Life Magazine © Time, Inc.*

Anton Lembede. *Drum*

Nelson Mandela. *Eli Weinberg*

separating gangsters and petty criminals from honest folk—
stood out clearly to Lembede as signs of degeneracy and cultural confusion. His tastes, Mda later recalled, "were very simple. The fads, fashions and foibles of sophisticated urban society did not appeal to him," but seemed instead to augur the
disastrous decline of the African people, caught in a vicious
cycle of degradation.[10] "Moral degeneration," Lembede wrote
in 1946 in one of his most pointed references to the alleged
sickness of African society,

> is assuming alarming dimensions . . . [and] manifests itself in
> such abnormal and pathological phenomena as loss of self-
> confidence, inferiority complex, a feeling of frustration, the
> worship and idolization of whitemen, foreign leaders and
> ideologies. All these are symptoms of a pathological state of
> mind.[11]

Africans had become a derelict nation, uncertain of their cultural identity, their rights, or their place in relation to the rest
of mankind. There could be no cure for these evils except
African freedom, and no means to the achievement of freedom other than a ruthless struggle grounded in the inspiration
of a well-devised ideology, a credo addressed to the deepest
strivings and needs of the African spirit.

Lembede believed that in Africanism he had evolved a philosophy which could offer Africans just such a psychological
antidote. The most basic ingredient in the prescription was
a new and aggressively positive self-image compounded of
pride in the past, confident expectations for the future, and an
emotional, burning love for the African's God-given blackness.
Of these elements, the last seems to have come most spontaneously to Lembede, who was, according to all accounts, an in-
curable romantic by nature, fond of pointing to his own lowly
origins as a peasant sprung from Africa's "black soil." "Look at

10. A. P. Mda, "The Late Anton Muziwakhe Lembede, M. A. (Phil)
LLB," *Azania News*, 25 August 1966.
11. A. Lembede, "Policy of the Congress Youth League," *Inkundla ya
Bantu*, May, 2nd fortnight, 1946, reproduced in Karis and Carter, vol.
2, pp. 317–18.

my skin," he is said to have often exhorted his colleagues, "it is black like the soil of mother Africa."[12]

The first duty of African leaders, Lembede held, was to teach Africans not to be ashamed of being black. Nature had endowed the black man "with all the elements of power, of creation and of nobility," and it was his duty "not to allow himself to be swamped by the tide of doctrines of inferiority," which were no more than a cunning fabrication of the white man, devised to facilitate his exploitation of the man of color.[13] Civilization was the heritage of all mankind and not the exclusive attribute of people of any one race or nation. Africa had been the cradle of civilization at the time of Egypt's glory: who could doubt that someday her time for greatness and world leadership would come around again? In the meantime, Lembede advised Africans to heed the words of Paul Kruger: *Wie zich een toekomst scheppen wil, mag het verleden neit uit het oog verleizen* (One who wants to create the future must not forget the past). Africans, he wrote in 1945,

> have still to erect monuments to commemorate the glorious achievements of our great heroes of the past ... Shaka, Moshoeshoe, Hintsa, Sikhukhuni, Khama, Sobuza and Mosilikazi etc. In their times and environment and under the circumstance in which they lived, these men served their people and did their duty nobly and well.[14]

Africans had to accept "the bitter and painful realization" that their continent had slumbered for centuries, Lembede noted in a letter to Ruth First in 1945.[15] Yet it was historically and philosophically unsound to maintain that Africa's subject condition and place in the world were immutable. Looking

12. Charles Lakaje, untitled MS, 1970, p. 18.
13. "Last Message of Late Mr. A. M. Lembede, M.A., L.L.B.," *African Advocate,* August–September, 1947 (Gubbins Library).
14. A. Lembede, "Some Basic Principles of African Nationalism," *The Bantu World,* 7 April 1945, and *Inyaniso,* February 1945, reproduced in Karis and Carter, vol. 2, pp. 314–16.
15. Letter from the ANC Youth League (Transvaal) to the Secretary [Ruth First] of the Progressive Youth Council, 16 March 1945, reproduced in Karis and Carter, vol. 2, p. 316. This letter is unsigned, but the style is unmistakably Lembede's.

beyond the bleakness of the immediate political environment, Lembede's thoughts soared to the grand plane of human destiny, clearly borrowing from the writings of western romantic nationalists. Each nation, like each organism in nature, he argued, was unique, having its own peculiar character and "its own peculiar contribution to make towards the general progress and welfare of mankind."[16] This destiny was God-given and was in fact a divine mission which each nation was bound by fate to carry out. Although Africa's ultimate cultural contribution was still unknown, hope for the future was summed up in the ancient Latin dictum: *Ex Africa semper aliquid novi* (Always something new from Africa).

On the political plane, Lembede professed a clear and unshakeable vision of Africa's destiny. However hidden, thwarted and unrecognized this destiny had been heretofore, the lessons of history showed clearly, he said, that like other great races and peoples of the world, Africans were destined to be one united and independent people, taking their rightful place in the world family of nations. In the unfolding pattern of world history, all Africans comprised one nationality, united by color. "Africa is a blackman's country," he wrote in a piece for the *Inkundla* in 1946;

> Africans are the natives of Africa, and they have inhabited Africa, their Motherland, from times immemorial; Africa belongs to them. Africans are one. Out of the heterogeneous tribes, there must emerge a homogeneous nation. The basis of national unity is the nationalistic feeling of the Africans, the feeling of being Africans irrespective of tribal connection, social status, educational attainment, or economic class.[17]

In an earlier *Inkundla* piece in October 1945 he had spelled out the rationale of his pan-African vision more explicitly. The uniting of all tribes into one nation was a sine qua non for liberation and progress, he argued. The great nations of the world all numbered their populations in the tens or even hun-

16. Lembede, "Some Basic Principles of African Nationalism," in Karis and Carter, vol. 2.
17. Lembede, "Policy of the Congress Youth League," in Karis and Carter, vol. 2.

dreds of millions. What was the Union of South Africa with her mere ten million inhabitants? The Xhosas, Basutos and Zulus numbered only a few million each. What could they hope to achieve in comparison with the world's great powers? In Africa as a whole, however, there were over one hundred thirty million Africans, a number comparing favorably with other large countries of the world. Given a sufficiently strong will to unite, Africans had all the essential properties of a single nationality because, Lembede maintained, perhaps borrowing from Montesquieu, all people who were products of the African environment with its unique climate, topography, and other regional features, were necessarily "dominated by the same spirit." Giving vent to the tendencies which had led many of his contemporaries to label him a hopelessly impractical thinker, Lembede went on to declare that

> The African natives then live and move and have their being in the spirit of Africa; in short, they are one with Africa. It is then this spirit of Africa which is the common factor of cooperation and the basis of unity among African tribes; it is African Nationalism or Africanism. So that all Africans must be converted from tribalism into African Nationalism, which is a higher step or degree of the self-expression and self-realization of the African spirit, Africa through her spirit is using us to develop that higher quality of Africanism. We have then to go out as apostles to preach the new gospel of Africanism and to hasten and bring about the birth of a new nation. Such minor insignificant differences of languages, customs etc. will not hinder or stop the irresistible onward surge of the African spirit.[18]

This spirit of Africanism, Lembede added, always anxious to impress upon Africans the necessity for self-reliance, could

> realize itself through, and be interpreted by, *Africans only*. Foreigners of whatever brand and hue can never properly and correctly interpret this spirit owing to its uniqueness, peculiarity and particularity.[19]

The driving force behind Africanism had to be an ardent

18. A. Lembede, "National Unity Among African Tribes," *Inkundla ya Bantu*, October, 2nd fortnight, 1945.
19. Ibid.

love for Africa, her people, her soil, her past, her future. "The tie that will bind all Africans together under the banner of Africanism will be the passionate and glowing love for Africa—our motherland—and her Freedom," he wrote in the *Inkundla* several months before his sudden death in 1947. Going on to quote Joseph Mazzini, the nineteenth-century Italian nationalist whose impassioned writings could not have failed to strike a responsive chord in his own emotional nature, Lembede admonished Africans

> "Love your country. . . . It is the home which God has given you, that by striving to perfect yourselves therein, you may prepare to ascend to Him. It is your name, your glory, your sign among the people. Give to it your thoughts, your counsels, your blood. Raise it up great and beautiful—and see that you leave it uncontaminated by any trace of falsehood or servitude; unprofaned by dismemberment.

"Oh!" If these inspiring words of Mazzini could only "sink and soak into our minds and hearts!" Lembede rhapsodized. If only nationalism could be

> pursued with the fanaticism and bigotry of religion, for it is the only creed that will dispel and disperse the inferiority complex which blurs our sight and darkens our horizon. The inferiority complex is a psychological malady; the opium that dulls our mental faculties and represses our physical energy. We must therefore verily believe that we are inferior to no other race on earth; that Africa and ourselves are one; that we have a divine mission of unifying and liberating Africa, thus enabling her to occupy her rightful and honorable place amongst the nations of the world. We must develop race pride.

Then in a final peroration, underscoring his conviction that nationalism held the key to the mobilization of Africans for political action, he declared that "the dynamic human energy that will be released by African nationalism will be more powerful and devastating in its effects than . . . atomic energy."[20]

Lembede's intensive study of history and philosophy had freed his mind from any blind tendency to conform to the

20. A. Lembede, "In Defence of Nationalism," *Inkundla ya Bantu,* 27 February 1947.

thinking of those around him and had stirred in him a fervent desire to create something in the philosophical realm which was new and uniquely African. He sometimes spoke, for example, of the need to give Christianity in South Africa a more indigenous base by incorporating into it certain aspects of African traditional religion. The originality of many of his political formulations is debatable in light of their obvious debt to the writings of western philosophers, but the total thrust of his ideas in the South African context was something quite unprecedented.[21] Few of his contemporaries were intellectually prepared to grasp, let alone accept, his new perspectives, however, and even Lembede himself sometimes betrayed a degree of uncertainty about where his ideas were leading and a reluctance to break completely with the liberal integrationist values of the past. The resulting picture was therefore often one of considerable confusion and inconsistency, in spite of the public image of boldness and supreme confidence projected by Lembede and his Youth League peers.

The concept of a metaphysical "African spirit" breathing unity and a sense of grand destiny into blacks throughout the continent carried a certain emotional appeal, but as the basis for a political creed it was too abstract to arouse much enthusiasm among Lembede's less mystically-inclined contemporaries. Presumably hoping to appeal to individuals of all temperaments—or perhaps representing a compromise between Lembede and his more down-to-earth colleagues—the Youth League's *Creed,* drawn up in 1944, commended to members a belief in both "the divine destiny of nations" and "the scientific approach to all African problems."[22] It was the

21. Some have wondered whether Lembede might have been influenced by the writings of early West African nationalists, but no evidence has yet come to light to support this speculation. His strong grounding in European philosophy is evident in his master's thesis, "The Conception of God as Expounded By or as it Emerges From the Writings of Great Philosophers—From Des Cartes to the Present Day."

22. The *Creed* is contained in the *Congress Youth League Manifesto,* March 1944, reproduced in Karis and Carter, vol. 2, pp. 300–308.

latter principle, however, that enjoyed the most support from the action-oriented organizers of the League, while the appeal to "destiny" was regarded at best as rhetoric, and was for the most part ignored in formulations of Youth League policy subsequent to Lembede's death—until its delayed revival in the late 1950s as an element in the pan-Africanism of the PAC.

Dilemmas of African Cultural Identity

Equally beguiling to the emotions but elusive as a foundation for policy was the idea which Lembede often expounded in his public speeches, that Africans had to build towards the future by selectively "borrowing" what was best from other cultures. Like so many other nationalists of the non-European world he spoke with glowing optimism of the possibility of choosing from among those attributes of the "materialistic West" and "spiritualistic East" those elements best suited to the development and modernization of Africa's own particular traditions. The end product would be something unique in the history of world civilization, for "Africanism and its development to higher forms" did not imply "mere superficial or artificial mimicry with no social roots," but rather a process of growth and change founded on the conscious selection of those foreign elements which could be most beneficially adapted to Africa's own cultural foundations.[23]

These foundations in their economic aspects had an affinity with socialism, and politically were not unlike democracy, said Lembede, but spiritually, the traditional African world view was diametrically opposed to that of European or western culture.[24] For whereas Europeans took an individualistic view of life, seeking selfishly after power, success and fame—thereby continually plunging themselves into conflict—the African regarded the universe

23. Quoted in P. L. Gqobose, "The Father of Africanism in Azania (South Africa), " *The Africanist*, March 1969. Probably quoted from a later oral account by Mda.
24. Lembede, "Some Basic Principles of African Nationalism," in Karis and Carter, vol. 2.

as one composite whole; an organic entity, progressively driving towards greater harmony and unity, whose individual parts exist merely as interdependent aspects of one whole, realizing their fullest life in the corporate life, where communal contentment is the absolute measure of values.[25]

The African's traditional philosophy of life thus revealed a striving towards greater human unity and social responsibility and was in essence more humane than that of the European. It was on these indigenous foundations, Lembede asserted, anticipating the later West African philosophers of negritude, that the culture and values of a New Order would rise once Africans were free to guide their own development and progress as a race.

In all these theories, and in his more general efforts to devise a formula for the mental emancipation of the oppressed, Lembede was groping toward a concept of cultural nationalism which, had it taken hold among the intellectuals of the Youth League generation, would have represented a highly significant innovation in the development of black South African political thought. As it turned out, Lembede's concern with the process of cultural change, like his concept of the "African spirit," did not make a lasting imprint on the thinking of most of his intellectual contemporaries. Although some in the Youth League did occasionally lapse into Lembedesque language in later years, especially in invoking the injunction against "wholesale borrowing and importing of foreign ideologies into Africa"—a reference to communism, which Lembede had always opposed as alien to Africa—it seems clear that on the whole, most of Lembede's colleagues were decidedly uninterested in what many felt was the luxury of his abstract speculations on culture.

Lembede's interest in rediscovering and emphasizing indigenous African culture and values represented a break with the white-oriented perspectives which had dominated the thinking of most African intellectuals up to his time, and it was perhaps not surprising that very few were willing to venture

25. *Congress Youth League Manifesto,* in Karis and Carter, vol. 2.

into the new ideological territory which Lembede was attempting to pioneer. The disillusionment brought on by the downgrading of the African franchise in 1936 and by the failure of the government to fulfill its promises of the early war period had bred a spirit of new militance in African intellectuals, but had fallen short of destroying their ingrained attitude toward cultural assimilation. No matter how insistent Africans might be that civilization was the heritage of all mankind, and that it had no "color," the assumption was still firmly lodged in their minds that progress meant the one-way absorption by Africans of modern, or western, or "white" patterns of culture. That integrationist goals still exercised a strong hold on Lembede's Youth League contemporaries is clear from the thinking of as radical a nationalist as A. P. Mda, who in August 1944 wrote a piece in *The Bantu World* attacking the white cliché that Africans should be discouraged from "running before they had even learned to crawl." "It is wrong," wrote Mda,

> to measure human progress by adopting the comparative method. It is wrong to say, for instance, that it took the Europeans 2000 years to assimilate, build up and develop Western civilization, and therefore the Africans should go through a like process. . . . The present day standards of civilization are the culmination of a long process of development. But *that a "standard civilization" has been attained today is an evident fact. The question, therefore, is not whether the Bantu should develop a new civilization. The question is whether or not the Bantu are capable of assimilating Western civilization upon the background of their historic past.* The question is one of "capacity" rather than one of "rate." I argue that the Bantu, in common with other peoples of the earth supposed to be primitive, have an infinite capacity for assimilating "any" civilization at "any" rate, provided that they are given the proper environment. . . . The meteoric rise of Japanese power, the almost phenomenal advancement of the American Negro, and the still more spectacular progress of the primitive peoples in the Soviet Union, should remove any lingering doubts as to the correctness of my assumptions.[26]

26. *The Bantu World,* 12 August, 1944. Emphasis added. Mbata recalls that the early Youth Leaguers had no strong feeling that contradictions might arise between western culture and the culture of a free, predominantly African-run South Africa (interview).

The notion toward which Lembede was moving, that Africans too had a culture, which was different from European culture yet equally valid as an expression of human values, was not a concept that could easily displace the resilent assimilationist dream. Educated Africans still thought almost exclusively of proving their worth in terms of the wholesale pursuit of "white" methods, skills, standards and values. Once the Afrikaners began to make good on their threat to use the African education system to "keep the Bantu essentially Bantu" in the 1950s, many educated Africans were to cling all the more stubbornly to the goal of cultural integration. Only with the emergence of independent Africa and the formulation of sophisticated new "black" philosophies in America and the Third World in the 1960s were historical and intellectual currents to gather sufficient momentum to break through the bulwarks of assimilationist thinking.

Who Owns South Africa?

When the Youth League ideologues left culture aside and came to the more directly political sphere, they were again beset by conflicts of emotion against intellect, and "rebel" impulses against "realist" perspectives inherited from the preceding generation. In defining the content of African nationalism, Lembede and the League had clearly moved beyond the conception of nationalism held by the ANC's old guard, for whom the "building of a nation" still carried only the limited connotation of eliminating divisive tribal loyalties. The Youth Leaguers too were dedicated to burying tribal parochialism and creating a sense of one ethnically homogeneous African "nation," but they did not stop, as did most older Congress leaders, at the anomalous concept of a nation within a nation. They went on to assert, albeit in language which was sometimes tinged with doubt, that Africans comprised not a nation within the boundaries of South Africa, but in fact were, by right of indigenous origins and preponderant numbers, the nation, and the only nation, entitled to claim and to rule South Africa.

"The starting point of African Nationalism is the historical or even pre-historical position," declared the Youth League *Basic Policy* of 1948:

> Africa was, has been and still is the Blackman's continent. The Europeans, who have carved up and divided Africa among themselves, dispossessed by force of arms the rightful owners of the land—the children of the soil. . . . Although conquered and subjugated, the Africans have not given up, and they will never give up their claim and title to Africa. The fact that their land has been taken and their rights whittled down does not take away or remove their right to the land of their forefathers.[27]

Such forthright assertion of the Africans' right to ownership of Africa had scarcely been heard in the ANC since the brief intoxication of some elements with Garveyism in the 1920s.[28] The implications were revolutionary: if Africans were the rightful owners of the country, whites would have to be made to vacate the seats of power and relinquish what they had stolen.

Action for the achievement of African rights was the League's incessant demand. But action to achieve what concrete political goals? If Africans were South Africa's rightful rulers, what place would there be for whites in a future political order? When it came to putting on record any aims less vague than "true democracy" or "national freedom," the Youth Leaguers, and even the brash Lembede himself, seem to have found it difficult to maintain the same tenor of radical thinking. Even the League's slogan of "Africa for the Africans," revived from Garveyist days, was usually asserted with the modifying amendment of "Africans for humanity, and humanity for God." The limited number of public references to specific objectives in the League's public statements in fact suggest that its leaders' underlying conception of political change still revolved around ideas of reforming, rather than totally scrapping, South Africa's existing system for the distribution of power. Like leaders of older political generations,

27. "Basic Policy of Congress Youth League," 1948, reproduced in Karis and Carter, vol. 2, pp. 323–31.
28. The best account of Garveyist influences in South Africa appears in Walshe, *The Rise of African Nationalism*, pp. 163–69.

they appear to have conceived of change primarily in terms of the extension of rights to Africans, not in terms of an African seizure of power which would result in turning the tables on whites. Two conditions, declared the Youth League *Basic Policy* of 1948, were necessary for "the achievement of true democracy": the "removal of discriminatory laws and color bars," and admission of the African into "full citizenship of the country so that he has direct representation in parliament on a democratic basis." "Self-government," Ngubane had written earlier, could not mean the same thing to an African in West Africa and in the Union, where whites had come to stay. To the African in South Africa, he wrote,

> self-government . . . means sitting side by side with the white-man in Parliament, in the Cabinet, on the Bench and in every aspect of South African life. It means the acceptance of the African as an equal partner . . . in the business of the State.[29]

Expressing a far more radical view, however, was a letter written several years later by Joe Matthews of the Fort Hare Youth League and published in Ngubane's paper, *Inkundla ya Bantu.* "We are not asking for a greater share to be given to the African in the running of the country," he wrote. "We are without apologies going to fight for a S.A. which will be ruled by the majority i.e. by the Africans. We intend to struggle for a return of sovereignty to the rightful owners of the country. . . . Young men and women at college," he continued, must begin therefore to "see themselves as part of a national army preparing themselves for their destiny which is to rule this country and indeed the continent."[30]

When Youth Leaguers were confronted with the question of what place whites ought to occupy in an ideal future South African society, detached rational considerations clashed in their minds with deep-rooted emotional reactions to white domination. On the one hand, there was a generous tendency to suppose that whites might ultimately be forced or persuaded

29. *Inkundla ya Bantu,* 18 September 1944.
30. J. G. Matthews, "The Significance of the African Nationalist Programme," *Inkundla ya Bantu,* 5 November 1949.

by Africans to accept the principle of equality and partnership, or even the logic of eventual African majority rule. According to this perspective, white prejudices were not hopelessly immutable but were as subject as any other attitudes to the conditioning forces of reason, law, morality and changing evaluations of self-interest. No necessary and ineradicable connection existed between whites as humans of a certain physical type and the particular attitudes evidenced, however universally, by white South Africans. It was possible, therefore, to dissociate people from their attitudes and see the struggle as one not against whites as such but against white domination.

Alongside and in conflict with this optimism stood the more pessimistic and emotional judgment that whites were somehow inherently evil in their intentions and behavior toward Africans—an evaluation which occurred repeatedly in Youth League literature of this period, often in conjunction with contradictory implied predictions of future racial reconciliation. In this more pessimistic outlook, all white motives were regarded with the utmost suspicion, the historical record of whites in South Africa was characterized with the most damning of epithets, and even the efforts of liberals stood condemned as an eyewash to deceive the outside world and lull Africans into a false sense of hope. Describing such views, which were most often voiced by the more radical nationalists like Lembede, Ngubane noted in 1944 that

> the progressive decline of living conditions for the African has given rise to feelings of great suspicions of the Whiteman's motives. Poor health services, low wages, shortage of land for Africans, the color bar, inferior education and the consistent assertion of White superiority over the African in every aspect of life are all regarded as one huge plan to undermine the African's resistance to disease, weaken his will to be free and are, therefore, an indirect attempt to exterminate the African people with a view to making South Africa a hundred percent Whiteman's country.[31]

If whites had proven themselves to be as destructive, evil and duplicitous over the course of nearly three hundred years as

31. J. Ngubane ["Twana"], *Inkundla ya Bantu,* 17 July 1944.

this view suggested, what reasonable hope could there be of finding a place for them in a future just society?

These conflicting opinions about the true nature of whites and the prospects for future racial harmony coexisted uneasily in Youth League circles and probably also in the thinking of many if not all of the several dozen individuals who comprised the League in its formative years. A certain degree of mistrust of whites characterized the outlook of everyone in the group, though a number were willing to modify their mistrust far enough to maintain that *some* well-intentioned whites did exist, and a few Youth Leaguers with leftwing connections (David Bopape and William Nkomo, for example), even favored open cooperation with whites who had demonstrated their commitment to the cause of equality. Others in the League, typified by Ngubane at this period of his own political development, took the position that "good" whites existed but had to be excluded from participation in the struggle in order that the African could build up his spirit of self-reliance. Once the African had put his political and psychological "house" in order, according to this view, he could go out to meet his white sympathizers from a position of strength and could work with them to iron out the details of a future egalitarian order. Finally, among the full-fledged "rebels" in the League were those, including Lembede, who scorned the entire notion of "good" whites as irrelevant and harmful to the nationalist cause. Liberal whites, they argued, had been responsible for stifling the spirit of a self-reliant nationalism among Africans for generations; any concession to or association with liberals was, therefore, a flirtation with the enemy, however well-motivated or "friendly" that enemy might believe himself to be. After freedom, any whites who accepted an African government could stay in South Africa; those who rejected majority rule could leave.

Given this variety of viewpoints it is not surprising that the framers of the League's official policy statements were often compelled to resort to ambiguities and compromises. Taking the position that "good" whites existed but exercised no significant influence, the *Basic Policy* of 1948 declared:

The majority of Europeans share the spoils of white domination in this country. They have a vested interest in the exploitative caste society of South Africa. A few of them love Justice and condemn racial oppression, but their voice is negligible, and in the last analysis counts for nothing. In their struggle for freedom the Africans will be wasting their time and deflecting their forces if they look up to the Europeans either for inspiration or for help.

Coming out more explicitly against the extreme nationalist position, but still vague on the precise future legal status of whites, the *Basic Policy* went on to assert in a key passage,

Now it must be noted that there are two streams of African Nationalism. One centres round Marcus Garvey's slogan "Africa for the Africans." It is based on the "Quit Africa" slogan and on the cry "Hurl the Whiteman to the sea." This brand of African Nationalism is extreme and ultra-revolutionary. There is another stream . . .(Africanism) which is moderate, and which the Congress Youth League professes. We of the Youth League take account of the concrete situation in South Africa and realize that the different racial groups have come to stay. But we insist that a condition for inter-racial peace and progress is the abandonment of white domination, and such a change in the basic structure of South African society that those relations which breed exploitation and human misery disappear.

"Africans could admit the Europeans to a share of the fruits of Africa" after freedom, said the *Basic Policy* in an earlier passage, on the condition that "the Europeans completely abandon their domination of Africa . . . agree to an equitable and proportionate re-division of the land . . . [and] assist in establishing a free peoples democracy in South Africa in particular and Africa in general."[32]

A number of practical considerations must have contributed to the ambiguity regarding whites that emerges from these statements. Firstly, there was undoubtedly a feeling that it was unnecessary and even unwise to be too specific about the nature of an ideal future society when the major task at hand was

32. "Basic Policy of Congress Youth League," in Karis and Carter, vol. 2.

simply to get Africans united and moving toward action. A cordial relationship with older Congress leaders was also important to the League, and too radical a stand on issues of little immediate urgency could easily have upset what was usually at best a delicate truce with the senior ANC. Lastly, it seems doubtful that educated Africans giving unemotional consideration to the future in the 1940s would have been likely to feel confident about the possibility of South Africa's government and economy being managed without whites. Of all the territories of black Africa, only Liberia and Ethiopia were then self-governing, and it was common for the backwardness of these two countries to be pointed out in South Africa media. Looking elsewhere in the world, black South Africans could note with satisfaction the emergence of several new nonwhite nations immediately following World War II, including India and Indonesia, but models of modern independent non-European states were still few in number. The historical milieu in the 1940s, it might therefore be said, did not lend much psychological reinforcement to the proponents of black power; in such an environment it took a visionary with the impractical bent of a Lembede to talk publicly of hypothetical nations, states, and systems which had never existed and ask "why not?"

Over and above considerations of practicality regarding the role and the future of whites, compulsions of a more subtle moral nature contributed to the divided mind of many members of the League. Africans were battling against race prejudice and discrimination: could they in good conscience, and given the Christian ideals many had been taught to cherish, think of turning the tables on whites and of creating an order in which a white skin would automatically single out an individual as a target of suspicion and abuse? Emotionally, there was a temptation to vent feelings of bitterness and hatred against whites; but intellect and upbringing dictated restraint. Even to suggest that the achievement of equality for the African would entail a loss of economic and political status for the European could expose one to accusations of "anti-white" vindictiveness or desire for revenge—clearly sentiments which

were unethical according to the canons of black middle class
Christian morality.

Lembede's inclinations here were toward cynicism, and he
appears to have taken few pains to prevent his public statements being labelled "anti-white." From some of his opinions
expressed on the ethics of nationalism, it seems likely that he
felt that many accepted tenets of political morality were largely
the products of white propaganda. A nationalistic outlook
among subject peoples, he wrote in 1946, for example, was so
threatening to imperialist powers that they spent

> enormous sums of money . . . on propaganda against na-
> tionalism which is dubbed . . . as "narrow," "barbarous," "un-
> cultured," "devilish," etc. Some alien subjects became dupes of
> this sinister propaganda and consequently became tools or in-
> struments of imperialism for which service they are highly
> praised, extolled and eulogized by the imperialistic power and
> showered with such epithets as "cultured," "liberal," "progres-
> sive," "broadminded," etc.[33]

In Lembede's view, it was the African nationalist's duty in the
face of such self-serving defensive "white" definitions of
right and wrong to adhere all the more single-mindedly to his
own moral standards and priorities, which placed love of
Africa and defense of African interests at the pinnacle of ethical values. Africa belonged by divine right to Africans, and
they had died in their thousands, fighting against overwhelming odds, to defend this right over the course of three centuries. Having been brought up in Zululand, Lembede reflected
the perspectives of the Zulu peasantry for whom the memory
of white conquest was fresh and bitter.[34] If it was "anti-white"
for Africans to carry forward their historic struggle, then Lembede was prepared to be condemned as "anti-white." Some
in the League were in agreement with this outlook; others
rejected it with varying degrees of vehemence. Something of

33. Lembede, "Policy of the Congress Youth League," in Karis and
Carter, vol. 2.
34. Ngubane makes this connection in Lembede's case, and calls
Lembede's outlook a "heroic" one, typical of many Zulus. J. Ngubane,
unpublished autobiography and interview.

the ingrained morality of liberalism and the new moral perspective of nationalism probably vied for ascendance in every Youth Leaguer's mind and heart, eventually leading each to his own particular position in the ideological alignments of the following decade.

"Going It Alone"

The question of whether "good" whites (or "good" Indians or Coloureds) existed became more than just a theoretical consideration when Africans had to face the choice of whether or not to accept organizational support proffered by non-Africans. In the view of Lembede, Mda, and a majority of the other early Youth Leaguers, interracial cooperation was a stage which could not be reached until Africans had achieved a far higher degree of cohesion and self-confidence. Every racial group in South Africa occupied a different place in the social and economic structure and consequently had its own distinct problems and goals. Whites had an overriding interest in preserving their dominant position, and even other nonwhites had special interests to protect. In any joint effort between Africans and other nonwhites, each group would be out primarily to promote its own interests and would not hesitate to use other groups in pursuit of its own ends. If Africans were weak and uncertain of their own goals they would be the losers in this game. "As long as the African people are not welded into a compact organized group," wrote Ngubane in 1944, "they will never realize their national aspirations. When they meet other non-European groups, they will be an unwieldy encumbrance, serving the purpose of being stepping-stones for the better organized groups."[35] Once Africans had pulled themselves together as a community, most Youth Leaguers felt, they could meet the representatives of other races on a footing of equality and cooperate in specific actions where each group had a similar goal, recognizing that it was unrealistic to expect a

35. J. Ngubane ["Twana"], "A Nation Building Itself," *Inkundla ya Bantu,* 31 January 1944.

complete communality of interests. As Lembede put it in 1946,

> cooperation between Africans and other Non-Europeans on
> common problems and issues may be highly desirable. But this
> occasional cooperation can only take place between Africans as a
> single unit and other Non-European groups as separate units.
> [Complete] Non-European unity is a fantastic dream which has
> no foundation in reality.[36]

Not only did the Youth League reject cooperation between
the ANC and other nonwhite political organizations, or at least
oppose it as premature in the 1940s, but it also rejected cooperation with communists of any race on the grounds that the
ideologies of communism and nationalism were in fundamental conflict. Lembede argued that race-conscious nationalism
was the only creed potent enough to inspire Africans to action,
but that communists would always work to undermine
nationalism because of their commitment to the theory of class
conflict and to "internationalism"—which in practice in South
Africa meant subordinating African group interests to the
interests and views of the white-led Communist party. The hostility of Lembede and most members of the League towards the
Communist party was therefore unremitting. The Communists returned the dislike, using their press to attack Lembede
and what they called the "narrow" and "chauvinistic" ideology
of nationalism.[37]

36. Lembede, "Policy of the Congress Youth League," in Karis and
Carter, vol. 2. Unity of Africans, Coloureds, and Indians was a declared goal of the radical Non-European Unity Movement founded in
1943.

37. The Communist Party of South Africa, at the bidding of the
Communist International, had in the late 1920s briefly adopted the
ideological position that South Africa should become "an independent Native republic, as a stage towards a workers' and peasants'
government." This slogan was widely rejected by white communists,
and was dropped after several years. For discussions of this early
unsuccessful attempt to reconcile African nationalism and communism, see E. Roux, *S. P. Bunting* (Cape Town, 1944); H. J. and
R. E. Simons, *Class and Colour in South Africa;* M. Legassick, *Class and
Nationalism in South African Protest: The South African Communist Party
and the "Native Republic," 1928–34* (Syracuse, 1973); and A. Lerumo
[M. Harmel], *Fifty Fighting Years: The Communist Party of South Africa
1921–1971* (London, 1971).

The League Calls for Action

However uncertain Lembede or the League may ultimately have been about the precise nature of the political or social system which the future era of "national freedom" would usher in, they were in no doubt about the short-run requirements of the struggle: mass organization and a new emphasis on action. A concern with these urgent priorities in turn raised the entire question of the relationship between African leadership and its potential mass following. Among many older African leaders of the "realist" tradition, this relationship had long been perceived as one of elite advocacy and mass passivity: "the people" patiently toiled, suffered, and nursed their grievances, leaving it to their better-placed and better-educated brethren to represent their claims and complaints to the ruling authorities in the form of deputations, conference resolutions, and policy manifestos. Appropriate as this approach might have been in earlier decades when mass political consciousness was in an embryonic stage, it was a political style which, in the eyes of younger African intellectuals, had become thoroughly obsolete by the 1940s. The urban working class was growing rapidly, and small-scale riots and strikes bore witness to mounting African frustration over inadequate wages, housing and transport. A massive African mineworkers' strike in 1946, though quickly suppressed, proved that it was not impossible to mobilize workers. Wartime propaganda had highlighted the sham of white "trusteeship"; the people were coming of age politically. "Conditions were ripe for the rise of powerful mass people's movements," Mda later recalled. "Granted a new clear-cut outlook, a clear program of struggle, and the development of new methods of struggle, the African National Movement could make unprecedented steps forward."[38]

Because of a preoccupation with what he took to be the confusion and demoralization of the urban African, Lembede was particularly adamant on the need for militant ideology as a precondition for organization and action. In the past, he ar-

38. *The Africanist*, May–June 1955 (Carter–Karis collection).

gued, the masses had never rallied to the ANC, in part because
its cautious leadership had never offered them an appealing
program of action and had never even accurately embodied
their truest aspirations for self-determination. Most importantly, the ANC had never adequately preached a "nation-
building" faith—a faith in the Africans' own worth, a pride in
their past, a sense of self-reliance and confidence in their ability to determine their own future. This was what orthodox
nationalism offered, and this was why for Lembede, and to a
greater or lesser degree for others in the League, it seemed to
be the key which might unlock the "repressed energies" of the
people, freeing them for effective action. In this light, the all-
inclusive, non-ideological character of the ANC, often praised
by older leaders as one of its major strengths, appeared to
Lembede as a fatal weakness. Only when the ANC ceased to
run like an ideological omnibus, as Ngubane put it, stopping
"at every station to pick up all sorts of passengers," could it
hope to shed its ineffective leadership and begin to evoke a
response in the hearts of ordinary people.[39]

In portraying the ANC's deficiencies thus, and in prescribing nationalist ideology as a cure, Lembede was proceeding on
a fundamental assumption which was to mark him as an ar-
chetypal "rebel" and to link him closely with his intellectual
disciples of the following decade. This assumption, which he
seems to have held unquestioningly, was that the "natural" or
true instincts of "the people" were toward nationalism and
away from the liberal reformism of the African petty
bourgeoisie. Although Lembede apparently never explicitly
analyzed this "natural nationalism" of the masses, it emerges in
his writings as a compound of popular instincts which are both
positive and negative. Powerful negative undertones were implicit, for example, in Lembede's parallel between African
nationalism and atomic energy. America had just resolved its
conflict with Japan through the use of the atomic bomb—but at
what price in innocent lives? Might not nationalism, insofar as
it aroused passions of hatred and vengeance, also inflict suffer-

39. J. Ngubane ["Kanyisa"], *Inkundla ya Bantu*, 13 August 1947.

ing on innocent people and mean a subordination of moral to political ends? Such considerations weighed heavily with older African politicians of liberal inclination confronted with Lembede's demand that the ANC espouse an unabashed nationalism. It was wiser, they felt, to proceed more cautiously and responsibly, to address appeals to reason rather than emotion—and also to guard against the serious possibility that uncontrolled popular outbursts might set back the African cause by evoking still stronger white repression. Lembede's response was to dismiss such misgivings as excuses for cowardice and inactivity on the part of African leadership. If negative or destructive impulses among the masses were a danger, in his view it was the task of African leadership to transform these into a positive nationalism emphasizing the high ideals of love, justice, self-respect and unity. The African needed guiding principles which he could feel in his soul. Given heroic and idealistic leadership, his passion for justice could never sink to mere vengeance, nor his sense of righteous indignation degenerate into simple hatred. A clearly articulated ideology, appealing to the higher instincts of all Africans, would be the binding force linking leaders in an invincible alliance with the masses.

Whether the "natural" striving of the masses for unity and nationalist self-assertion was already conscious or still merely latent was a question on which Lembede was compelled by conflicting evidence to take an ambivalent position. At times his writings heavily stress what he took to be the abject and demoralized outlook of the urban African. At other times he belligerently took the opposite position—characteristic also of the next generation of "rebel" nationalists—that the masses were ready for action but that the leaders were reluctant to lead, hesitant to harness the people's pent-up revolutionary energies. The first view suggested a need for patient programs of political education aimed at gradually eroding popular ignorance and apathy. Youth League spokesmen occasionally did call for such a strategy of patient consciousness-raising, and older Congress leaders, hoping to tone down the League, often tried to encourage activities channelled in this direction.

Lembede, however, with strong support from some of his colleagues, resisted any emphasis on gradualist approaches and instead took the position that insofar as political education was required to arouse popular consciousness, it would come through action itself.

Experienced Congress leaders like Xuma, and A. W. G. Champion in Natal, while basically sympathetic to nationalism as a philosophy, warned Lembede and the League that it would be a great mistake to think Africans could "march barefoot" against their enemies; organization had to precede action or the ANC might weaken or destroy itself through impetuous bravado. A case in point was the League's adamant defense of a boycott policy toward the government's schemes for separate and indirect political representation for Africans. As the 1940s wore on, much of the conflict between militant Youth Leaguers and the ANC old guard came to center around this issue. Should Africans accept the Natives' Representative Council, urban advisory boards, the Transkeian *bunga* (tribal council) and indirect representation by a handful of whites in Parliament, or should they try to wreck these "dummy institutions" by boycotting them?

By the late 1940s virtually all politically discerning Africans recognized these forms of representation as ineffectual sops, but it was by no means clear whether the ANC stood to gain by trying to destroy them. Older leaders argued that election boycotts were bound to fail because most African voters would not understand or agree with their purpose, and that in the absence of politically sophisticated candidates for the NRC the Council would fall into the hands of acquiescent political "good boys." In the Youth League's view, it was of no consequence who occupied the Council seats or who sat in Parliament to "represent" Africans; not only was a boycott correct in principle, but if leaders would make an all-out appeal to the African electorate, they might actually succeed in wrecking these notorious "toy telephones." Africans were ready to act, Lembede told a meeting of the ANC National Executive in February 1947; the problem was that the leaders lacked the courage to lead. It was false to claim that the people were unready for boycotts. If an appeal was made, he declared, he was "almost sure" that 50 percent of the electorate would respond.[40] The ANC elder "realists" were unconvinced. The League's case for non-cooperation, they felt, was based on abstract reasoning, not on the here-and-now realities of African political life and the existing level of popular political consciousness. Not until the adoption of the 1949 *Programme of Action*—by which time Malan and the Afrikaners had come to power and the NRC was virtually defunct anyway—did a solid majority in Congress swing to the support of a militant policy of non-cooperation.

It is important to appreciate that when the Youth League challenged the Congress old guard, as in the controversy over boycotts, more was frequently at stake than immediate questions of ideology and strategy. Often such controversies masked, and only thinly at best, conflicts of a deeper and more personal nature between competing generations of African leadership. Thus in Lembede's writings some of the most vicious language is aimed not at whites but at leaders of the older generation, whom he derides as "traitors and quislings" to be "destroyed,"[41] "purged . . . forcibly hurled out and thrown overboard."[42] ANC tradition and African social custom accorded wisdom, deference and leadership to age. Not surprisingly in the rapidly changing social and political conditions of the 1940s, these traditions seemed obsolete to younger men in the ANC, many of whom felt themselves to be better educated than their elders and more attuned to the prevailing moods of politicized and action-oriented youth. The result therefore was often a struggle within a struggle as established leaders maneuvered to safeguard, and younger members to assail, protected positions of power within the organization. In the boycott controversy, the reluctance of the ANC's leadership to reject "collaboration" with the government became for the

40. "Minutes of the National Executive Committee of the ANC," February 1-2, 1947, reproduced in Karis and Carter, vol. 2, pp. 266-72.
41. *The Bantu World*, 27 May 1944.
42. *Inkundla ya Bantu*, 31 May 1944.

Youth League a symbol of the obsolete strategies of the older generation; boycott and non-collaboration became the symbols of youth's new mental emancipation from the outworn perspectives of the past. Whether boycott was or was not a realistic practical issue around which to rally mass support assumed secondary importance beside the question of the principles at stake—principles which were real, to be sure, but which at the same time served to bolster the rival leadership claims of a new political generation.

The 1949 Programme of Action

In terms of professional prestige and standing in African public life, Lembede possessed the essential qualifications the ANC looked for in its highest officials, and had he lived longer he might eventually have found himself in a position of authority in Congress from which to carry out, or to modify, his ideas in practice. But ill health plagued his adult years, and in July 1947 he died suddenly at the age of thirty-three of a cause never disclosed (and perhaps never known) by his doctors, but probably related to an intestinal malfunctioning for which he had previously undergone at least one serious operation. The period of his active participation in politics was extremely short, amounting to less than four years in all, and at the time of his death it was by no means clear whether African leadership would eventually be won to an ideology of more radical nationalism. The Youth League, while officially subscribing to many of Lembede's doctrinal formulations, was never a tightly disciplined group and included in its membership individuals of widely differing political inclinations. Lembede therefore left behind a handful of nationalist thinkers of his own stripe, most notably Mda, who succeeded him as Youth League president, but no well structured group of disciples prepared to popularize his theories or build them into the ideological basis for a practical plan of action. The philosophical threads he had woven together into a new and indigenous brand of nationalism gradually began to unravel again as African leadership pursued its uncertain quest for a formula which would end the harshness of white rule.

At its annual national conference at Bloemfontein in December 1949, the ANC dropped Xuma from the presidency, elected an energetic Youth Leaguer, Walter Sisulu, as Secretary General, and adopted a radical *Programme of Action* championed by the Youth League. These events opened a new phase in African politics, and brought the impatient mood of the younger generation to the fore over the doubts and objections of the Congress establishment. This coup by the Youth League militants left some important questions unanswered, however.

The *Programme of Action* called for civil disobedience, strikes, boycotts and stay-at-homes, and thus unequivocally committed the ANC to a new strategy based on extra-legal tactics, mass action, and the principle of non-collaboration; but on what specific ideological principles this new action phase would rest was not altogether clear.[43] The *Programme* pledged the ANC to the goals of "national freedom," "political independence," and "self-determination," but left these terms undefined. By 1949 all but the most conservative members of Congress were prepared to accept a platform based on the ultimate objective of one-man-one-vote. But by what political process and over what time span did the ANC hope for this objective to be attained, and what would be the fate of non-African minorities? "Congress realizes that ultimately the people will be brought together by inspired leadership, under the banner of African Nationalism with courage and determination," declared the *Programme's* final clause; but precisely what the content of that nationalism would be was left for each member of the ANC to define privately.

In later years the "rebel" group committed to a revival of Lembedist nationalism within the ANC were often to cite the 1949 *Programme* as a "nation-building" plan true to the principles of Africanism. The *Programme*, wrote Mda in 1954, had both immediate and longer-range "nation-building" aspects, the latter being directed at the gradual unification and politicization of Africans and the building of their power resources

43. *Programme of Action*, reproduced in Karis and Carter, vol. 2, pp. 337–39.

through economic, cultural, and educational self-help.[44] (Among the proposals endorsed in the *Programme* were the establishment of an African Academy of Arts and Science, the promotion of African business ventures, the establishment of an African press, and the promotion of adult education.) But if most members of the ANC recognized in these ambitious proposals of the *Programme* a commitment to the Lembedist notion of mass psychological conditioning for pride and self-reliance, the recognition was not made explicit in the wording of the actual document of 1949. In all likelihood, a strong belief in the primary importance of such ideological conditioning of the masses was confined to a small core group of Youth Leaguers around Mda himself. In spite of the *Programme's* endorsement of African nationalism as the "banner" under which the ANC would march forward, Lembede's belief that there could be no directed mass action without the inspiration of a clearly articulated "nation-building" ideology was not, by 1949, a conviction widely shared among most members of Congress. What mattered to most militants was that the conservative Congress old guard had been overthrown and its approaches discredited because of a demonstrated failure to produce results. After the 1949 conference, the way was finally clear for bolder political action, and it was for action—not ideological theorizing—that the ANC and its new leadership now geared itself.

44. "Comment on Programme of (1949) African Nationalism," a paper presented at a January 1954 Youth League training seminar in Natal (Treason Trial, documents presented in evidence). This paper is unsigned but is clearly by Mda, who was a participant in the seminar, according to the seminar organizer, M. B. Yengwa (Yengwa testimony, trial transcript, p. 17579).

4

The African National Congress in the 1950s

Apartheid Triumphant

The impact of racial discrimination in South Africa changed both quantitatively and qualitatively after the coming to power of Daniel F. Malan's National party in the general election of 1948. Malan and his followers were determined to refashion South African society according to Afrikaner ideals of racial purity and segregation, and at the same time to end once and for all any possibility that the country might ever move toward an extension of economic and political rights for blacks at white expense. During the first Nationalist government, 1948–1953, the rhetoric of trusteeship fell by the wayside as one repressive measure after another was advanced in Parliament and passed into law, sometimes with little more than token protests from the United party opposition.

Mixed marriages were outlawed in 1949, and the following year penalties were imposed for all sexual relations between whites and Coloureds (thus extending the Immorality Act of 1927, which banned sex between whites and Africans). The Population Registration Act of 1950 required the classification of all individuals by race, in order to make the prohibitions on race-mixing enforceable. Launching their massive plan to implement residential segregation in every corner of the country and to prevent the expansion of Indian businesses into areas coveted by whites, the Nationalists pushed through the Group

Areas Act of 1950, setting in motion the zoning by race of all urban areas in respect to ownership, occupancy, and trading rights. Turning to public services, the Reservation of Separate Amenities Act of 1953 struck down any lingering adherence to the principle of "separate but equal," making it legal for services to be discriminatory and removing the discretion formerly vested in the courts to pass judgment on the suitability of nonwhite facilities. Also onto the statute books in 1953 (one year before the American Supreme Court decision against school segregation began to move the United States into the civil rights era), came the momentous Bantu Education Act, prescribing tight government control of all African schools, with a view to the long-range implementation of apartheid. By removing administration and curriculum planning from missionary oversight, it was clear that the Nationalists intended to eliminate "liberalizing" influences from African education. New stress on vernacular instruction and the segregation of black schools by language group pointed to a longterm plan to stop the erosion of tribal identity among Africans and to substitute for the erosion process a calculated policy of *re*tribalization so that whites might better divide-and-rule. Finally, added to these sweeping measures for the reordering of society, was the Malan government's most ominous piece of political weaponry: the Suppression of Communism Act of 1950, giving the Minister of Justice a wide array of powers to silence critics and cripple extra-parliamentary opposition groups. To those who opposed the new direction of government policy, it was by no means clear how or when the Afrikaner juggernaut could be halted.

Continuity and Change in the ANC

The ANC entered the 1950s with its leadership divided among nationalists of varying ideological hues. Among the older generation, men of a liberal bent predominated, and there was a sprinkling of Marxists who had managed to balance their immediate loyalties to the cause of African rights with a longer-term loyalty to construction of a socialist order. Among younger leaders, distinctions between orthodox and liberal nationalists, Marxists and non-Marxists, were more difficult to draw.

Passage of the 1949 *Programme of Action* had taken a toll among senior leaders in the liberal camp, with men like Xuma in the Transvaal and the Reverend James Calata in the Cape preferring to lapse into inactivity rather than identify themselves with the aggressive new spirit of Congress militance. Members of the prewar old guard who remained in key leadership posts included Professor Z. K. Matthews in the Cape, Dr. Silas Molema, the national treasurer, and Dr. James Moroka of the Orange Free State, whom the Youth Leaguers had precipitously thrust into the ANC presidency to replace Xuma. The liberals were soon to find their most eloquent and popular spokesman in Chief Albert Lutuli, elected Dr. Moroka's successor as President General in December 1952. With one foot in the ANC and one outside stood the veteran liberal R. V. Selope Thema, editor of *The Bantu World* and leader of a breakaway "National-Minded Bloc" which opposed the growing influence of communists and Indians in Congress decision-making. Defeating Thema for the presidency of the Transvaal ANC in 1951 was J. B. Marks, the communist trade unionist who had gained prominence in Congress through his leading role in the impressive 1946 African mineworkers' strike. Also in the communist camp were Moses Kotane and Dan Tloome, both active members of the ANC National Executive Committee elected in 1949, and David Bopape, secretary of the Transvaal executive committee. After the Communist party was banned in 1950, African communists turned naturally to Congress, of which most were already members, seeing in it the best remaining outlet for their radical energies.[1]

---

1. At a national conference a few months before its dissolution in 1950, the CPSA expressed this attitude toward the racially-based Congresses: "The national organizations [i.e. the ANC, the South African Indian Congress, the Coloured Franchise Action Council, etc.], to be effective, must be transformed into a revolutionary party of workers, peasants, intellectuals and petty bourgeoisie, linked together in a firm organization, subject to a strict discipline, and guided by a

Finally, opposed to both the cautious reformism of the liberals and the white and "foreign" connections of the communists, stood an as yet not fully distinct faction of orthodox nationalists, the ideological heirs of Lembede. A. P. Mda was to remain the foremost figure in this "rebel" faction throughout most of the 1950s, although chronic illness prevented his active participation in organizational work from 1949 onwards. It was out of this group that the Africanist movement eventually took shape.

In each of these ideological camps, a handful of leaders was surrounded by a much larger number of less articulate partisans, and at the peripheries, each camp faded off into the others. While liberals and communists borrowed the language of orthodox nationalism, orthodox nationalists professed a vague socialism; communists employed the Christian idiom of liberalism and here and there a liberal might be found praising the colorblindness of communists. Among politically conscious activists looking for theoretical moorings, there was a tendency to drift in and out of ideological camps as first one set of perspectives and then another seemed best to illuminate the perplexities of the African predicament. To the casual adherent or even the member of many years standing, the ANC seldom if ever presented an impression of ideological clarity or uniformity, let alone dogmatism. Yet within its inner leadership circles ideological pressures and counter-pressures were

definite program of struggle against all forms of racial discrimination in alliance with the class-conscious European workers and intellectuals. Such a party would be distinguished from the Communist Party in that its objective is national liberation, that is, the abolition of race discrimination, but it would cooperate closely with the Communist Party. In this party the class-conscious workers and peasants of the national group concerned would constitute the main leadership. It would be their task to develop an adequate organizational apparatus, to conduct mass struggles against race discrimination, to combat chauvinism and racialism in the national movement, to develop class-consciousness in the people, and to forge unity in action between the oppressed peoples and between them and the European working class." *Report of the Central Committee to the National Conference* of the CPSA, January 6–8, 1950, para. 121, as recorded in the *Report of the Select Committee on Suppression of Communism Act Enquiry* (S.C. 10/1953), pp. 214–5.

important factors both in policymaking and leadership selection. During the 1950s, as most orthodox nationalists gradually coalesced into a distinct movement which would eventually break off as the racially exclusive Pan Africanist Congress, nonracial nationalists and communists drew together into an alliance around the principles of multiracialism—or "progressive" nationalism as they sometimes called their ideology to distinguish it from the orthodox or "extreme" nationalism of the Africanists.

Following an infusion of younger leadership committed to extra-parliamentary tactics, and under the government's relentless pressure to implement apartheid and intimidate all political opposition, the ANC after 1949 underwent a major transformation which left it different in size and character from the ANC of the prewar era. Its first nationwide campaign of passive resistance, the Defiance Campaign of 1952, brought a fourfold increase in membership (from 25,000 to 100,000),[2] and even though the enlistment of dues-paying members fell off again after 1953, the foundation had been laid for a mass movement potentially capable of affecting national politics through the force of organized numbers. In the public speeches of older leaders, shades of the traditional pattern of elite advocacy were still sometimes discernible, with African grievances being catalogued, followed by reasoned appeals to whites' supposed sense of justice and fair play. But for the most part African leadership reflected the evolution to a bolder style. The role of leaders was no longer seen as one of communicating to whites but rather as attracting and guiding a growing mass following. Timid attitudes toward mass action were gone, and in their place had grown a determination to use the power of African numbers—in strikes and other demonstrations of strength—to wring changes out of white South Africa.

New dilemmas of action and ideology accompanied this

2. Figures given by Albert Lutuli in an interview with Carter in 1953. Of the 100,000, 60 percent were in the Cape, he said. Leo Kuper in *Passive Resistance in South Africa* (New Haven, 1957), p. 146, gives the pre-Defiance Campaign membership of the ANC as 7,000.

change in the primary focus of leadership. Action had to be centered around issues capable of inspiring mass enthusiasm, and the choice of such issues—from among the multifarious selection being generated by oppressive government legislation—lay predominantly with African leadership, not with the masses themselves. Also confronting African leaders were ideological choices: what political principles was the ANC to preach in order to maximize its strength and insure its unity? The 1949 *Programme of Action* had proclaimed that the ANC would advance "under the banner of African nationalism," but precise definition of this nationalism had been avoided in the interests of unity. Lembedists continued to adhere to a concept of nationalism emphasizing race-consciousness and African self-reliance. To nationalists of the ANC mainstream, on the other hand, such an emphasis seemed perilously close to a black version of Afrikaner ideology. If they believed in "nationalism" at all it was in a broadly defined "South African nationalism" which was dedicated to the building of a united multiracial "nation" in which the equal rights of all races would be constitutionally guaranteed.

Like the nonracial nationalists, African communists rejected what they called the "chauvinistic" goal of an exclusively African state, not because they saw such an objective as necessarily immoral or unrealistic, but on the grounds that the ultimate aim—the overthrow of capitalism—had to be defined in terms of class rather than race. Constraints faced the communists in projecting their ideological views within Congress, however. It had never been easy for the Communist party, even in the days of its legal existence, to rally significant numbers of ordinary unschooled Africans around the sophisticated principles of Marxism; after the 1950 Suppression of Communism Act, open espousal of communist views became a crime punishable by banning, fines, or imprisonment.[3] Na-

3. Under the terms of the Suppression of Communism Act, it became possible for the minister of justice to ban any individual considered dangerous to the state. Banning orders were of different types, and could prohibit the banned person for a set number of years from attending meetings, belonging to particular organizations, writing or

tionalists were free to promote their viewpoints openly; for communists, no such luxury was possible.

Responsibility for defining the ANC's ideological position at the opening of the decade lay with its senior leadership, and in particular with Dr. Moroka, a liberal of the old guard with no flair for either philosophy or strategy. In a position of equal potential influence as Secretary General was Walter Sisulu, one of the original Youth League founders, but a man whose bent was more practical than ideological. In the Youth League itself, the semi-retirement of Mda after 1949 left a dearth of strong leadership at the top. The result was a period of drift and realignment in the ANC during which none of the three definable ideological camps proved strong enough to impose its stamp on the organization as a whole.

The Suppression of Communism Act, long threatened and finally passed in June 1950, had the effect of temporarily tangling the lines of internal conflict in African politics. The act did not stop at declaring the Communist party illegal, but went on to define a communist, *inter alia*, as any person who aimed "at bringing about any political, industrial, social or economic change within the Union . . . by unlawful acts," a definition so broad as to constrain nearly any form of extra-parliamentary opposition. There was every reason to believe that the government intended to use the new law to paint all African political activity as leftwing subversion or "statutory communism." In the face of this common threat, an instinctive solidarity arose between the ANC and the doomed Communist party, and the two staged joint demonstrations against the act at the

---

being quoted in publications, communicating with other banned persons, leaving a particular magisterial district, and, later, under new provisions providing for house arrest, leaving his or her own house at any time (24-hour house arrest) or from 6 p.m. to 6 a.m. (12-hour house arrest). Bans were issued widely from 1952 onward, and affected many leaders of the ANC. In 1969, the Institute of Race Relations reported that a total of 853 nonwhites and 126 whites had been issued banning orders in the period 1950–1969. See M. Horrell, comp., *A Survey of Race Relations in South Africa* [1969] (Johannesburg, 1970), p. 41.

time of its passage. The partnership was an awkward one, however, marked by mutual suspicion. White communists faced the prospect of becoming politically impotent, but were excluded on racial grounds from membership in the ANC—an organization which many of them regarded as hopelessly unrevolutionary in any case. Anti-communists in the ANC who had never been happy over the presence of leftwing elements in the freedom movement had now to face the likelihood that communists would try to increase their influence even further in those political organizations which were still directly or indirectly accessible to them. Thus, just when the government's offensive began to intensify, anti-government forces appeared poised on the verge of an internal struggle which might seriously set back consolidation of the gains made by the ANC in 1949.

As in 1949, when the annual conference of the ANC had left crucial ideological terms undefined, African leaders coped with the potential clash of ideologies after 1950 by judiciously avoiding the question and appealing for unity in action against the common foe. "I do not think we differ concerning our ideas of the aims of African Nationalism," Nelson Mandela, then a 34-year-old lawyer in Johannesburg, declared optimistically in a December 1951 presidential address to the Youth League; nationalism's aim—stirring but vague—was a "free, independent, united, democratic and a prosperous South Africa."[4] The speech was both frank in admitting internal conflicts and evasive about how these differences might be resolved. Some in the League, said Mandela, had suggested that the language of nationalism was not sufficiently uniform and that nationalism came in different "brands," but this was wrong, for fundamentally African nationalism was one:

> in any case the very nature of [the] national movement to which we belong makes it impossible to expect [an] absolutely identical approach. The very nature of the National struggle and the manner of its organization make it impossible to achieve what is

4. N. Mandela, "Presidential Address to the Youth League," in *African Lodestar*, December 1951 (Carter-Karis collection).

perhaps possible to achieve in a Party. African Nationalism has to my mind been sufficiently concretized and its aims are, for the present historical stage, clear. Any attempt to go beyond this might well be unconstructive and will merely [delay] the consideration of what our answer should be to the immediate crises facing our people. . . . Expressed in what is perhaps an oversimplification, the problem of the Youth League and Congress today is the maintenance of full dynamic contact with the masses. . . . We have a powerful ideology capable of capturing the imaginations of the masses. Our duty is now . . . to carry that ideology fully to the masses.[5]

Such differences of opinion as did exist, he maintained, were really over concepts of action—how to take the ANC's message to the people—not over the content of the message itself.

There was a note of studied ambiguity in this formulation, and it was a note which would continue to characterize the ANC's ideological position throughout the decade. The ideology of Congress could be seen as "uniform" only if the lowest common denominator of its political principles was considered and all contentious viewpoints were dismissed as minor side issues. For better or worse, in the interests of holding together its wide spectrum of supporters, the ANC had settled again into the same vague "omnibus" ideological position which had been the object of Youth League attacks before 1949.

The Legacy of Liberalism

In spite of the drastic adjustment in tactics endorsed by the ANC's 1949 *Programme of Action,* the underlying political orientation of most Congress leaders appears to have shifted very little as a result of the advent of the Nationalist government and the younger generation's brief fling with radicalism. The use of militant rhetoric, borrowed first from African independence movements elsewhere on the continent and later from the vocabulary of socialism, sometimes gave the impression that substantial alterations were taking place in African con-

5. Ibid.

ceptions of the struggle; in fact, however, the thinking of most leaders in the ANC remained close in most essential respects to the pattern set by earlier generations.

As in the past, Congress continued to state the primary objective of Africans as the winning of political and civil rights within the basic framework of South Africa's existing parliamentary democracy. The Freedom Charter, drafted in 1955 and ratified as a basic policy document of the ANC in 1956, catalogued these goals in detail, demanding for all citizens the right to vote, to hold office, to enter the civil service, and to be equal before the law. It also called for the end of all discriminatory legislation and for freedom for all to travel, own land, trade, form trade unions, and receive education and other social services on a non-discriminatory basis. Underlying all these objectives was the complete rejection of race as a criterion of worth, and the acceptance of liberal democratic institutions as the ideal form of government.

Also in keeping with the liberal tradition, the ANC throughout the 1950s continued to project its aims as essentially reformist rather than revolutionary. The demand for universal franchise implied the transformation of South Africa into a state where predominant political power would rest in the hands of the African majority, a transformation which would clearly result in a dramatic change in the status and fortunes of whites; yet ANC policy as publicly articulated never acknowledged this inescapable revolutionary implication of the demand for "full democratic rights." Instead, spokesmen for Congress at the national level continued to call upon whites to "share" power, to "extend" freedom, and to allow nonwhites to participate as "partners" in government within the system as it stood. The ANC's goal, Lutuli was to write in his autobiography, "is not that Congress shall rule South Africa, but that all Africans shall fully participate in ownership and government."[6]

At street rallies, local Congress speakers did sometimes declare that the ANC stood for rule by Africans; but a person listening to Congress speeches on official occasions would have

6. Luthuli, *Let My People Go*, p. 82.

concluded that power in South Africa was an infinitely expandable pie, big enough that anyone could get a share without having to take anything away from anybody else.[7] Typical of this cautious view was a resolution taken at the Natal provincial conference of the ANC in October 1955, criticizing a clause in the Freedom Charter (which at the time had not yet been ratified by the ANC) which called for the country's wealth to be "restored to the people." The Natal conference noted that "this phrase creates the impression that something will be taken away from someone (maybe the 'Haves') and given to some other person (maybe the 'Have-nots'). We would prefer something like this: 'shall be shared equitably among all the people.'"[8]

How literally any follower—or leader—of the ANC took these pronouncements of moderation depended on a great variety of individual factors, including temperament, experience and degree of political sophistication. The most conservative members of the older generation still privately conceived of change as a gradual process in which "civilized" Africans might be assimilated into the system at a rate that would in fact pose no genuine threat to whites. Those who stood nearer to the orthodox nationalist position—but who were temperamentally "realists" more than "rebels"—tended to see the moderateness of the ANC's demands as a regrettable but temporary necessity, given the weakness of African organization. The phrase "Africa for the Africans," for example, had dropped out of use, Joe Matthews wrote to a colleague in the Cape in November 1954, "but it is our slogan [still]. . . . We are only keeping the slogan in reserve whilst we build our strength. *Akuncendi nto ukuqwebisa ungaphethanga nto* [It does no good to be arrogant before you have achieved anything]."[9]

7. For the former view, see for example the police notes from the Sophiatown, Johannesburg, rally of 8 January 1956 (Treason Trial, documents presented in evidence).
8. "Conference Resolutions: Annual Provincial Conference, African National Congress, Natal Province, Held in Durban, October 1955," p. 1 (Carter-Karis collection).
9. Letter from Joe Matthews to T. E. Tshunungwa, 9 November 1954 (Treason Trial, documents presented in evidence).

Underlying ANC policy was a streak of political pragmatism which stood in pointed contrast to the type of heroic romanticism that had inspired Lembede to rhapsodize about pan-African utopias. In the perception of most ANC leaders, the principal arena of power was still white politics, and any strategy for African mass action had to be fashioned with this reality in mind. Although the National party was returned by white voters in 1953, hope still existed that a subsequent election might remove the Afrikaners from power. The 1950s, wrote Lewis Nkosi, a Johannesburg journalist, were "a time of infinite hope and possibility; it seemed not extravagant in the least to predict then that the Nationalist Government would soon collapse."[10] Most of the men in leadership positions in the ANC were sensitive to the range of racial attitudes prevailing among whites, and they naturally devoted much speculation to the possibility of a shift among whites away from the Nationalist hard line. If demonstrations of African strength could not force the government to make concessions to African demands, it was generally reasoned, such demonstrations might nonetheless succeed in swinging white opinion toward a more conciliatory stance. Testifying at the Treason Trial in 1960, by which time he had already considerably altered his assessment of political "reality," Mandela described his outlook on this question at the time of the 1952 Defiance Campaign:

> I visualized that if the Defiance Campaign reached the stage of mass defiance, the government would either say to the ANC . . . we will repeal these laws, we will remove discrimination and from now on everybody in this country . . . is entitled to vote for members of Parliament . . . or if the government refused to take this attitude, we would expect the voters, because of this situation, to say we can't go on with a government like this; we think that this government should make way for a government which is more sensible, more responsible. A government which will change its policy and come to terms with these people, and then they would vote it out of power.[11]

10. L. Nkosi, *Home and Exile* (London, 1965), p. 23.
11. Mandela testimony, Treason Trial transcript, pp. 15794–95. The famous case of *Crown vs. F. Adams and Others*, better known as the Treason Trial, began with the arrest in December 1956 of 156 leaders

Sisulu also expressed optimism about the possibility of a swing away from white extremism as late as 1957, when he wrote in an article that "as far as the Nationalist Party is concerned, any serious analysis will reveal that it has reached its high-water mark. There is no possibility of the Nationalists growing stronger than they are at present."[12]

Given this view of strategic possibilities, it became axiomatic that the ANC should retain its nonracial interpretation of the struggle. The ANC could not afford to antagonize any of the swing elements of white opinion if its objective was to woo as many whites as possible away from support of the Nationalist government and thereby eventually to isolate what was assumed to the minority of whites who were bedrock racists. If one rejected this concept of strategy—as the "rebel" Africanist faction of the ANC eventually did—then one could argue against the moderate formulation of Congress goals. But if one accepted the view that Africans had to win support from anti-government whites, it was then necessary to phrase African demands in terms that appeared to pose the least possible threat to white interests.

Thus Congress spokesmen, while endorsing majority rule in principle, often made a point of denouncing "black domination." All whites in South Africa might deeply fear democracy, but in terms of universal principles of political justice, they were really only justified in fearing unfair *domination* by others. This, the ANC was optimistically prepared to assure whites, could never be the intention of Africans. The argument often repeated was that Africans had suffered too much under racial domination to wish ever to substitute their own for the Afrikaners' version. "Democracy" and "domination," it was im-

---

of the ANC and its allied organizations. By 1958 charges had been dropped against all but 30 "first-string" accused. These 30 remained on trial, charged with contraventions of the Suppression of Communism Act, until March 1961, when all were acquitted. See below, pp. 106–7 and 173–74.

12. W. Sisulu, "South Africa's Struggle for Democracy," *Africa South* 1, no. 2 (January–March 1957): 31.

plied, were mutually exclusive since the latter had the connotation of coercion or dictatorship. There could be no simple
equation of democracy with majority rule; democracy implied
representative government and the guaranteed freedom of
all, including minorities, to enjoy not just political but also
cultural rights. "All national groups shall have equal rights!"
declared the Freedom Charter,

> All people shall have equal right to use their own languages and
> to develop their own folk culture and customs;
>
> All national groups shall be protected by law against insults to
> their race and national pride;
>
> The preaching and practice of national, race or colour discrimi-
> nation and contempt shall be a punishable crime.[13]

In keeping with its attempt to downplay a perception of
politics strictly in terms of race, the ANC took a similarly liberal
approach to the question so fundamental to orthodox
nationalist ideology: "Who owns South Africa?" Rejecting the
claim of Lembedists that South Africa was rightfully the exclusive property of its indigenous people, the ANC took the position that all races which had made South Africa their home
were entitled to claim at least part-ownership. "South Africa
belongs to all who live in it," declared the preamble of the
Freedom Charter, "black and white." "I am not prepared to
concern myself with such questions as 'Where have you come
from?' . . . 'Did you come from the north?' or 'Did you come
from Europe?'" Chief Lutuli told a white audience in 1959.

> It is not important. What is important for our situation is that we
> are all here . . . and no one desires to change it or should desire to
> change it. And since we are all here, we must seek a way whereby
> we can realize democracy, so that we can live in peace and har-
> mony in this land of ours.[14]

13. "The Freedom Charter," 1955, reproduced in Karis and Carter,
vol. 3, pp. 205–8.
14. A. Lutuli, "Freedom Is The Apex," an address at a public meeting
in 1959 organized by the Congress of Democrats, reproduced in Karis
and Carter, vol. 3, pp. 456–63.

From such a perspective it followed that the freedom struggle in South Africa could not be regarded in the same way as independence movements in other African countries. Countries to the north faced the clear-cut task of throwing off foreign rule; but in South Africa one could not speak of whites as "foreigners."

Ultimately, for men of religious upbringing like Lutuli, Z. K. Matthews, James Calata, and others of the generation born around the turn of the century, Christian morality was the touchstone of all political policies, just as it had been for most Congress leaders of the Xuma era and earlier. Of all the implicit ideological assumptions underlying the outlook of the ANC, this was perhaps the most firmly rooted. An aggressively anti-white stance could perhaps be ruled out on grounds of practicality alone, but more important to the genuine Christian—and there were many in the ranks of the ANC—no African organization could ever be regarded as *morally* justified if its appeal for support was based on the policy of an eye for an eye. Even those who saw no possibility of a voluntary change of heart and who felt that whites would eventually have to be forced by one means or another to grant rights to blacks nevertheless held to the view that for African political action to be morally justified, means had to be consistent with ends. As long as the goal was a multiracial system, and racial exclusiveness was the evil to be fought, it was the duty of black leadership to avoid race-oriented appeals so as to show all South Africans, and the world, that Africans were sincere in their desire for cooperation and reconciliation. This linking of means and ends was seen not only as moral in an abstract sense, but also as "realistic" because it took account of the potentialities for good and evil in human nature. "The pain of not being [an orthodox] nationalist lies in the cold realism of it," wrote Ezekiel Mphahlele, expressing well the sentiment in Congress circles.

> We are aiming at a common society and to prove that multi-racial societies can thrive and become a glorious reality in Africa. The black nationalist in a multi-racial context appeals not only to the

most dangerous, because corroding, element of human nature among his people but also to the worst hedgehog qualities of those who would like to crush him. . . . We who look forward to a South Africa with a non-racial society where there won't be any need for minority fears, appeal to the nobler element of human nature, even when we know that the white ruling class is far gone.[15]

Even for those whose political convictions had no particular religious foundation, the moral position of the ANC was an important strategic consideration. International interest in South Africa had grown considerably from Xuma's time onward, and the United Nations appeared to be a promising instrument for pressuring the South African government with the force of adverse world opinion. Whites might have the firm upper hand in power and material resources, but Africans could retain at least some degree of leverage in the struggle to the extent that they could maintain a moral advantage in the eyes of the world. Keeping this moral advantage in the 1950s depended on maintaining a race policy which was moderate and free of emotionalism. As Sisulu expressed it in 1959,

> Nothing has brought greater credit to the ANC in the eyes of Africa and the world than its steadfast refusal to respond to the vicious persecution of the Nationalists and their predecessors in the Union Government by a blind and irrational "anti-Whiteism." It has shown the African people to be larger-minded than, and morally superior to, their oppressors; it strikingly refutes the ridiculous claims of "White South Africa" about alleged African "immaturity" and "unreadiness for self-government."[16]

Two years later, after the ANC had been banned and almost completely crushed as an organized movement within South Africa, Lutuli could look back with pride and approval on these efforts to keep the race conflict free of any appeal to baser human instincts; in a candid defense of the ANC's prin-

15. E. Mphahlele, *The African Image* (New York, 1962), p. 74.
16. W. Sisulu, "Congress and the Africanists," *Africa South* 3, no. 4 (July–September 1959): 33.

ciples, he told an audience in Oslo when accepting the Nobel
Peace Prize in December 1961:

> How easy it would have been in South Africa for the natural
> feelings of resentment at white domination to have been turned
> into feelings of hatred and a desire for revenge against the white
> community. Here, where every day in every aspect of life, every
> non-white comes up against the ubiquitous sign "Europeans
> Only," and the equally ubiquitous policeman to enforce it—here
> it could well be expected that a racialism equal to that of their
> oppressors would flourish to counter the white arrogance to-
> wards blacks. That it has not done so is no accident. It is because,
> deliberately and advisedly, African leadership for the past fifty
> years, with the inspiration of the African National Congress. . . .
> had set itself steadfastly against racial vaingloriousness. We knew
> that in so doing we passed up opportunities for an easy dem-
> agogic appeal to the natural passions of a people denied free-
> dom and liberty; we discarded the chance of an easy and expe-
> dient emotional appeal. Our vision has always been that of a
> non-racial democratic South Africa which upholds the rights of
> all who live in our country to remain there as full citizens with
> equal rights and responsibilities with all others. For the consum-
> mation of this ideal we have laboured unflinchingly.[17]

Cooperation with the Indian Congress

The ANC's resistance to racially-based nationalism was still
further reinforced once it began to seek organizational alliances across the color line in the 1950s, first with the South
African Indian Congress and later with Coloureds and anti-
government whites. These alliances, made initially with the
object of boosting the ANC's organizational capacity, eventually also had a profound effect on the shaping of African ideology, for once the ANC had embraced the strategy of a multiracial united front, the adoption of any more racially exclusive
creed became politically impossible. The alliances thus

17. A. Lutuli, "Africa and Freedom," in *The Road to Oslo . . . and Beyond!* (London, 1962?), pp. 12–13, reproduced in Karis and Carter,
vol. 3, pp. 705–15.

cemented the ANC's traditional integrationist leanings and helped to close off more orthodox nationalist alternatives.

The South African Indian Congress was an old organization which traced its origins to the early attempts of Mohandas Gandhi to mobilize Natal Indians against race discrimination in the 1890s. Like the ANC, the SAIC had undergone a radicalization during the years of the second World War. The bourgeois conservatism and narrow concern with purely sectional issues which had characterized most Indian politics in South Africa since the days of Gandhi gave way to a new outlook in the mid-1940s as younger militants combined forces to oust the discredited leaders of an older generation. In both the Transvaal and Natal, the two provinces where South Africa's Indian minority is concentrated, leadership passed to men of radical inclinations, the most important figure being Dr. Yusuf Dadoo, a member of the Central Committee of the Communist party, who was elected president of the Transvaal Indian Congress in 1945. Under the leadership of Dadoo and Dr. G. M. Naicker in Natal, Indians began to show greater concern with the plight of Africans and to consider the possibility that Indian interests might best be served by making common cause with other nonwhites. In late 1946 the SAIC helped finance a trip by Xuma to the United Nations, and in March 1947 Xuma, Dadoo and Naicker issued a "Joint Declaration of Cooperation," a document which became known informally as "the Doctors' Pact."[18]

The real turning point in African-Indian political relations came in 1949, however, after a horrifying race riot in Durban in which 50 Indians and 87 Africans were killed and many others died later of injuries.[19] At the level of day-to-day relations, antagonism ran deep between ordinary Africans and the class of highly visible Indian merchants who dominated the retail trade of black urban areas in Natal and the Transvaal. Indians kept aloof from Africans socially and frowned on intermarriage to such an extent that it was virtually unheard of.

18. Reproduced in Karis and Carter, vol. 2, pp. 272–73.
19. See K. Kirkwood and M. Webb, *The Durban Riots and After* (Johannesburg, 1949).

Urban Africans, consumed with grievances and frustrations of every kind, found in Indians a ready target for their aggression, and the Durban riot was one result. The death and destruction of the riot came as a grim lesson to both Indian and African leaders that relations between their groups were in urgent need of repair. For Indians a double threat loomed. Not only had the riot revealed Indian vulnerability to the wrath of Africans, but the attacks against Indian property rights launched during the Smuts regime now seemed likely to intensify under the Nationalists, who had plans for segregating all commercial and residential areas by race. The logical approach for Indians on both fronts was to seek closer cooperation with Africans, who also stood to lose in the scheme for "group areas," and whose leaders, at least, appreciated the futility of making Indians a scapegoat for the whites who were ultimately responsible for African oppression.

In addition to moral support and potential diplomatic support from the government of newly independent India, South African Indians had two valuable resources to offer Africans: organizational experience, including expertise gained over several decades in the management of Gandhian passive resistance campaigns, and money. The value of Indian experience may not have been fully apparent to African leadership in 1949, but the need for new financial sources was urgent and clear. The problem of inadequate funds, never solved in the prewar years of modest Congress organizational effort, now posed the most immediate constraint as the ANC laid plans for implementation of the *Programme of Action.* Dr. Xuma during his presidency had often met the operating expenses of Congress privately from the proceeds of his medical practice; Dr Moroka and Dr. Molema were willing to follow suit up to a point, but the expenses of the movement were multiplying rapidly. If Africans were to follow through a policy of confrontation with the government, money would be needed for bail, lawyers, and aid to workers dismissed in strikes. Paid organizers were required if Congress was to build itself into a genuine mass movement. Meeting in February 1950, two months after the passage of the *Programme of Action,* the National Executive

Committee for the first time took the step of voting a salary to the Secretary General: the royal sum of £5 per month.[20]

The men in charge of day-to-day Congress operations were therefore in a position to appreciate the advantages of closer African-Indian cooperation from more than merely an idealistic point of view. Indian financial resources, while not very great in absolute terms, were considerable when compared to those available to the ANC acting on its own. Moreover, the Indian community, for all its comparative wealth, was so small—or at least so concentrated around the single center of Durban—that it appeared to constitute no long-term political threat to the numerically far superior African population. As the ANC gathered momentum in the period following the conference of December 1949, what might ordinarily have been considerable opposition to an alliance with the SAIC from within the more general Congress ranks had no opportunity to materialize. Organizational cooperation with Indians was a departure from African tradition, and some Congress conservatives opposed it for that reason alone. Some used the argument of tradition to mask a simple dislike of Indians, or pointed to the leftwing connections of various Indian leaders as evidence that cooperation would provide a cover for communist efforts to subvert the ANC. ANC provincial leaders in Natal, who had disapproved of the Doctors' Pact, expressed doubts that their followers would accept a political partnership with Indians.[21] But at the ANC's Johannesburg head office

20. About $14. "Minutes of a Meeting of the Executive Committee of the African National Congress Held at Headquarters, No. 2–3 New Court Chambers, 44 Commissioner Street, Johannesburg, on the 5th February, 1950" (Treason Trial, documents presented in evidence).

21. Writing to the ANC Secretary General on 30 June 1947, H. S. Msimang expressed the disapproval of the Natal ANC executive of Xuma's action. The pact, Msimang implied, reflected a spirit of cooperation only at the leadership level; Dr. Naicker, who had signed for Natal Indians, "represented a Province in which he had, insofar as my Executive Committee is aware, done nothing to foster the spirit of cooperation. . . . Our Executive Committee has refrained from declaring what it knows to be the universal feeling of the Africans in this

these arguments carried little weight when measured against the pressing need to strengthen ANC organization at the center using all available resources. Cooperation was a practical policy—and furthermore it was living proof of the ANC's utter contempt for the principle of racial segregation.

In late July 1951 the national executive committees of the ANC and the SAIC met and agreed to form a Joint Planning Council to coordinate preparations for a national campaign of civil disobedience. Representatives of the Franchise Action Council, an organization of Coloureds in the Cape, were also present and pledged support. The famous Defiance Campaign, modelled on Gandhian passive resistance, was launched the following June. ANC membership soared, and over 8,000 defiers, the vast majority of whom were Africans, courted arrest. Towards the end of the campaign top African and Indian leaders were arrested and stood trial together, charged under the Suppression of Communism Act. All were found guilty but received suspended sentences. While the campaign could not be counted a success in terms of its stated goals—the repeal of discriminatory laws—it was unquestionably the most impressive campaign ever organized by the ANC and served to forge its alliance with the SAIC into a permanent relationship.

The Congress Alliance

Having accepted multiracial alliances in principle, the ANC now moved to enlist support from other non-African groups, and by 1953–54 it had formed working relationships with the South African Coloured People's Organisation (SACPO, the successor to the Franchise Action Council), and the South African Congress of Democrats (COD), a small organization of radical whites. Launched during the course of the Defiance Campaign, the COD hoped to organize anti-government pres-

---

Province as it would not like to hasten a rupture within the ranks of Congress." (Papers of James Calata, Carter-Karis collection). Feeling remained strong on this issue in the 1950s, although the Natal Congress accepted the policy of cooperation after A. W. G. Champion was replaced as provincial president by Albert Lutuli in 1951.

sure among liberal-minded whites, but found its potential constituency divided almost immediately by the new Liberal party
which was established at about the same time. With its few
hundred members almost completely concentrated in Johannesburg and Cape Town, the COD never became a force to be
reckoned with in the context of white politics in spite of its
initial high hopes. Its following was accurately described by
one member as being drawn from three main groups: "youth
and students who are less full of racialism than their elders;
intellectuals who are more influenced by arguments, ideas and
appeals to principles; [and] white groups themselves
threatened by racialism and religious prejudice—so far mainly
Jews. . . ."[22] Since most of the COD's leading activists were
former members of the banned Communist party, its image
was distinctly leftwing.

Cooperation between the ANC and these groups increased
during the planning stages of the two-day multiracial Congress
of the People, which met at Kliptown near Johannesburg in
June 1955. The Congress of the People, a huge open-air meeting attended by about 3,000 people, took the form of a mock
national convention and those present voted clause by clause to
adopt the Freedom Charter, a statement of principles and aims
drawn up by an assorted group of activists from what by this
time was known as the Congress Alliance. Following the Congress of the People, a multiracial National Consultative Committee was established to meet regularly for the purpose of
coordinating the allied organizations with the activities of the
ANC. The committee met in Johannesburg and included representatives from the SAIC, COD, SACPO and the multiracial
South African Congress of Trade Unions (SACTU), in addition to those from the ANC. In spite of government bans re-
stricting many leaders, informal as well as formal contacts between the allied groups increased during these years, culminat-
ing in an intense spirit of camaraderie during the period of the
epic Treason Trial in the late 1950s when leaders from all the

22. "D. H.," "The Social Basis of the European Political Groups,"
Liberation, no. 17, March 1956, pp. 8–12.

Congresses sat side by side through years of wearying testimony.[23] Justifiably regarded as a unique achievement by its architects, this unity of action and spirit among the Congress allies made the 1950s the high-water mark of multiracialism in South Africa.

The formation of the Congress Alliance was remarkable enough given the animosity between all South Africa's racial groups historically, but it was particularly remarkable in light of the strong Youth League stand in the 1940s against multiracial cooperation and cooperation with the Communist party. Had orthodox nationalists of Lembede's stripe ever secured firm control of the ANC, their views would almost certainly have precluded any form of close cooperation with the South African left and, probably, with any of the political organizations representing non-African minorities.[24] As it turned out, however, the apparent Youth League "coup" of 1949 was followed by the formation of the multiracial Congress Alliance over the years 1950–55, an interesting historical volte-face and one which was thereafter to become the basis for much mutual recrimination among African politicians. How did this change of course come about?

In explaining the ANC's ideological development over these years, one must look for clues in the evolution of political thinking among the young "rebels" of 1949. For at the same time that these former colleagues of Lembede were moving into positions of influence in the senior Congress, most were also modifying their political opinions to such an extent that they eventually moved out of the bounds of orthodox nationalism and closer toward the nonracial "realist" position more traditionally associated with the ANC. This modification in their

23. Of the 30 first-string accused in the trial, 24 were African, 3 were Indian, 2 were white, and 1 was Coloured. Of the original 156, 105 were African, 21 were Indian, 23 were white, and 7 were Coloured.
24. Some leaders of the ANC have speculated that had Lembede lived longer, he might have modified his views and accepted cooperation with other groups and with communists, but, of course, the truth of this cannot be determined.

thinking was not a sudden development but one which took place over a number of years and which needs to be seen against the background of other trends in South African society in the early years of the Nationalist era. Analysts hostile to communism have tended to see this ideological change of course among Africans as the outcome of a well-coordinated communist intrigue aimed at capturing the ANC and turning it to communist ends, but such an explanation fails to do justice to the complexity of the forces shaping African political thinking.[25] The influence of Marxist class perspectives on key ANC leaders during these years was unquestionably strong, but communism's net effect was less to sway Congress from its chosen path than, as we shall see, to reinforce some of those elements in Congress thinking which were most firmly rooted in the Christian-liberal tradition. To understand the de-radicalization of the "rebel" generation of 1949, it is necessary to examine some of the characteristics of African urban society in the 1950s.

Apartheid and the African Middle Class

"The fifties were important to us as a decade because finally they spelled out the end of one kind of South Africa and foreshadowed the beginning of another," wrote Lewis Nkosi reflecting on his years as a writer for *Drum* magazine in Johannesburg. It was, he went on to observe,

> a decade in which it was still possible to pretend to the viability of extra-parliamentary opposition. While there was a fantastic array of laws controlling our lives it was still possible to organize marches to police stations, to parliament, to the very prisons holding our political leaders. It was possible to go to the same universities as white students; there were racially mixed parties enjoyed with the gusto of a drowning people; it seemed at the least obligatory to assume an air of defiance against Government and authority.[26]

25. See, for example, J. Ngubane, *An African Explains Apartheid* (London, 1963), and E. S. Munger, *Afrikaner and African Nationalism* (London, 1967).
26. Nkosi, *Home and Exile*, p. 8.

Johannesburg, of course, registered the changing national mood more rapidly than smaller population centers and was thus not typical of the political environment of the country as a whole; nor was the select world of writers, white universities, and multiracial social gatherings part of the experience of the average African. Yet this was the milieu in which the ANC's politics took shape because this was the world of its national leadership. Without some consideration of this milieu no balanced view of African politics in the 1950s would be possible.

At the vastly expanded level of local branches, especially in the eastern Cape where popular loyalty to the ANC was stronger than in any other area of the country, the years around the Defiance Campaign saw a notable influx of working class men and women into leadership positions.[27] At the provincial level, too, there was considerable representation by workers, though the men elected provincial presidents were almost always middle or upper-middle class. Where policy decisions were made, however, at the level of the National Executive Committee—from which the National Working Committee in Johannesburg was drawn—by far the heaviest representation was from the higher strata of African society, defined in terms of education and occupation. Of the 23 men elected to the National Executive Committee in 1952, for example, more than half were in occupations generally recognized as "elite": these included two lawyers, five doctors, three ministers, one university professor, and one prominent Johannesburg businessman.[28] In matters where administrative ability, financial responsibility, and articulateness were required, the ordi-

27. Women rarely held executive positions in ANC branches but focused instead on the activities of the ANC Women's League and later the Federation of South African Women, a multiracial adjunct to the Congress Alliance. The 10 African women who were among the original 156 defendants in the Treason Trial included 3 who were or had been factory workers, 1 domestic servant, 1 typist, 1 dressmaker, 2 teachers, and 3 housewives. See A. Sampson, *The Treason Cage* (London, 1958), and *South Africa's Treason Trial* (Johannesburg, n.d.) (Carter-Karis collection).

28. "Annexure 'C', The Annual Report of the National Executive Committee of the African National Congress," December 1955 (Carter-Karis collection).

nary unlettered African first turned, naturally enough, to
whoever among his educated brethren were willing to assume leadership. But also naturally enough, the leadership of
men thrust forward in these circumstances was as likely as not
to mirror their own perspectives and preoccupations as a class
as much as the interests of the masses of Africans they purported to represent. However broad the ANC's working class
support may have become during its decade of mass action
(and amorphous "support" is all one can speak of since formal
membership was never large after 1953), its ideological position remained nearly as firm a reflection of middle class thinking as it had ever been in the days of Xuma and earlier. But it
was a middle class now beleaguered as never before.

The policy of the United party under Smuts had aimed to
assuage the frustrations of more "advanced" Africans by offer-
ing them privileges which set them apart from the mass and
gave them a status closer to that of Europeans. The National
party, however, rejected all approaches to the African based on
the premise of eventual assimilation into an egalitarian common society. Instead, the blueprint for apartheid promised a
step-by-step closing off of every avenue of middle class
privilege left open under Smuts: exemption from pass and
curfew laws, freehold property rights in urban areas, access to
superior education through liberal mission schools and "open"
white universities, and the token representation of "qualified"
voters in Parliament and provincial councils. One general effect of this onslaught on African rights was to drive more well-
to-do Africans back onto the mass of their dispossessed coun-
trymen. The more rigid the ceiling barring African mobility
into the dominant society, and the more harsh the leveling
process imposed by a government determined to protect the
interests of its lower class white constituency, the more the
recognition of an identity of interests between all strata of
African society was bound to develop. African university
graduates were "like passengers seated most comfortably in
some first-class, water-tight cabins of a sinking ship; therein
enjoying the luxuries that surround them," Ntsu Mokhehle,
then a Youth Leaguer at Fort Hare, told the Fort Hare

graduating class in a 1949 speech, one year after the accession
to power of the Malan government:

> Other passengers are seeing how to save the ship and how to save
> themselves. Water is entering everywhere excepting in our in-
> tellectual watertight luxury cabins. Nevertheless the ship is sink-
> ing. Our African National and Continental ship is sinking in the
> stormy sea of politics. It is high time the African intellectuals
> came out of their intellectual luxury cabins—for the ship does
> not only sink with the "red natives" . . . as we seem to think; it is
> sinking with us—illiterates and graduates alike.[29]

Looking up to white authority had failed to bring fulfillment
for the African middle class; the only alternative was now to
look down in the hope that the dispossessed masses might lend
their strength to the struggle for racial equality.

Neither the elite's new-found community of interest with
lower class Africans nor the resentment of Afrikaner cruelty
altered a fundamental psychological feature of the African
predicament, however: all standards of achievement, status,
and worth in South Africa were standards imposed or inherited from the dominant society of whites. Exploitation and
discrimination might bring the African to hate all whites as
oppressors, but at the same time, for almost any African who
had given up traditional ways in favor of a modern life-style,
self-esteem was inextricably bound up with the successful ac-
quisition of white culture—in every aspect from material possessions and occupational skills through forms of etiquette and
leisure pastimes. Much or all of the prestige accorded to well-
educated or wealthy Africans by their communities was recognition of their success in becoming "like whites." And ultimately (as a reading of African news media throughout this
period confirms), the most prized source of prestige and esteem was the recognition of African worth and achievement *by*
whites themselves.[30]

---

29. N. Mokhehle, "A Sinking Ship," reproduced in *The Commentator*
(Lesotho), July 1968, p. 15.
30. Brandel-Syrier, studying the elite of African society in a Reef
township in the late 1950s and early 1960s, observed that: "The elite
were frequently described as 'those who, at social functions, can be

Against this background, the importance of the Congress Alliance can be assessed in more than its purely political context. Although smallest in membership of the allied organizations, the white Congress of Democrats served a highly symbolic function for those Africans in the ANC who were able, through personal contact with it, to feel at least some measure of the recognition and status denied Africans by white society at large. It mattered little that the men and women in the COD constituted a radical fringe whose views were rejected by 99.99 percent of their fellow whites; they were willing to treat blacks as equals, to mix with them socially, and to take them seriously as human beings. Such recognition by a handful of nonconformist "progressives" could hardly outweigh the burden of contempt from all the rest of white society, but it did have a profound effect on the racial perspectives of many Africans in the ANC. For many, association with whites had the effect of demonstrating that Africans could be just as capable as whites. In most cases, moreover, COD whites were free of the paternalistic air of *noblesse oblige* which had for so long characterized the relations of most white liberals with Africans. Contact with such people—an experience not generally available to Youth Leaguers of the 1940s[31]—proved to be of crucial importance for a number of important African politicians, including Sisulu, who later observed in an article defending the Alliance that

---

seen to talk with Europeans.' It was in such European contacts that the elite found confirmation and justification of their social prestige. But in addition, from such contacts, they derived much of the power and influence they could command. For, after all, . . . the Europeans were still the source of all privilege, and whoever had the ear of Europeans was assured of certain benefits. Other less-privileged and less well-connected Africans had to appeal to him to intercede for anything they needed and for any project in which a European could be of assistance. . . . In this intermediary position between black and white the elite could, therefore, command and manipulate a source of actual or potential power." M. Brandel-Syrier, *Reeftown Elite* (London, 1971), p. 105.

31. An exception was Mandela, who befriended radical whites and Indians as a law student at the University of the Witwatersrand in the mid-1940s. See Benson, *The African Patriots*, pp. 120–23.

most Africans come into political activity because of their indignation against Whites, and it is only through their education in
Congress and their experience of the genuine comradeship in
the struggle of such organizations as the Congress of Democrats
that they rise to the broad, non-racial humanism of our Congress
movement.[32]

Joe Matthews, another ANC leader whose early tendencies
toward orthodox nationalism underwent a marked change,
later elaborated on this "maturation" process:

As far as any young African is concerned . . . he first comes up
against the oppression which we suffer as a people, . . . and he
straight away comes up against various choices. . . . One thing he
learns is that he can't fight alone, . . . and I think that it is in
contact with politically minded people that you then first come
up against problems which demand more than the initial antagonism. The question of how did [the whites] get here? . . .
Why are we not fighting them? Where are the weapons? . . . As
these things come up, the political bodies or body which one has
identified with provides certain answers, which may or may not
be satisfactory. They may not entirely meet the feelings of a
person. . . . But then . . . you can't wait for all your misgivings or
ideas about things to be settled before the struggle demands
reactions. . . . As soon as you do that, you start coming into contact with those who are also engaged in these problems. . . . You
start meeting, for instance, people whom you'd never thought
you'd meet. You meet white people who say they entirely support
you . . . and you feel, well, I don't think there can be such whites,
but anyway, here they are. And then you see them being arrested, you see things happening to them, you see them banned.
. . . There are all sorts of factors operating: the political movements, . . . the immediate needs of the struggle, the postpone-
ment of certain misgivings because of the needs of the immediate
struggle, contact with people. All these operate to produce not a
modification, . . . modification suggests that you had a complete
set of ideas which was then modified . . . but this is not the case.
You start with one or two basic ideas: you have been clapped
[punched] by somebody . . . or you've just got a vague idea which
you have grown up with, in which your parents or other people
have said, "oh, the white people this, the white people that." And
that's all you've got. And from that you start to learn more, you

32. Sisulu, "Congress and the Africanists," p. 34.

start to build up, you start to understand a bit more and so on. And another great teacher is of course the reaction of the oppressor. . . . When you discover the physical forces at the disposal of the oppressor, this also has a tremendous influence on determining your strategy and your tactics.[33]

Thus however personal in some respects the motives of some African leaders may have been in seeking a political association with whites, other reasons could always be advanced in justification of the relationship. The tactical needs of the struggle seemed to require resources which only non-Africans could offer. "Rebel" attitudes were appropriate for the immature and inexperienced, but the exigencies of the real-life liberation movement demanded a "realistic" recognition of the need for allies. Multiracial associations where a premise of equality and mutual respect prevailed could be seen as a challenge to the government, moreover. The more relentlessly authoritarian the measures of the National party became, the more an attitude of defiance against all authority seemed "obligatory," as Nkosi put it, especially among young intellectuals. Everywhere, he observed,

> members of my own generation, both black and white, were beginning to disaffiliate from a society organized on a rigid apartheid design. We began to sense that we were being deprived of a profounder experience; a sense of a shared nationhood. Stories began to filter to the press of mixed racial couples taking part at University dances; of white youths from the rich white suburbs defying the law and roaming black townships by night, of new clubs and jazz haunts where free racial mixing took place on an unprecedented scale.[34]

All such mixing, in the minds of those who engaged in it, "assumed . . . the proportions of a vast conspiracy against the state,"[35] and stood as a gesture of individual self-affirmation in the face of white South Africa's crushing conformity to the norms of social segregation. A new and better society was in the

33. Interview with Matthews.
34. Nkosi, *Home and Exile,* pp. 40–41.
35. Ibid., p. 25.

making, and however microcosmic its size, it seemed to shine as a beacon, lighting the way to a better future.

The motives of the radical whites who welcomed the multiracialism of the Alliance were equally complex and included, like those of the Africans, a mixture of altruistic and personal emotional reasons. Participation in the campaigns of the Alliance gave the radical white an opportunity to strike a blow, however feeble, against government policies, to protest against an entire system outrageous to the sensitive conscience. It was an opportunity to make friendships across the color line, to lighten an onerous burden of guilt, and demonstrate to the scornful and unbelieving that multiracial cooperation in South Africa was not a utopian dream. The Congress Alliance, declared a 1958 editorial in the radical journal, *Liberation*, because of the "truly equal and fraternal relationships" it had established between its constituent member organizations, provided "an inspiring preview of the free South Africa of tomorrow."[36]

Africans who objected to cooperation with the COD were often to charge that whites had entered the Congress Alliance

36. Few can convey the emotionalism of the white democrat's commitment as well as Alan Paton. Writing of a student Christian conference at Fort Hare in 1930, but conveying sentiments which must have been even more intense by the 1950s, Paton observed: "Though white and black slept separately at the conference, they ate together. . . . On the Sunday morning there was a joint communion service. . . . To some it was the deepest experience of their lives; they could hardly control the tumult of emotions that threatened to overwhelm them. Spiritual and invisible unity is very fine, but visible unity stabs at the heart and takes away the breath and fills one with unspeakable and painful joy, unspeakable because glory is unspeakable, painful because it is all a dream, and who knows how many years must pass and how many lives be spent and how much suffering undergone before it all comes true. And when it all comes true, only those who are steeped in the past will have any understanding of the greatness of the present. The emotion of joy was all the deeper because all fear had gone, the white fear of the black, the black fear of the white, gone at the sight of black and white kneeling humbly before the Lord of them all, here in this very countryside where their forefathers had fought implacably against each other in the bitter frontier wars." A. Paton, *South African Tragedy* (New York, 1965), p. 125.

in order to convert it to the ideology of communism, yet this was probably not a primary factor behind the participation of most members of COD. If the Alliance provided a sympathetic forum—rare in the hostile environment outside Congress circles—in which white Marxists could proselytize for a class interpretation of the South African struggle, this was an added virtue of the Alliance for them, but not necessarily its main attraction.

The Congress Alliance and ANC Ideology

The transition from being an all-African movement to leading a multiracial alliance of organizations brought subtle developments in the ideological orientation of the ANC, loosening the allegiance of its national leaders to certain values and strengthening their allegiance to others. First to undergo a process of modification was the fierce emphasis on African self-reliance which had been such a mark of Youth League thinking in the 1940s. Looking back after the joint campaigns of the early 1950s, it seemed to former Youth Leaguers like Mandela, Sisulu, Oliver Tambo, and Joe Matthews, that their earlier insistence on Africans "going it alone" had been the product of an adolescent phase in their lives, reflecting a political naivete and a subconscious feeling of inferiority which they had now outgrown.[37] Equally naive, they felt, had been their rabid prejudice against communists, many of whom, subsequent experience had shown, were among the most intelligent and hard-working fighters for the African cause. Far from being an obstacle in the path of Congress, veteran communists like Marks, Kotane, Tloome, and Dadoo were among those who consistently contributed the most to the inspiration and organization of Congress actions. Older Congress liberals, who had been conditioned to reject communism as a philosophy but who had never been particularly affected by a

37. Interviews with Joe Matthews, Duma Nokwe, and Charles Lakaje.

sense of the ideological incompatibility between nationalism and communism, had long appreciated the contribution of individual communists both to the ANC and to the trade union movement, and through the influence of older leaders in the late 1940s, Congress had several times rejected Youth League moves aimed at expelling members of the Communist party. Once thrown together with African and Indian communists in a day-to-day working relationship, particularly during the Defiance Campaign, former orthodox nationalist Youth Leaguers discovered virtue in this tolerant attitude of their elders which they had earlier rejected.

Not only did personal contact with communists lead to a cooling of the hostility which a number of key Youth Leaguers had felt so strongly in the 1940s, but experience, discussion and reading also led some of them to begin to incorporate elements of Marxist thinking into their own perception of the South African situation. Missionary-bred liberals might wring their hands in horror over the excesses of Stalinist Russia, but where could one find a better example of the ravages of capitalism than right in South Africa? Cold war propagandists could warn about the Soviet threat to Africa, but what about the yoke of western imperialism which Africa at that very moment was struggling to throw off? "Today Ngubane and others talk of 'Communists' and all that nonsense," wrote Joe Matthews in a letter to an ANC colleague in Natal in 1956. "Who is oppressing the Africans in Afrika? Who has colonies here in Afrika? Who is murdering Africans in Kenya? Who is extending passes to our women? Who have made us slaves in the land of our birth? Is it communists?"[38] Congress reports began to be increasingly shaded with the vocabulary of anti-colonialism and phraseology borrowed from leftwing publications. The communist press, particularly the weekly *New Age,* anxious to make common cause with the Congress movement, easily filled the long-standing void which had resulted from the ANC's

38. Letter from Joe Matthews to P. H. Simelane, 14 May 1956 (Treason Trial, documents presented in evidence).

inability to finance and manage a newspaper of its own.[39] This service to the ANC, and the dozens of other favors, large and small, which radical whites on account of their relative wealth and influence were able to offer their African allies, inevitably created a debt which Africans could repay only by lending their support to the pet causes of the white left—the peace movement and propaganda efforts on behalf of the Soviet Union and China. It seemed a small price to pay and hardly constituted a commitment on any issue close to the immediate struggle in South Africa.[40] In other words, in the view of most of its supporters in the ANC leadership, the alliance was primarily a tactical, not an ideological one; it was simply a "realistic" effort to tap every readily available resource in the African's favor.

Where commitments to a future social and economic order for South Africa were concerned, the ANC remained firmly wedded to the liberal ideals for which it had always stood. It visualized a redistribution of wealth to blacks, but not an attack on class differences as such. It stood for a reallocation of land to give Africans their just share, but would never have countenanced the abolition of private land ownership. A controversial clause of the Freedom Charter called for the nationalization of mines, banks and monopoly industries, but this was seen as taking place within the framework of a predominantly capitalist system. "It is certainly not Congress policy to do away with private ownership of the means of production," Lutuli

39. Other regular communist publications were *Liberation* and *Fighting Talk*. *New Age* was the successor paper to *The Guardian, Clarion, People's World,* and *Advance,* all banned in succession under the Suppression of Communism Act.

40. In an interview with the Carter team in 1964, Z. K. Matthews expressed the view that communist-inspired resolutions on foreign affairs, made at various ANC conferences in the mid- and late-1950s, meant nothing to most members of the ANC and were regarded as a nuisance by many. Occasionally, direct conflicts of interest did become apparent. For example, according to Joe Matthews in an interview with the Carter team in 1964, at the time of India's border dispute with China, *New Age* took the side of China, embarrassing the ANC, which counted India as its staunchest international ally.

declared in a long written submission to the Treason Trial judges. "The African business community has a full place in Congress and I personally regard African business enterprise as something to be encouraged."[41] After an exhaustive effort by government prosecutors to prove that the ANC had become a communist organization, the judges were compelled by the evidence to find the accused "not guilty."

The issue of whether or not the ANC had become dominated by communists tended to obscure the related question of how membership in a multiracial alliance as such had affected the ideological stance of African leadership. In 1949 the Congress had stood poised between conflicting interpretations of African nationalism, the Youth League pressing for the Lembedist conception of an all-African "nation," and others emphasizing the traditional ANC policy of a non-exclusive "South African nationalism." Rank-and-file opinion, always highly susceptible to suggestion and manipulation by Congress leaders, was not decisive in resolving such questions of abstract principle. More important by far was the drift of mood and opinion at the level of national leadership, which in turn meant primarily leadership in the Transvaal where the Congress head office and the heaviest concentration of its important leaders were situated. Once African leadership at this level had, for the variety of reasons already examined, accepted the principle of cooperation with non-Africans, the direction in which the ANC would move in defining its nationalism became a foregone conclusion and the Lembedist conception fell out of favor.

Leaders of the Indian and white Congresses were, naturally enough, among the strongest proponents of the principle of a "shared nationhood." We have seen how the nightmare of the Durban riots of January 1949 pushed Indian leaders toward a policy of partnership with Africans. Among anti-apartheid whites the Defiance Campaign aroused a somewhat similar reaction. Rioting in Port Elizabeth and several smaller centers

41. "Statement Taken from Chief Albert J. Lutuli," Treason Trial lawyer's brief (Carter-Karis collection).

towards the end of that campaign showed that urban Africans were in a volatile mood which could easily spill over into anti-white violence. To those few concerned whites who made a point of following the internal politics of the ANC, there seemed to be a possibility that a racially exclusive and threatening nationalism might gain ascendancy—unless whites themselves acted to forestall such a development. The founders of the COD felt that their action represented an important step in this direction. The COD's significance, editorialized *Liberation* in November 1953,

> is not in its numbers—for at this stage it has not many—but in the fact that it kills the idea that the issue in South Africa is a racial one of white versus non-white. It is nothing of the sort; and the addition of an organized body of white persons who stand four-square with the liberation movements for equal rights and opportunities for all will serve to underline the truth: that this issue is one of principle.[42]

Five years later, after the Nationalist government had been returned to power with a stronger majority than ever and it seemed that all efforts to woo whites away from apartheid had failed, the COD could still argue that its support for the ANC had been productive because it had nevertheless "broken down, probably for all time, the exclusive and accepted Black and White camps of South African political life . . . and [had] also shaken the basis for the development of Black nationalist chauvinism amongst the non-European people themselves."[43]

In accepting the Congress of Democrats as its ally, the ANC was confronted from the start with the adamant insistence of COD whites that the struggle be seen as one of conflicting principles and not conflicting races. In defining "the enemy," Africans were expected to focus their hostility on the Nationalist government, never on whites as such.[44] If any

42. "The Crisis of Leadership," unsigned editorial in *Liberation*, no. 6, November 1953, pp. 1–6.
43. "Where Do We Go From Here?", Congress of Democrats, 1958 (Gubbins Library).
44. Controversy on this point came to a head at the time of the 1958 general election when the ANC, probably under pressure from its

African accused all whites indiscriminately of being enemies of black freedom, he was castigated by white radicals and by his peers as a "racialist"; if he raised his accusation to the level of a political principle, he was condemned in shrill tones as a "chauvinist" or a "black fascist." These labels were not applied facetiously. The radical white behaved decently towards Africans and knew in his heart that he was different from other whites; he expected Africans to recognize this and acknowledge it in their politics. If Africans refused to accept the bona fides of democratic whites, how could there be any hope for South Africa's future as a multiracial country? For the sake of preserving a working relationship which in many respects seemed so beneficial, Africans in a position to articulate policy for the ANC found themselves adopting a similar attitude of aversion to anything which might be labelled "racialistic." At the lower levels of ANC organization, local leaders and platform speakers still sometimes lapsed into the language of orthodox nationalism. At street rallies in the mid-1950s, for example, during the ANC's campaign against the removal (under the Group Areas Act) of Africans in Johannesburg's Western Areas, tempers often boiled up and sentiments of "Africa for the Africans" were sometimes expressed.[45] But at the level of national leadership, orthodox nationalism as a means of rallying mass support was a weapon which by the late 1950s had fallen into near-total disuse, and this eschewal of nationalist language at the top inevitably affected the stance

---

allies, adopted the slogan "The Nats Must Go" in trying to organize an election stay-at-home protest. The protest was a failure, and critics argued that, among other reasons for the lack of popular response, the anti-Nationalist concept of the struggle—and indeed the whole focus on white politics—lacked mass appeal. See, for example, K. Shanker, "Congress and the Multiracial Conference," *Analysis*, no. 1, February 1958 (Gubbins Library).

45. Speeches made by ANC members during the Western Areas campaign provided much grist for the prosecutors in the Treason Trial, who were hoping to prove that the ANC had advocated violence against the state. See the trial transcript, *passim,* and police notes from public rallies during the campaign, included in the documents presented in evidence.

and popular image of the ANC at lower levels. The ideological norm set in the prewar period by Christian influences and the weight of paternalistic white liberal opinion had been superseded by a new norm, set now by radical whites who openly espoused mass action but whose definition of political "reality" once again distracted Africans from making their own objective assessment of where black interests lay.

The Youth Leaguers of the 1940s had been divided in their feelings towards white sympathizers, sometimes arguing that a distinction had to be drawn between "good" and "bad" whites, and at other times denouncing all whites as obstacles in the path of African self-realization. With the establishment of the Alliance, those who tended toward the latter view eventually gravitated into the dissident faction known as the Africanists, while the main weight of opinion among Congress leaders remained on the side of cooperation, whether symbolic or tactical, with sympathetic non-Africans. Tradition, circumstances, and the ANC's customary pragmatism all combined to reinforce this rejection of the Africanist alternative. We have already seen how the traditions of Congress and the psychosocial strivings of the African middle class inclined African leadership towards a preference for multiracialism and integrationism in principle. In practice, even those who harbored some lingering doubts about the true intentions of whites and Indians could nevertheless appreciate the immediate benefits of multiracial cooperation; one could argue convincingly that the financial, logistic and press support which accrued to the ANC as a result of the Alliance were vital to its functioning as a mass movement. Added to these considerations were the opinions and perspectives of the ANC's partners themselves, particularly the whites with their deep-seated fear of racially-defined nationalism. As time went on, the pressure of all these considerations intensified until the principle of multiracialism itself, from initially being mainly a matter of pragmatic "realism," hardened into an ideological absolute to which each partner in the Alliance was irrevocably committed. As criticism from Africanist "rebels" became more and more strident over the course of the 1950s, the commitment of Congress leadership to the Alliance became more rigid in response, each side claiming that its position was representative of the true interests and aspirations of the African masses.

5

The Africanist
Movement, 1951–1958

Mda Inherits Lembede's Mantle

Lembede's premature death in 1947 deprived orthodox nationalism of its most prestigious theorist and spokesman, but by the time the ANC began its mobilization for the Defiance Campaign in 1951, the ideological seeds which Lembede had planted were beginning to germinate. While the national leadership of Congress in Johannesburg grappled with the day-to-day problems of planning, managing and financing a nationwide action campaign, small groups of nationalist-minded Youth Leaguers scattered across the country mulled over the implications of the *Programme of Action*, debated the issues raised by the ANC's new association with the Indian Congress, and confided to one another a growing dissatisfaction with the ambiguity of the ANC's ideological course. Drawn together around the pivotal personality of Mda, and holding stubbornly to Lembede's cardinal principles of self-reliance, psychological emancipation, and faith in the goal of a black-ruled South Africa, these members of the League gradually coalesced into a small but significant faction within the larger Congress.

Over the following years, the reaction of the ANC leadership to this Africanist group alternated between scorn for what was seen as its "armchair intellectualism" and disgust and alarm at its overt appeals to African race-consciousness. Indeed, the nihilistic undertones of this rebel brand of nationalism constantly threatened to rise to the surface, and had the Africanist group not come under the guiding influence of Mda, it would probably have failed to attract any significant support among educated Africans—which in turn would have spelled its early demise as a political force.

Mda had distinguished himself among his Youth League colleagues from the start as a gifted theoretician and strategist, and when Lembede died, leadership of the League had passed without dispute into his hands. Reviewed and revised under Mda's ideological stewardship, the ideas of Lembede took on a new luster and were rounded out into a more complete political philosophy. The closeness of Mda's friendship with Lembede and the nature of their intellectual partnership had always made it difficult to demarcate with precision the line between Lembede's ideas and Mda's own contributions to nationalist theory, and there were some in the League who believed that Lembede had derived much of the ideology of Africanism from Mda to begin with.[1]

Like Lembede, Mda grew up in a rural district and received his early education in Catholic mission schools.[2] Born in the African reserve area of Herschel in the eastern Cape in 1916, he had an early introduction to politics from his father, a shoemaker, who served in the area as a headman or petty chief. Accompanying his father on horseback to the local *pitsos* (Xhosa public meetings), Mda learned the rudiments of political debate at a young age and absorbed some of the spirit of peasant proto-nationalism which would later lead him to assert that Africans were the only true "owners" of South Africa. Both Mda's parents had attended primary school, and his

1. Mda in an interview in 1970 described his relationship with Lembede as one of continuous mutual interchange, with Lembede providing the major input from outside reading and himself supplying the main impetus in applying Lembede's philosophical abstractions to the concrete situation in South Africa.

2. Biographical data on Mda is drawn from his interview with the author, a biographical sketch in *The Bantu World,* 16 August 1947, and numerous articles in *Inkundla ya Bantu* by and about Mda, 1944–49.

mother, like Lembede's, was a teacher, it still being possible in those days to qualify as a teacher on the basis of a mere five or six years of formal schooling. From primary school at Herschel, Mda entered Mariazell, a Catholic institution in the Transkei, where he took a teachers' training course. Being short in stature, he experienced some initial difficulties in finding a teaching position and had to accept a clerical post with the Native Affairs Department at Sterkspruit, near Herschel; eventually, however, he was hired by a Catholic primary school in Germiston and moved to the Transvaal to take up that position in 1937 at the age of twenty-one. The following year he transferred to a church school in Orlando township in Johannesburg, where he remained for the next nine years.

At the time Mda moved to Johannesburg, the ANC was weak and divided and political initiative had temporarily passed to the new All African Convention which had been formed in 1935–36 to protest the downgrading of the African franchise. When the AAC met at Bloemfontein in December 1937, Mda attended but found the organization devoid of substance and inspiration. The Communist party also disappointed him, though he was attracted to the Marxist critique of capitalism and avidly absorbed the writings of the Russian revolutionaries. Marxism, however theoretically valid it might be in a European context, seemed to him to offer no solid foundation for black liberation in the South African setting. Turning to the ANC, Mda saw more promising prospects and threw himself into organizing for the Congress in Orlando. After Xuma became ANC President General in 1940, Mda's talent and energy gained increasing recognition and by the time the Youth League was founded in 1944, he was already a member of the Transvaal Executive Committee and thus a person of some standing in the senior Congress.

When Lembede arrived in Johannesburg to serve articles with Seme in 1943, Mda was studying privately to earn a bachelor's degree from the University of South Africa. Lembede had embarked on his master's thesis, and found in Mda the ideal testing-ground for his experiments in philosophy.

Where Lembede was primarily emotional in his approach to life, Mda was shrewd and pragmatic. Each found in the other a match for his own intellect and intense political consciousness, and together they formulated the basic principles which became the core of the Youth League's ideology.

From the time of Lembede's death in July 1947 until the passage of the *Programme of Action* in December 1949, Mda worked himself into a state of near-collapse physically and mentally in an effort to build up the League and give it an orthodox nationalist perspective. In 1948 for the first time, due to Mda's efforts, the League began to spread beyond the immediate area of Johannesburg and the Reef. Jordan Ngubane and several colleagues, after a false start some years earlier, launched a Natal branch, and Mda personally established a branch near his home at Herschel after returning there in 1948 to begin private study for a law degree. 1949 saw branches founded in the Cape at Port Elizabeth, East London, Cradock and Cala.[3] But the most important of Mda's organizing efforts during his presidency of the League centered on the University College of Fort Hare in the Cape, at that time the country's principal center of higher education for Africans. Since graduates of Fort Hare were the cream of South Africa's black intelligentsia, and Africans who were trained as teachers at Fort Hare later took up positions in schools all over the country, capturing Fort Hare for the Youth League was one of Mda's major strategic objectives. After making contact with Godfrey Pitje, a young lecturer in anthropology, Mda encouraged the establishment of a Youth League branch at the college by sending Pitje a steady stream of policy pronouncements and organizing suggestions.[4]

In November 1948 the Fort Hare Youth League branch was formally launched with Pitje as chairman and Joe Matthews, then a student, as secretary. Up to that time, the All African Convention had dominated political life on the campus, but

3. *Inkundla ya Bantu,* 18 September 1948 and 27 August 1949.
4. Two of Mda's letters are reproduced in Karis and Carter, Vol. 2, pp. 319–23.

after the establishment of the Youth League, the AAC gradually found itself eclipsed by the ANC. The resuscitation of the Congress under Xuma, the unsettling effects of the war, and the shock of Malan's victory over Smuts in April 1948 had all roused the Fort Hare student body to a new pitch of political concern, and the passive politics of the AAC could no longer slake the thirst for action. When the draft proposal for a program of action came up before the annual Cape provincial conference of the ANC in June 1949, and then before the national conference at Bloemfontein in December, it was members of the Fort Hare League who took the lead and together with Mda and the League's Transvaal leaders—Tambo, Sisulu and Mandela—most forcefully pressed for the program's adoption. What was widely recognized as a victory for the Youth League was also a personal triumph for Mda, whose tireless organizing had helped bring young militants to Bloemfontein in force, and who as a member of the drafting committee had held out against any watering down of the program's nationalist language or its call for strong action.

Mda took a spirited interest in the jab and thrust of political infighting in the ANC, but he also felt that the African struggle would be a protracted one in which patient and systematic building would have to take precedence over immediate problems of tactics. Economic forces, and the strategies adopted by whites, might be beyond the power of African leadership to affect—but Africans could build, and had to build, their own strength in anticipation of a future time when circumstances might tip the power balance in their favor. As Mda saw it, success in the long run depended on the laying of a strong ideological foundation which could eventually serve as the basis and the inspiration of a unified mass movement. He saw the Youth League as a means to this end, a movement which could attract young intellectuals, indoctrinate them, and send them forth into the ranks of the senior Congress as agents of orthodox nationalism. The Congress then, inspired by nationalism, would guide the masses to victory when the time was ripe.

Like Lembede, Mda was sensitive to the psychological dimensions of the African's plight, and he saw orthodox nationalism as both a way of defining the goals of the struggle clearly and as a means of mobilizing Africans to throw off their complexes of dependence and inferiority. In an interesting commentary on the political effects of mass media on young Africans in the 1950s, he observed that

the introduction of pictorials and monthly journals in which Africans feature prominently [has] revolutionized the entire field of journalism among Africans . . . [and has] struck deep into the social life of the African people in towns in particular. . . . These welcome changes [have] had an immediate impact on the psychological makeup of our people, more especially the youth. The resultant feeling among vast sections of our people [is] that of self importance. . . . This . . . fact has been of immense value. When people begin to realize their own intrinsic importance as human beings, they are on the road to full nationhood. It is only one little step to a consciousness of rights, and to an awareness of the anomalous position under which vast sections of the people are denied elementary democratic rights. No doubt the monthly journals and pictorials have served in no small way to destroy the sense of inferiority and futility which has eaten into the very vitals of our national life, generation after generation.[5]

Mda believed that the task of liberation would ultimately be twofold: first white domination would have to be broken; and second, the democratization of society would have to be achieved and safeguarded by the masses, lest an African triumph turn out to benefit only an elite. To insure mass support for an eventual assault on white domination and to insure that the masses would settle in the end for nothing less than full democracy, nationalism had to be fostered as a popular ideology—not merely as a set of values cherished by intellectuals.

5. A. P. Mda ["Sandile"], "African Youth and the Pictorials," *The Africanist,* May–June 1955 (Carter-Karis collection). He is referring to magazines like *Drum* and *Zonk.* On the "debit side," he notes, "these journals reflect a spineless liberalistic philosophy which lacks dynamic power and a creative drive. . . . The journals glorify the fads and foibles of the most degenerate classes among the Western Nations—the indolent, dissipated and debauched rich, whose mode of life and silly sophistications make no real appeal to the oppressed colonial people who are seeking a new way of life."

"The next twenty years will see the growth of the African Nationalistic Movement, and its increase in volume, clarity and striking power," he wrote in *Inkundla* in August 1949.

> In order to keep the movement constantly progressive and mass-based, we shall have to begin now setting our objectives clearly before the African intellectuals and the vast mass of toilers and peasants. It is important for us to realize that the tasks of the movement will not end with the winning of African National Freedom. In the course of our forward advance to National Freedom there will be created the democratic forces which will ensure the establishment of a true democracy and a just social order.[6]

A just social order, he had stressed in another piece in *Inkundla* earlier in 1949, did not merely mean the end of the color bar, for the legal abolition of discrimination

> might under certain circumstances very well mean that the African middle class joined hands with the European, Indian and Coloured middle class in order to impose further chains and to exploit the black peasants and toiling millions. . . . The African masses are their own Trustees. We are inclined to suspect those who talk of Trusteeship [of leaders for the masses] on our side, of holding out a hand of friendship to the European middle class. It has happened before in many Colonial territories even in Africa. It must not happen here. A militant and progressive African Nationalistic Movement will ensure that there shall be no deal among the African elite which will betray the cause of the Millions of the illiterate and semi-literate African peasants and toilers.[7]

The interests of the masses could be safeguarded, Mda argued, only by making socialism a goal of the nationalist movement. Nationalism should aim, he wrote in a later document known as "The Analysis," not just at "full political control by the workers, peasants and intellectuals," but also at "the liquidation of capitalism" and the "equal distribution of wealth." These goals did not differ substantially from those put forward

6. A. P. Mda, "Statement to the Youth League of Congress," *Inkundla ya Bantu,* 27 August 1949.
7. A. P. Mda, "African Nationalism: Is It a Misnomer?" *Inkundla ya Bantu,* 28 May 1949.

in South Africa by communists and Trotskyists (the latter being represented by certain intellectuals in the Non-European Unity Movement), but neither of these ideological schools, in Mda's view, had appreciated the indispensability of orthodox African nationalism as the inspiration of militant leadership and the essential catalyst of mass action. As he saw it, communists were shackled by their association with whites, and Trotskyists limited their activities to passive theorizing. Only African nationalists had the potential to blend correct theory and practice into a powerful alliance of leaders and masses.[8]

Mda's concept of the struggle was grounded on the assumption that South Africa was moving toward some kind of revolution in which Africans would forcibly seize power from whites. "The Analysis," while vague on just how this transfer of power might take place, put heavy emphasis on the need to build the African liberation movement with this end in view. The rural areas, Mda believed, would ultimately be as important as the cities in overthrowing white rule, and he urged nationalist leaders to consider the careful building of a "revolutionary basis in the reserves," and "careful cultivation of revolutionary leadership from the ranks of the [rural] intellectuals," elsewhere in "The Analysis" defined as clergy, lawyers and teachers, "progressive farmers and progressive traders."[9] In

8. Although contemptuous of the Trotskyists for their passivity, Mda professed an admiration for Trotsky. "I refuse to associate [them] with Trotsky," he wrote to Pitje in a letter dated 10 November 1949. "Leon Trotsky was a man of action: he was a doer, a thinker, a theoretician and an orator" (Carter-Karis collection).

9. Treason Trial transcript, pp. 9888–89. The story of "The Analysis" is an interesting one. A handwritten document of some twenty-four pages, it was produced by Mda shortly before the ANC annual conference of December 1951 which adopted the plan for the Defiance Campaign. Mda was in poor health, and had gone into political semi-retirement in Herschel to recuperate and to study for his law degree. According to a close friend of Mda's in this period, an outline plan for the Defiance Campaign was brought to Mda in Herschel before the conference by Mandela. Mda was critical of the plan on the grounds that it did not conform to the "nation building" strategy of the *Programme of Action*. He produced instead, and gave Mandela, a document outlining a general strategy for the building of nationalist cells of leadership in both the urban and rural areas. Harsher repres-

the cities, the growing proletariat was ripe for the message of nationalism. "This section is . . . full of a new militancy and an unbounded hope in their future," Mda wrote,

> But the group lacks a faith in its destiny, a mental and moral discipline flowing from a creed of redemption, a dynamic creative creed of nation-building and liberation. African Nationalism supplies this new dynamic creed and Africanism should provide the great intellectual discipline in their lives. The forces of genuine African Nationalism should create [a] powerful revolutionary basis in the larger towns first (in a few of them to start with) and gradually widen and broaden their influence. . . . Trade unions should be given an Africanistic orientation, and . . . the workers should be regarded priority number one in all industrial areas.[10]

---

sion by the government was foreseen in the document, and Africans were counselled to develop the core of an underground movement which would prepare for guerrilla tactics. Mandela reported Mda's plan to the National Executive Committee when it met in Bloemfontein, but the proposals were considered too dangerous and were never discussed in the open conference. The document was later sent to T. E. Tshunungwa, a friend of Mda's in Queenstown, with instructions to mimeograph it for distribution. Tshunungwa never completed the job, and when police raided him several years later they seized the document, which was unsigned. It was presented in evidence against Tshunungwa at the Treason Trial, where portions of it were read into the record (document T. E. T. 70., pp. 9887–97). It was identified as being in Mda's handwriting (pp. 11059ff), and Tshunungwa acknowledged the circumstances under which he had received it (pp. 18309–10). Mda was not a defendant in the trial and could not be questioned on the contents. Unfortunately, the original hand-written document does not appear among the Treason Trial documents on microfilm, so this account of the document's contents must rest on the portions, perhaps twenty percent of the original, which were read into the trial record. Pitje recalled in an interview with Thomas Karis in 1964 that "The Analysis" as presented in the Treason Trial was substantially the same as the presidential address delivered by Mda to the Youth League when it met on the eve of the Bloemfontein conference of December 1949. This speech, the original of which is also a "lost document," caused a sensation in the League at the time, and made a profound impression on P. K. Leballo, Z. B. Molete, Peter 'Molotsi and other Youth Leaguers who were later to cluster around Mda in the Africanist movement. Molete and 'Molotsi were high school students at the time (interview with Z. B. Molete).

10. Treason Trial transcript, p. 9889.

Considering the meager size and strength of organized nationalist forces in 1951, these notions of wide-scale recruitment of peasants and workers represented a long-range scheme more than an immediate plan of action. While Mda spoke in terms of advancing on all fronts simultaneously, in practical terms he saw the need to turn first to the urban intelligentsia as the potential cutting edge of a broader nationalist movement. Missionary institutions and colleges, and in particular Fort Hare, were producing a growing supply of intellectuals with no place in either white or tribal society, he wrote in "The Analysis"; liberalism had ceased to appeal to this group, yet it sought the "strong discipline of a philosophy." Nationalism was the logical creed to replace liberalism. The "Africanistic Movement must gain intellectual conquest of [the] African intelligentsia," he added, for from their ranks revolutionary leadership would be produced.[11]

Mda placed a high value on the development of popular mass leadership having the "correct" nationalist outlook, but he did not seek a high position for himself in the ANC after his retirement from the Youth League presidency in December 1949. He turned his attention instead to the cultivation of the nucleus of nationalist intellectuals which he regarded as so essential. His own personal inclinations were not towards platform oratory or marching at the head of protest demonstrations. The role which best fit his conception of the struggle, and most aptly suited his own talents, was that of the backroom analyst and strategist, the political tutor willing to sit through all-night sessions with groups of hand-picked disciples, lecturing and arguing for the nationalist viewpoint. If orthodox nationalism was to take root as a political creed—and as a positive ideology rather than a nihilistic doctrine aimed at "driving the white man into the sea"—the first concern, he felt, had to be the recruitment and ideological training of a dedicated cadre of organizers who could serve as the core of an ever-expanding movement. To these disciples would fall in due

11. Ibid., p. 9890.

course the work of mass mobilization—after the senior ANC had first been completely won over to a militant nationalism.

The Bureau of African Nationalism

When the Transvaal leadership of the ANC allied with the Indian Congress in 1950–51 and began to lay plans for a resistance campaign based on Gandhian-style civil disobedience, Mda was among those who regarded the new role of Indians with mistrust. The resolutions of the Herschel Youth League forwarded for consideration to the 1951 Cape provincial conference, reflecting Mda's suspicions, urged that African-Indian cooperation be limited to specific points or questions of common concern, and "that the principle of subsidizing Congress struggles by other bodies and parties be rejected in favor of a genuine Congress struggle based on its own efforts."[12] In the Transvaal at about the same time, a group of older conservatives, alarmed at the departure from the ANC's all-African tradition, had broken from the ANC and reconstituted themselves under the leadership of R. V. Selope Thema into what they called the "African National Congress (National-Minded Bloc)." The group was given a build-up by *The Bantu World*, then edited by Thema, but it gained no significant popular support and gradually faded from the scene. Equally "national-minded" but critical of the tactics of Thema's followers, Mda and a number of other "rebel" nationalist intellectuals decided to stay within the ANC fold, support the Defiance Campaign, and agitate as best they could for their position by publishing and distributing propaganda. One result was the formation of an informal group called the "Bureau of African Nationalism," centered in East London in the Cape where a number of Youth Leaguers had access to a duplicating machine.

The first bulletin of the Bureau of African Nationalism, written by Mda under the pseudonym of "Africanus," came

12. "Resolutions," African National Congress (Herschel Branch), 1951 (Carter-Karis collection).

out in January 1952. It was followed by a series of similar circulars published throughout the Defiance Campaign carrying pieces by Mda, T. T. Letlaka (then provincial president of the Youth League in the Cape), J. N. Pokela (a disciple of Mda's from Herschel), C. J. Fazzie, and other Cape Youth Leaguers. It also carried occasional anonymous pieces by Robert Sobukwe, a teacher in the Transvaal town of Standerton who as a student in 1948–49 had taken a leading role in the Fort Hare Youth League. The members of the Bureau saw themselves as a watchdog group overseeing the conduct of the Defiance Campaign to insure that there would be resistance to any attempt by non-Africans to reinterpret the goals and methods of the struggle endorsed in the *Programme of Action*. In the Transvaal, where ANC leaders had put a damper on the expression of nationalist sentiments for fear of affronting the Indian Congress, a similar wariness prevailed in militant Youth League circles.

Among the recipients of the Bureau's circulars in the Transvaal was a teacher named Potlako Kitchener Leballo, an energetic and vocal member of the Orlando Youth League. With others in the ANC who shared an orthodox nationalist outlook, Leballo greatly resented the leadership role taken in the Defiance Campaign by Indians and communists. This antagonism towards "non-African" elements, rather than subsiding after the campaign, intensified during 1953 when the white Congress of Democrats was formed and welcomed into the expanding Congress Alliance, and several Transvaal leaders who were friendly with white communists (including Walter Sisulu, Duma Nokwe, Alfred Hutchinson and Henry Gordon Makgothi) were invited to visit Eastern Europe. By 1954 opposition to the ANC's increasingly close ties with Indians and whites had crystallized in Orlando, the largest of the African residential areas southwest of Johannesburg. In March 1954 Leballo was elected chairman of the Youth League's Orlando East branch.

When considering the Cape-based Bureau of African Nationalism and the Transvaal-based movement to which it helped give rise, it may be useful to digress briefly to comment on regional variations in the character of African politics. Tensions between the Cape and the Transvaal, so much a feature of white South African politics for nearly a century, were also a perennial factor among Africans. Johannesburg is the largest city in South Africa, and the one where discrepancies between white wealth and black poverty stand out most starkly. Like major cities everywhere, it tends to attract a disproportionate share of the country's most ambitious individuals and it has always drawn to itself a high proportion of the more skilled and educated Africans, who in turn form the most politicized— and often the most frustrated—stratum of black society. For Africans inclined toward politics, Johannesburg has provided a somewhat more hospitable environment than most smaller South African cities. Its city administration, at least in the 1940s and 1950s, was relatively tolerant on the issue of free speech; if one lost a job in Johannesburg because of political activity, it was usually possible to find new employment; and, most importantly, since the number of politically active Africans in Johannesburg was always high, outsiders of similar inclination were often drawn there by the prospect of finding sympathy and safety in numbers. In the postwar period, these factors combined to make Johannesburg fertile ground for radicalism.

Yet where political consciousness ran deepest and strongest on a mass level in the 1950s was not Johannesburg or the Transvaal but the eastern Cape, the region of South Africa with the longest experience of mission education and political rights for Africans. Thus, while the headquarters of the ANC was always in Johannesburg, the area of the strongest and best organized Congress support was the eastern Cape, where the continuing strength of liberal traditions gave a tone of moderation to even the most militant anti-government campaigns. The politically-minded African based in Johannesburg tended to regard the Cape as conservative, or, more often, he tended to neglect it altogether in his thinking and to slip into the fallacy of equating the country as a whole with Johannesburg. Cape leaders tended to react against this attitude and to regard the Transvaal as too impractical and parochial in its planning of national campaigns. The influence of Transvaal communists was also regarded with disapproval by some Cape leaders, but this disapproval never became outright alarm because it was always obvious in the Cape that communism as an ideology had no particular appeal to the mass of Congress supporters. Most importantly, Cape leaders valued unity within the ANC far more highly than they valued uniformity on ideology or policy, and as a result, their criticisms of the ANC national office were generally muted ones. If the Cape took a position at variance with the national office, it was usually a "watchdog" position, not a position of open criticism.

During the Defiance Campaign, these tensions between Johannesburg and the Cape were present at times, but of all the regions in the country, the Cape rallied most strongly to the call for passive resisters. Thousands of volunteers went to jail, and thousands more joined the ANC to give their support.[13] Skepticism about supposed communist influences in the Transvaal was sometimes voiced, and the bulletins of the Bureau of African Nationalism were the most open expression of this sentiment; but even in the case of the Bureau, the position taken toward the Transvaal leadership was that of watchdog, not of challenger. In the more acid soil of Johannesburg, however, the plant of nationalist dissent grew somewhat differently. The protagonists were in striking range of one another; quarrels became more personalized. White and Indian radicals were visibly in evidence, identifying themselves with the African cause and lending their support and advice. Rumors travelled like lightning and opinions polarized rapidly. The rest of the country seemed far away. To Leballo and those around him, it mattered little that the Defiance Campaign had scored its most spectacular successes in the Cape, where white or Indian influences had never entered the picture. The Transvaal was the immediate reality, and there it seemed that orthodox nationalism was confronting its deadliest enemies.

13. Of the 8,057 arrests made in the campaign, 5,719 were in the eastern Cape, and only 1,411 in the Transvaal. See Karis and Carter, Vol. 2, p. 420. Also see above, p. 112, fn. 2.

Leballo and the Orlando Africanists

When Lembede had called on Africans in 1947 to embrace the cause of nationalism, "with the fanaticism and bigotry of religion," he had aptly anticipated the spirit of Leballo's politics. Never had a struggling young movement found a "true believer" bursting with such faith and zeal. As a thinker, he came nowhere near the intellectual level of Lembede or Mda, but by temperament he was a born "rebel," ready at the slightest provocation to challenge any accepted political norm, black or white. Had Mda's efforts netted a dozen more individuals of Leballo's type, South Africa's subsequent history might possibly have been different. For better or worse, however, Leballo was a political rara avis, unique in personality and style. Born in Basutoland in 1924, he grew up just over the Basutoland border, near Modderpoort in the Orange Free State, where his father was a priest at an Anglican mission. At the outbreak of World War II, Leballo was a boarding student at Lovedale, a leading missionary institution in the Cape. Drawn by the prospect of adventure and heroic deeds, he dropped out of Lovedale in 1940, overstated his age by two years (he was then sixteen), and enlisted in a nonwhite unit of the South African Army. As a driver in a transport unit he saw action in Ethiopia against the Italians and in North Africa against the Germans, and appears to have made his first political mark by taking part in a mutiny against the army's color bar regulations.[14] After demobilization he returned to Lovedale to complete a teacher training course, but was soon involved in agitation against the school authorities. Following a student strike in 1946 he was expelled, but finished his training course at Wilberforce Institute in Evaton and took up teaching in the Transvaal.

The Youth League had attracted Leballo on his return from the war, for it mirrored his own disillusionment and frustra-

14. Interview with Leballo. By Leballo's own account, he was rescued from a sinking ship in the Mediterranean, captured by the Germans and sent to prison camps in Germany, court-martialed and given a death sentence for his part in a mutiny, discharged by the South Africans, and enlisted by a unit of the British Army in which he bore arms.

tion and did not mince words in identifying whites as the enemies of African freedom. Politics as such attracted him. He had a taste for leadership, but his real appetite was for combat per se, and politics offered him a boundless field of battle. Lembede's emotional patriotism struck a responsive chord in his own makeup, and Mda's audacity and brilliance inspired him to extremes of hero-worship. What Leballo lacked in intellect or originality of thought he more than made up in stamina, physical courage and single-minded devotion to the political line handed down from Lembede and Mda. If his interpretation of that line was sometimes a little crude, he could at least take comfort in the knowledge that his own thinking was close to what he conceived to be that of the common man. If Mda's place was in the back room or on the platform before "highbrow" audiences, Leballo's calling was to the streetcorners and the hustings where intellectual principles became transformed into the slogans and emotionalized appeals of a would-be mass movement.

After teaching for several years in Pretoria, Leballo moved to Johannesburg in 1952 and quickly became involved in ANC politics in Orlando, participating in meetings of both the Youth League and the senior Congress. During this period, he also appears to have served a brief jail sentence on a fraud conviction, as well as for participation in the Defiance Campaign. Unable to accommodate himself to the restrictions of the teaching profession, he moved through a succession of jobs and eventually settled into working for Paul Mosaka, one of Johannesburg's few moderately successful African businessmen. First selling funeral insurance for one of Mosaka's companies, and later working for Mosaka's African Chamber of Commerce, Leballo sped around the townships of Johannesburg on a company motorscooter, mixing politics with business wherever he went. He was not quite the type of university-educated intellectual Mda had envisaged as the cutting edge of the Africanist movement, but by the time the rift in the ANC began to take clear shape in the aftermath of the Defiance Campaign, Leballo had become the central figure in a growing Transvaal group of orthodox nationalists and was therefore not a person whom Mda could afford to ignore. In any case, Leballo had the makings of an effective propagandist, and it seemed probable that he would be useful in winning over the ANC's rank and file to support of a nationalist line.

Leballo based his bid for office in the Orlando East Youth League on the demand that the ANC return to the "go it alone" principle of the pre-Alliance period and enforce the boycott of urban advisory boards and other government-initiated "dummy institutions"—a policy endorsed in the 1949 *Programme of Action* but never actively implemented by the ANC.[15] He denounced as "eastern functionaries" the Youth League leaders who had accepted invitations to the communist-sponsored World Youth Festival in Bucharest in 1953, and painted lurid pictures of foreign ideologies swamping the true doctrine of "Africa for the Africans."[16] Coming at a time when the ANC was facing both increased government harassment and a general post–Defiance Campaign letdown among the rank and file, this brazen display of disloyalty was more than some members of the provincial executive of the Transvaal Youth League could tolerate. Leballo was therefore notified in May 1954 that he was being expelled from the League and his Orlando branch committee suspended pending an investigation. The dispute dragged on for several months, no formal procedure for dealing with it was ever adopted, and eventually, sometime in November 1954, several members of the provincial executive of the Youth League resigned in protest, including Joe Molefi and Nana Mahomo, who were sympathetic to Leballo's views.[17]

Up to this time orthodox nationalists in the Transvaal had been conscious of being a distinct group unified around their opposition to the alliance policy. Now they began to consider their position more seriously and to organize in earnest for the

15. See above, pp. 80–81.
16. See for example *The Bantu World*, 13 March and 1 May 1954.
17. See N. Mahomo, "The Rise of the Pan Africanist Congress of South Africa" (MA thesis, Massachusetts Institute of Technology, 1968), p. 43, where the author describes the resignations as the catalytic event preceding the establishment of the Africanist Cencom.

propagation of their opinions. It was obvious that an open break with the ANC would achieve nothing. The more promising course of action seemed to be the one always advocated by Mda: tight organization of Africanist nuclei which would agitate and recruit support within the ANC itself. Leballo and his inner circle of associates accordingly began to refer to themselves secretly as the Africanist Central Committee or "Cencom," and in November 1954 they brought out the first mimeographed issue of a journal called *The Africanist*.[18] Appearing periodically thereafter and drawing on many of the same contributors who had suported the earlier Bureau of African Nationalism, *The Africanist* became a focal point for nationalist agitation and criticism of the ANC's policy of multiracialism. Open rupture in the ANC was still four years away, but the lines of conflict were being drawn with increasing clarity.

What sort of men made up the initial Africanist inner circle, and what differences set them apart from their protagonists in the leadership of the ANC? Why did they become "rebels" who deviated from the ideological norm? In terms of class background the Africanists as a group did not differ substantially from the group of men leading the ANC. Each group had its share of university graduates and men of lesser educational attainment, and each its mixture of city and country-bred men.

18. Opinion now varies among former members of the Africanist movement about exactly who was a member of the Cencom, and we can only conclude that its composition changed between 1954 and 1958, and that membership was not a very formal matter. Leballo has recalled its membership as including, besides himself and Mda (who was living in Herschel in this period but who paid frequent visits to Johannesburg), J. N. Pokela and Robert Sobukwe (who were teachers in Standerton), Peter 'Molotsi (a clerk in a law office and later on the staff of *The Bantu World*), Selby Ngendane (a law clerk), and Victor Sifora (a teacher and previously the Transvaal president of the Youth League). Others sometimes mentioned as members include Zephania Mothopeng (a teacher at Orlando High School), Peter Tsele (a Pretoria doctor), Nana Mahomo (then a clerk), Abednego B. Ngcobo (a University of Natal law student), Peter Raboroko (a teacher at Orlando High School), Joe Molefi, Z. B. Molete, and Philemon Makhetha.

In ethnic terms, ANC leadership had a strong representation of Nguni-speakers (Xhosas and Zulus), whereas Africanist leadership was heavily Sotho. But both A. P. Mda and Robert Sobukwe were Xhosa, and a number of non-Nguni were very prominent in the ANC, including Moses Kotane and Z. K. Matthews.

More important than any measurable criterion of class, education, or ethnicity were psychological differences which distinguished the Africanists as a group from the type of men in control of the ANC. Exactly how these psychological differences were in turn related to differences in background must remain largely a matter for speculation. Probably significant is the fact that a high proportion of leading Africanists had grown up in the Orange Free State and the Transvaal, the regions of South Africa where black-white relations are the most strained and the concentration of Afrikaans-speaking whites is the heaviest. In the provinces of Natal and the Cape, that is, in the home areas of the Nguni-speaking groups, English-speaking whites predominate and race relations are less stark, in part because of missionary influences. Africans who grow up in the northern provinces can on the whole be expected to feel more hostility to whites than do Africans from the Cape and Natal.

Almost without exception, the Africanists were men who had come at a relatively formative age under the strong influence of Mda's impressive personality and intellect, but the same could be said of a number of the most important figures in the ANC as well—including Mandela and Sisulu, who continued throughout the 1950s to be on close personal terms with Mda at the same time he was working to undermine them politically. What caused some to cling permanently to the idée fixe of orthodox nationalism as preached by Mda and Lembede, while others temporarily accepted it and then set it aside? An ingrained mistrust of whites based on childhood experience and parental precept, the memory of a parent or teacher humiliated by whites, a need to assert the independence and intellectual equality of Africans and demolish the stereotype of the African as the perpetual "tutee" of other "superior" races —the ultimate explanation of each individual Africanist's outlook would have to take into account such factors as these. When adult careers are considered, however, one pattern of experience is frequently encountered: the thwarting of a large number of the Africanist leaders in their ambitions for higher professional achievement.

As Kuper has noted, teaching was for many years the main profession open to African university graduates, given the restrictions placed on black entrance into technical, scientific, civil service, or business careers. Starting in the 1940s, however, very limited opportunities for entrance into medicine and law began to open up (almost all older African lawyers and doctors having qualified abroad); but the road to success in these professions was arduous and the number who achieved it was very small.[19] For those few who did succeed in qualifying—and it is important to note that in the top ranks of the ANC in the 1950s there were several doctors and four lawyers, including Nelson Mandela, Oliver Tambo, Duma Nokwe and Joe Matthews—the rewards were great. Not only did law and medicine bring more prestige and significantly higher income than teaching, but they also brought independence; for unlike teachers, who held their positions at the pleasure of a government department, lawyers and doctors had the option of being self-employed. Of the fifteen most consequential figures in the Africanist movement of the mid-1950s, eight were teachers, not counting Leballo who had abandoned teaching in 1952. Only one, Dr. Peter Tsele, had already achieved a position of high professional status at the time of his entrance into active national politics.[20] Of the remaining

19. See Kuper, *An African Bourgeoisie*, pp. 133–34.
20. The 15 Africanists referred to are Mda, Sobukwe, Letlaka, Pokela, Raboroko, Molete, Mothopeng, Sifora, Leballo, Tsele, 'Molotsi, Ngendane, Mahomo, Molefi, and A. B. Ngcobo. The first eight, who were teachers, all wrote in *The Africanist* under pseudonyms because political activity by teachers often brought dismissal or other sanctions.

Africanist leaders, one was a student and four were in clerical or other white collar occupations. Significantly, however, of the fourteen other than Tsele, no less than nine were aiming, or had aimed, at careers in law or medicine; two had begun medicine, and seven were hoping to qualify in law. Only two eventually succeeded;[21] the rest had their ambitions thwarted to one degree or another. For highly motivated men like these, the South African system threw up a formidable battery of obstacles. The result was not just a sense of frustration and generalized anger, but a deep determination to destroy the system root and branch, to solve for all Africans the problems which each had failed to solve for himself alone.[22] Politics offered the most direct opportunity to fight racial inequality, and may also have helped assuage the thirst for self-esteem, prestige and independence of action.[23]

No such analysis of private motives can serve as an explanation of political behavior; it can provide only a clue, in this case a clue to the temperamental differences which distinguished the "rebels" of the Africanist movement from the less iconoclastic leadership of the ANC. But insofar as the private ambitions of individual African intellectuals *were* a force in condi-

21. Mda and Letlaka, who qualified as lawyers. Sobukwe and Mothopeng, who did not begin law studies in the 1950s, both took up law after their release from prison in the 1960s. They are not included in the nine.

22. For the prototype of this analysis of the revolutionary personality, see E. Erikson, *Young Man Luther* (New York: W. W. Norton, 1962), p. 67.

23. As Brandel-Syrier notes in *Reeftown Elite* (pp. 105, 149–50), the opportunity for an African to get ahead occasionally presents itself in the form of patronage and favors from well-placed whites. But for the African who is too proud to accept such favors—or who is suspicious of white "friends" and avoids them on principle, as the Africanists did—even this narrow avenue of opportunity is closed. The overlapping perception of personal and political careers comes out in the remarks made frequently by Africanists that Mandela, Tambo, Nokwe, Sisulu and other ANC leaders were favorably disposed towards multiracialism because whites had helped them get ahead professionally or had aided them financially; whether these assertions are true or not, they indicate the connection in the thinking of many Africanists between political views and personal success or failure.

tioning the character of their politics—status-striving and frustration in the case of the Africanists, status-striving and a measure of success among ANC leaders—it can be said that the life chances of the African middle class (to use Kuper's phrase), do very directly influence the politics of black South Africa.

Without Mda to give form and content to their thinking, the founders of the Africanist movement would probably have dissipated their energies in fiery but fruitless outbursts. Whatever their deepest drives and aspirations were as individuals, the Africanists as a group were characterized by an intensity of emotion and political fervor rarely exhibited in the national leadership circles of the ANC. Some, like Leballo, were simply emotional by nature. Others, like 'Molotsi and Molete, had been converted to orthodox nationalist thinking while still in high school and had internalized it so thoroughly that any attack on nationalism came as an attack on their very identities. While some Africanists sought to bolster their emotional convictions with new knowledge garnered from reading and participation in political study circles, most looked primarily to Mda, and through Mda back to the ideas of Lembede, to get an intellectual lead and an arsenal of arguments to use in political debate. For Mda—one of those rare original thinkers who does not merely apply ideological formulae but himself fashions them in his own calculating imagination—the situation offered at least some promising possibilities. He felt that the effort to win the ANC over to orthodox nationalism would be a difficult one, but in his own thinking and in the thinking of his Africanist disciples, there was a self-conscious sense of destiny, a stubborn belief that nationalists would be vindicated in time, however small their initial numbers might be.

The Return to Nationalist Fundamentals

In their search for a political formula that could mobilize Africans into a successful mass movement, the Africanists lost no time in reviving the slogan "Africa for the Africans" and the fundamental tenet of orthodox nationalism which it expressed: the right of Africans to reclaim their "stolen" country. The Youth League's *Basic Policy,* authored by Mda in about 1948, had postulated that Africans were historically entitled to "ownership" of Africa, and the European conquest of the continent had not removed this inalienable right. Over and over in the pages of *The Africanist* this same theme was repeated: Africans claimed the right to rule Africa not just because they were the majority, but because they were Africa's indigenous people, the "sons of the soil." "Before the advent of European Imperialism to this land the African tribes ruled themselves and were the undisputed owners of the soil of Africa," wrote Letlaka.

> After fierce wars in defense of their fatherland the Africans were conquered and dispossessed of their land by European Imperialists. The African people to all intents and purposes were rendered homeless in the land of their birth. They could no longer own land but were merely herded into small reserves where a few held small plots of land with the grace of the white rulers. . . . The entire African nation was converted into a vast reservoir of cheap labor for the insatiable European-owned farms, mines and secondary industries. The immediate goal of the African Liberation Struggle, therefore, is clear and unequivocal. It is an *uncompromising reversal* of this unhealthy state of affairs. . . . The struggle for national emancipation, and *the regaining of all things that were lost as a result of White conquest of Africa,* is the cornerstone of Africa's struggle for liberation.[24]

Grist was added to the Africanists' ideological mill when the member organizations of the Congress Alliance undertook to summarize their political goals in the Freedom Charter. The Charter proclaimed in its preamble that

> We, the People of South Africa, declare for all our country and the world to know:
>
> that *South Africa belongs to all who live in it,* Black and White, and

24. T. T. Letlaka ["Nyaniso"], "An Aspect of the 1949 Programme," *The Africanist,* December 1956 (Carter-Karis collection). Emphasis added.

that no government can justly claim authority unless it is based on the will of *all* the people.[25]

Seizing on the ANC's declaration that South Africa "belonged to all," the Africanists launched a campaign to popularize the idea of exclusive African "ownership rights." "To whom does Afrika belong?" queried *The Africanist*. "Do stolen goods belong to a thief and not to [their] owner? Those Africans who renounce their claims over Afrika should not stand in the way of the people, for they will be crushed together with oppression."[26] Nor could whites claim any rights based on the argument that they had first settled in "empty" parts of South Africa:

> The African people have an inalienable claim on every inch of the African soil. In the memory of humanity as a whole, this continent has been the homeland of the Africans. . . . Their migration in their fatherland does not annul their claim to the uninhabited parts of Africa. No sane man can come to your house and claim as his the chamber or room you are not occupying. The non-Africans are guests of the Africans . . . [and] have to adjust themselves to the interests of Africa, their new home.[27]

Whites, they argued, had failed to make any adjustment which took into account the interests or rights of Africa's indigenous peoples, and thus the only course open to Africans was to fight back until the tables had been turned, the conquerors defeated, and Africa restored to the control of its "owners."

The Africanists were confident that in appealing to the African's sense of grievances at being dispossessed of his land they were speaking a political language which even the most unsophisticated could readily comprehend. To "evoke a deep-seated and lasting response, which could be harnessed to

25. "The Freedom Charter," in Karis and Carter, vol. 3. Emphasis added.
26. "Africanus" [unidentified], "Away With Foreign Domination," *The Africanist*, January–February, 1956 (Carter-Karis collection). Some Africans spelled Africa with a "k" to emphasize their rejection of European influences.
27. "The Guiding Star to New Africa," *The Africanist*, December 1956 (Carter-Karis collection).

a massive National Liberation Movement," wrote Mda in 1955, it was clear that the people would have to be roused "on the basis of African Nationalism which harked back to their past historic struggles, and which projected these to present and future conditions."[28] Jordan Ngubane in the days of the early Youth League had called nationalism "the political philosophy of the man in the kraal,"[29] the outlook of the peasant who was unconcerned with the frivolities of ideological and moral disputation and who knew only one reality: the expropriation of his land and livestock by the whites. Vestiges of this rural heritage were still present not far beneath the surface in nearly every urban African, particularly among the semi-urbanized lumpenproletariat of the Reef in whom peasant perspectives had yet to be submerged to any significant extent beneath more complex urban perceptions of the race conflict.

To reinforce this sense of an historic grievance and to evoke the memory of African resistance to white conquest, the Africanists, first in their public speeches and later in their house-to-house recruiting efforts, made frequent reference to the heroes of the tribal past—Moshesh, Tshaka, Hintsa, Sekhukhuni, Makana and a host of lesser figures. Although it was customary for African politicians to refer to "three hundred years" of white oppression, in fact the real confrontation of black and white, and the most bloody wars of conquest, had taken place much more recently, not in 1652 with the arrival of the earliest whites but in the mid- and late nineteenth century, a mere two or three generations removed from the 1950s. African resistance was still a matter of live tradition among the Zulu in Natal, the Sotho and the Pedi in the Free State and the Transvaal, and even among the Xhosa of the Cape, although their defeat had taken place earlier and their memories of conquest had been somewhat more blurred by subsequent social change. Whatever the tribal background of an African, he was likely to respond at least in some measure to an appeal to vindicate his forebears' defeat. Sometimes in polit-

28. *The Africanist,* July–August, 1955 (Carter-Karis collection).
29. *Inkundla ya Bantu,* 17 July 1944.

ical recruiting, Molete later recalled, an organizer might come across a person who seemed completely disinterested in politics.

> "What can you do with the white man?" That's what they would tell you. "The white man is all right; there is nothing that we can do." They would also use some of the texts from the Bible, some of them, in order to show how God dictated things to be; there's nothing that can be done about them. But here you would have to use methods of persuasion. You draw examples from as many sources as you can, show the fight that went on in our country. . . . The question of land, for instance, touches the African to the core of his heart. Now if you draw from the fights of Moshesh in defense of the land, every Mosotho respects Moshesh very much. Once you talk of Moshesh . . . he is bound to listen. Or you talk of Hintsa, you talk of all other heroes, Sekhukhuni and Tshaka and his warriors, that the land is the central point. Let us get back the land that was given to us by our forefathers.[30]

A struggle defined as a continuation of the traditional resistance to conquest was a struggle simplified and stripped of moral dilemmas. By stressing the alienation of African land, the complex question of white "ownership rights" in mining, industry and commerce could be brushed aside. If all whites were engaged, in Leballo's words, in "the maintenance and retention of the spoils passed on to them by their forefathers," then they were traffickers in stolen goods; none could escape responsibility for the original "theft."[31] If Africans were actually engaged in an all-out war of self-defense, then they were justified in using any means necessary to insure their survival and victory. Problems of accommodation or compromise did not enter the picture, nor did the problem of defining a role in the struggle for "sympathetic" whites. There were only two combatants in the conflict: "the conquered and the conqueror, the invaded and the invader, the dispossessed and the dispossessor."[32]

30. Interview with Molete.
31. P. K. Leballo, "The Nature of the Struggle Today," *The Africanist*, December 1957 (Carter-Karis collection).
32. Ibid. South Africa provides much corroboration for T. O. Ranger's thesis that modern African nationalism has been shaped by

ANC policy-makers were prepared to agree that nationalism couched in these terms had a strong potential appeal to ordinary Africans. Writing in *Africa South* in the late 1950s, Sisulu praised what he called the "wonderful example of political wisdom and maturity" shown by Africans in rejecting the "emotional mass-appeal to destructive and exclusive nationalism." "It would be unrealistic," he said, "to pretend that a policy of extreme nationalism must, in the nature of things, always be unpopular. . . . In certain circumstances," such an ideology could be "a dynamic and irresistible force in history."[33] Yet the ANC, he said, would continue to eschew such "Black chauvinism" as contrary to long-term African interests.

If the potency of an "Africa for the Africans" brand of nationalism was evident to the leaders of the ANC, why did they continue to reject it throughout a period when it might have made good sense politically to adjust to the rising mass temper and move in more radical directions? The answer, as we have seen, was twofold: first, such a course would have been a departure from the ANC's long tradition of moderation in the articulation of its goals; and second, such a move toward radical nationalism would have set the ANC in conflict with the strongly held views of its allies.

The Attack on the Congress Alliance

The Africanists would have blundered politically had they openly called on the ANC to renounce its own traditions per se. The ANC was an old organization by the 1950s and it derived much of its prestige from its aura of tradition. It was therefore important, even when attacking the ANC, to claim the sanction

---

forces of "historical memory." See his "Connexions Between 'Primary Resistance' Movements and Modern Mass Nationalism in East and Central Africa," *Journal of African History* 9, no. 3 (1968), Part I, and 9, no. 4 (1968), Part II. The "memory," of course, is a highly selective one. It filters out inexpedient details, for example that Africans fought as tribal groups and not as a united "nation," and may over-romanticize "all things that were lost as a result of white conquest" (Letlaka, fn. 24 above).

33. Sisulu, "Congress and the Africanists," p. 34.

of tradition and, if possible, to present the alleged wrongdoing of the Congress as revisionism, or a heresy somehow contrary to the "true" traditional principles of the organization.[34] The Africanists followed this pattern and claimed that their conception of nationalism was in the "true" spirit of African self-reliance as preached by the 1912 founders of Congress. That the generation of 1912 had also firmly believed in the liberal premises of integration and cooperation was an aspect of ANC tradition which the Africanists preferred to ignore.

The Africanists needed a clear-cut point on which the ANC's leadership was vulnerable and through which its entire handling of the liberation struggle could be called into question. The Congress Alliance was just such a ready-made point of attack, and starting from the first issue of *The Africanist* in late 1954, Leballo and his colleagues declared open war on the Transvaal leadership which had initiated the alliance. From that time onward, through the founding of the Pan Africanist Congress in 1959 and beyond into the post-Sharpeville era, multiracial political cooperation was to be one of the most divisive issues in black South African political life. While appearing to be primarily a question of tactics, the decision to accept or reject multiracial cooperation rested in fact on political choices which were fundamentally ideological. The debate that ensued therefore revolved around questions of both tactics and ideology, with the distinction between the two often becoming cloudy.

The Africanist attack on the ANC's alliance policy was characterized by much inflated rhetoric, but it deserves scrutiny because beneath its angry and exaggerated language lay some important insights.[35] The Africanists recognized that the deci-

34. Thema's "National-Minded Bloc" cited tradition as the basis of its critique of the African-Indian alliance of 1950–51, and Dr. Xuma in an attack on the Congress leadership in December 1955 called on the ANC to return to the traditions of the 1940s. See "Dr. Xuma's Letter Congress Would Not Read," *The World*, 28 January 1956, reproduced in Karis and Carter, vol. 3, pp. 242–45.

35. Except where specific references are given, the following description of the Africanists' position is drawn from issues of *The Africanist* between 1954 and 1959, and from the author's interviews with former

White crowd cheers the arrival of Malan at an election rally in Pretoria, April 1953. *Ernest Haas/ Magnum.*

Africans study election results outside the Johannesburg offices of the *Rand Daily Mail*, April 1953. *Ernest Haas/ Magnum.*

Executive Committee of the Pan Africanist Congress with A. P. Mda, Bloemfontein, September 1959. Front, l. to r. Abednego B. Ngcobo, Robert Sobukwe, A. P. Mda, P. K. Leballo, Howard S. Ngcobo. Back, l. to r. Jacob D. Nyaose, Elliot Mfaxa, Z. B. Molete, Peter 'Molotsi, Selby T. Ngendane, Hughes Hlatswayo. Missing from photo: Peter Raboroko, Zephania Mothopeng, C. J. Fazzie, Nana Mahomo. *PAC.*

sion to accept support from non-Africans had effectively closed Congress off from the option of an orthodox nationalist stand, and they hoped that the direction of ANC policies might be reversed if the motives of the various parties to the alliance could be portrayed in a sufficiently damaging light. Their attack therefore concentrated on exposing the Transvaal Congress leaders as dupes and stooges who had been taken in by clever representatives of the oppressor races. Indian leaders, and particularly the whites of the Congress of Democrats, were painted as a diabolical fifth column, feigning friendliness to the oppressed but actually bent on drawing the sting out of the African liberation movement.

To the Africanists' way of thinking, there was no essential difference between the radical whites of the COD and the old-fashioned white liberals who had always taken a benign interest in Congress. Liberals of the older type had always advised the ANC to water down its militancy and go in for less extreme forms of political action; the COD in contrast had encouraged Congress to engage in a whole variety of militant, if sometimes ill-conceived, action campaigns. And yet, argued the Africanists, the white liberal and the white radical shared the same underlying attitude toward African political initiatives: neither was willing to stand aside and let Africans chart their own course, because Africans left to define the struggle in terms of their own interests alone would inevitably come to define *all* whites as enemies. All whites, the Africanists maintained, including liberals and radicals, had an interest in the perpetuation of the status quo, no matter how intellectually committed they might be to the principle of racial equality. As members of a pampered and privileged group, no whites could ever work wholeheartedly for the total dismantling of the South African social order. Instead they would always try, consciously or unconsciously, to guide and control the African

---

members of the Africanist movement, including Mda, Leballo, Molete, 'Molotsi, Lakaje, Sifora, Letlaka, Raboroko, Mahomo, Molefi, Matthew Nkoana, and Ellen Molapo.

movement for freedom so that it would never become too destructive of their own long-term interests. "Our past experience," Sobukwe told the Africanists in 1959,

> has been that minority groups declare themselves sympathetic to our struggle. . . . But when they come into our movement they do not accept the program we have formulated ourselves. They present us with programs which protect their sectional interests. If I am building a house, if there is a friend who wants to help me I expect him to bring building materials with him to come and help me. I do not like him coming with already drawn up plans which will affect my original scheme.[36]

This urge among minority group sympathizers to prevent Africans from getting "out of hand," or turning "anti-white," said the Africanists, was as strong among white radicals as it had ever been among white liberals. Indians too had an advantaged position to defend, and offered to help Africans primarily in order to safeguard their own sectional interests.

How did these self-proclaimed "friends" of the African insure that the movement for liberation stayed within safe limits? Their methods, according to the Africanist analysis, were subtle and varied, but always pointed toward one objective: wooing African leadership away from the ideology of orthodox nationalism, the one ideology potent enough to be the basis of a successful revolution. The first step was to win the confidence of African leaders through profuse demonstrations of support and a program of wining and dining selected promising Africans at the posh homes of white Johannesburg radicals. This campaign of treating Africans to the dazzling attractions of white social life began in the early 1950s, about the time, according to the Africanists, when the Defiance Campaign had served a warning to whites that the movement for African liberation was in danger of getting "out of hand." Africans invited to these relaxed multiracial parties were easily swept off their feet by the glamour of associating with whites and being

36. Remarks made at the PAC inaugural convention, as recorded by Benjamin Pogrund, April 1959 (papers of Benjamin Pogrund).

in a social setting so exalted in contrast to the squalor of the African townships. Drinks flowed freely, in defiance of the law against serving "European" liquor to Africans; everyone present was on an immediate first-name basis, and the rigid sex taboos of South Africa's conventional white society could be freely flouted. Even African leaders of substance found it hard to resist the snob appeal of mixing with whites and the gratifications of having their superior education or talents recognized by white intellectuals.

The Africanists in the 1950s confined their public attack on social mixing mainly to sarcastic references to "cocktail parties" held in "Parktown and Lower Houghton," stylish white Johannesburg suburbs. A fuller picture of their attitudes emerged later in interviews, where the following comments were typical:

"Hobnobbing and consorting" was always condemned by the Africanists for ideological reasons; it led to the dilution of our ideology. . . . Going with white girls, going to mixed parties, this was what the intellectuals liked. A —— liked this treatment from the whites because he was rejected by the African people; he wasn't a big person with education. . . . Some of the nobodies liked to go to these parties because you got free drinks. The big men liked it because this was their type of society, on their level.

You can only [understand] this in terms of South African society. I mean you don't really know what apartheid means . . . you've got to stay in South Africa to know what it means. And to be accepted in white society . . . you are completely in a new world. You see these white chaps defying the laws . . . and money, good God!

Enjoying that type of life, of being able to be on a first-name basis with white women. . . . It just became so very glittering for them.

Once B—— got ahead professionally, he much preferred the company of Indians and whites to the company of ordinary Africans. He just had no time for them.

Here began the cancer that was ultimately to split the organization, because decisions were being arrived at in Lower Houghton by whites, Indians and the so-called African intellectuals, who were being treated to victuals and liquor and returned drunk with the sense of their self-importance to impose such decisions upon us.

So they found themselves really catapulted from the mass of African society into this.[37]

For a handful of the most promising leaders—promising in their open attitude toward whites and in their sympathy toward the ideas preached by some of the COD's earnest Marxists—there was a special bonus in 1953: paid trips to Europe to represent the ANC at the Bucharest World Youth Festival.[38] Once strong inroads into the Transvaal African leadership had been made using these methods, it was just a matter of time, the Africanists charged, until the ANC's allies had maneuvered themselves into positions of commanding strength within the Congress Alliance.

One objective of this campaign of subversion, said the Africanists, was to destroy the "nation-building" 1949 *Programme of Action* and replace it with the multiracialist Freedom Charter of 1955. According to the Africanists, most of whom had been active Youth Leaguers in the late 1940s, the tactics and goals outlined in the 1949 *Programme* were all directed toward one underlying objective: the conditioning of the

37. In an earlier political generation, the same resentment of "non-mixers" against "mixers" was revealed in the frequent attacks on so-called "tea drinkers." A. W. G. Champion, for example, attacked his critics in the 1940s in much the same vein: "Most of you waste time by going to drink tea with Europeans and Indians at the International Club, Joint Council, and the Communist Party where there are Jews and Jewesses with red cheeks. You do not care about your fellow Africans working with the road gangs. There you keep on cheating the whites that you are representing your own people while you hardly know of any of your people. It is nice for a person to say before Mrs. Palmer and Mr. Carey that he is the mouthpiece of the African people, but at the same time complain in the press that he does not get elected and given the position by the Africans of being a leader in their organizations" (undated translation of a Champion letter to the press, late 1940s, Carter-Karis collection).

38. See *Advance*, 22 October, 5 November, 19 November, 24 December and 31 December 1953, and *South Africans in the Soviet Union* (pamphlet published by Ruth First, Johannesburg, n.d., Carter-Karis collection). Also see W. Sisulu, "I Saw China," *Liberation*, no. 7 February 1954, pp. 5–9. Legislation was later passed making it illegal for South Africans to leave the country without passports.

African masses to "think nationalist." With the cementing of the Alliance, however, the Africanists argued, this objective had been carefully forgotten, and the *Programme of Action* officially reinterpreted as a mere "action program" aimed at pushing the ANC beyond the cautious methods of the Xuma era. In place of the "dynamic" nationalist doctrines of 1949, enemies of the Africans had pushed forward the diversionary Freedom Charter, which outlined an ideal future multiracial society but incorporated no plan for mobilizing the African masses for struggle. "The Freedom Charter is a political bluff," declared Leballo in the December 1957 issue of *The Africanist*.

> It promises a little wonderful heaven if not Utopia around the corner. The question is: How to get there? The answer is: There must be an immediate implementation of the *Programme of Action* of 1949 and the principles laid down therein, item by item, for the achievement of the aims of the envisaged little heaven or the very proposed Utopia around the corner. It is utterly useless to go around shouting empty slogans such as "The people shall govern," "The people shall share," without practical steps towards that government. We are merely being made tools and stooges of interested parties that are anxious to maintain the status quo.[39]

The Freedom Charter, according to the Africanist critique, had avoided the correct nationalist definition of the South African struggle as one of dispossessed versus dispossessors, and had attempted instead to define the conflict as one of "the people" against "a system." "Our people," said the Charter, "have been robbed of their birthright to land, liberty and peace by a form of government founded on injustice and inequality." "The truth is," said *The Africanist*, "that the African people have been robbed by the European people."[40] In the Africanists' view, nothing could be gained by trying to appease white opinion; all strategies that aimed at splitting, swaying, or neutralizing sections of the white population were counterproductive

39. Leballo, "The Nature of the Struggle Today."
40. P. Raboroko and Z. Mothopeng ["Ufford Khoruba" and "Kwame Lekwame"], "The Kliptown Charter," *The Africanist*, June–July 1958 (Gubbins Library).

because they would always conflict with the need to preach "unadulterated" nationalism to the masses. "The Africans are asked, through their spineless leaders," wrote Sobukwe in 1957,

> not to "embarrass" their "friends" and "allies,". . . [and] to "water-down" their demands in order to accommodate all the Anti-Nat elements in the country; in short, we are asked to "grin and bear it" so that our "friends" can continue "to plead for us." And we are told that in that way we shall achieve freedom. What rubbish![41]

By inveighing constantly against what was labelled the "anti-white," "inverted racialist," and "black supremacist" outlook of African nationalism, said the Africanists, white radicals had successfully created an image of nationalism as a crude, immoral ideology no different from the rabid racism of the Nazis or the Afrikaners. It made no difference to white radicals that Afrikaner ideology had grown up to rationalize and perpetuate the subjugation of the country's indigenous majority while African nationalism was a creed of liberation for those millions who were being oppressed; all whites feared the just wrath of Africans, the Africanists argued, and even the most anti-government whites were therefore prepared to go to great lengths to avoid facing the truth that the conflict would inevitably bring a head-on collision of blacks against whites. In their depths of self-delusion, sympathetic whites convinced themselves that the conflict was one of "principles" and not races, and that the African's enemy was "racialism" and not white South Africa. Africans had to try to understand the "inner compulsions" of radical whites, noted *The Africanist* in 1958.

> The first of these . . . is the instinctive tendency of every ruling class to uphold its economic interests as long as it possibly can. The second is the "missionary zeal" of the apostles of a new found ideology, who believing as they do in the inherent superiority of their brand of ideology over all others, . . . feel

41. R. Sobukwe ["Nzana"], "What of the Future?" *The Africanist*, December 1957 (Carter-Karis collection).

themselves compelled to spread their gospel and recreate the subject peoples in their own image, regardless of the chances of success.[42]

Because radical whites had succeeded in setting themselves up as the models and arbiters of political maturity for African leaders, charged the Africanists, it was not difficult for them to convince the "vulnerable" leadership elements in the ANC that orthodox nationalism was a mistaken political outlook. All that was required was to define "racialistic" views as immoral, and then to declare that nationalism was "racialistic."

What effect had the dealings between the ANC leadership and its allies had on the loyalty and enthusiasm of the Congress rank and file? Congress leaders had originally welcomed and encouraged support from non-Africans partly in order to strengthen the ANC financially and organizationally, and it was clear that relative to the previous decade the ANC in the 1950s had made huge strides toward becoming a mass movement. Nevertheless, in the estimation of its Africanist critics, the Congress had come nowhere near realizing its potential in membership or influence among Africans. In part this could be attributed to the ANC's lack of a press of its own, and to financial constraints which prevented the organization from taking fuller advantage of other forms of communication, including car transport, telephones, and the printing and distribution of flyers and pamphlets. But more importantly, the Africanists charged, the ANC, even when it was in direct touch with its followers, fell short of its potential because of its unwillingness to preach a clear-cut nationalism in political language which ordinary Africans would readily understand and accept. Moreover, they charged, the high visibility of the ANC's non-African allies had confused and alienated many Africans who might otherwise have been attracted to the ANC's program of militant political action.[43]

42. Raboroko and Mothopeng, "The Kliptown Charter."
43. This and other criticisms of the policies of the Congress movement are evaluated by Ben Turok, a former leader of the COD, in his *Strategic Problems in South Africa's Liberation Struggle: A Critical Analysis* (Richmond, Canada, 1974).

It was one thing, said the Africanists, for African intellectuals to feel at home in the racially-mixed circles of the Alliance leadership, and to assure themselves that no one in such circles was "dominating" anyone else—but what of the ordinary African? Leaders knew that the ordinary man in the street regarded whites with fear and mistrust. Furthermore, and more importantly, he also regarded them with deference, because every aspect of the South African system worked to instill Africans with a belief in their inferiority to whites. In school, church, and factory; through the laws and the white-owned media; in the national government, local civic affairs, and in day-to-day race relations at every level, one lesson was impressed upon the African incessantly: his total inability to manage his own affairs without direction from whites. Given the resulting African attitude of defeatism, the Africanists—like Lembede a decade earlier—argued that it was essential for leaders to restore African confidence and self-reliance. True nationalists, they said, recognized that the "most vital frontier in the war for national liberation . . . [was] the psychological frontier," and the battle one "against overwhelming spiritual forces seeking to inspire the African with a sense of his own unworthiness."[44] If Africans clung to their habits of deference and passivity, they might wait forever for other people to free them. It was essential for them to grasp the reality of their position: that they could obtain freedom only by their own efforts. African leaders had to preach this reality, said the Africanists, and to impress it on their followers they had to live it as well.

It was Lembede, the Africanists pointed out, who had best analyzed the psychological factor in the African's political struggle, and it was to his prescriptions that the liberation movement had to return. "The man we remember today was sensitive [to]. . . the spiritual factor in all battles," declared Victor Sifora at a memorial service to Lembede, held in Orlando by the Africanists in September 1956.

44. V. Sifora ["Black Savage"], "African Nationalism and the 1949 Programme of Action," *The Africanist*, January–February 1956 (Carter-Karis collection).

For him as for us, the slogan of African Nationalism was not, as it is not, a formula of hate but rather a formula of reconstruction, the reconstruction of the soul of the African without which all battles, moral, economical and political, must be lost. The formula foreshadowed a battle at a new level, with new weapons and new standards for living and action, the standards of love of ourselves and our own, love and faith in our cause. . . . The African Nationalist . . . does not believe that the fault, the cause of our fall and shame is with our stars. We believe strongly, like [Lembede] that [we] ourselves, for ourselves and by ourselves, hold the key to our salvation, to our progress and glory, whether the whiteman, his law, his government, his church are with us or not.[45]

According to the Africanists, the spiritual strivings of the African were directed toward the solution of his own problems of dignity, identity and freedom. The "broad humanism" on which the Congress leadership prided itself—the concern for the needs and the future of South Africa's non-African population—was, in the Africanists' estimation, an abstraction which had little or no meaning for the average African in his harsh daily struggle for existence. Such concerns were in fact a luxury of the intellectual and cosmopolitan elite. If the ANC's leadership claimed, as it did, that its policies enjoyed the support of the African masses, this could only indicate that it was a leadership hopelessly out of touch with the true feelings of the people. It might be easy enough, the Africanists argued, for an educated and sophisticated African leader to make a distinction between the vast majority of racist whites and the tiny minority of "negrophilistic democratic liberals,"[46] but the ordinary African could hardly be expected to make exceptions

45. V. Sifora, "I Will Arise . . . ," *The Africanist,* December 1956 (Carter-Karis collection). Lembede was greatly revered by the Africanists, many of whom were too young to have known him but learned of his ideas through Mda. Mda encouraged the building up of Lembede as a semi-mythical hero, and in 1955 Leballo's group organized the first "Lembede Memorial Service" in Orlando, an event which was repeated in several subsequent years on the anniversary of Lembede's death.

46. P. H. 'Molotsi ["Mphatlalatsane"], "The Stay-at-Home Expulsions in the A. N. C.," *The Africanist,* June–July 1958 (Gubbins Library).

for this tiny minority when he was deciding how to deal with white oppression. "Even if we grant the sincerity of the whites, Indians and Coloureds who want to collaborate with us," a spokesman for the Africanists told *Contact*, a Liberal Party paper, in early 1958,

> the fact remains that the only way in which white domination will ever be broken is by black force. When that day comes if we have to stop and ask ourselves whether a particular white man was a friend of ours in the past, then we will never be able to act. After it is all over we will grant all those who accept African hegemony their full rights as private citizens of an African State.[47]

Just as it was impractical to urge Africans to distinguish between "good" and "bad" whites, the Africanists argued, so too was it contrary to African instincts to welcome the Indian as a sympathizer and a comrade in the struggle. In the Transvaal, and particularly in Natal, said the Africanists, the urban African knew the Indian only as an exploiting shopkeeper and an economic competitor, not as a fellow member of the oppressed. Indian leaders found it easy to declare their solidarity with African leaders, as in the famous Xuma-Dadoo-Naicker "Doctors' Pact" of 1947; but in the day-to-day dealings between Africans and Indians, the latter retained their attitudes of superiority and continued their exploitation of Africans unabated. The politics of the South African Indian Congress, the Africanists charged, were the self-interested politics of the Indian "merchant class," concerned with fighting the Group Areas Act and forestalling a strategy of African economic boycotts which might cut into the livelihood of Indian traders. "The down-trodden, poor 'stinking coolies' of Natal who, alone," declared Sobukwe,

> as a result of the pressure of material conditions, can identify themselves with the indigenous African majority in the struggle to overthrow white supremacy, have not yet produced their leadership. We hope they will do so soon.[48]

47. *Contact*, 8 March 1958.
48. Address to the Inaugural Convention of the PAC, 4–6 April 1959, reproduced in Karis and Carter, vol. 3, pp. 510–17.

Thus in the ANC's acceptance of a multiracial alliance and the Africanists' rejection of it, two fundamental interpretations of political "reality" were in conflict. Where the ANC weighed heavily the financial and organizational needs of the liberation movement at the center, the Africanists looked primarily to the problems of fashioning a propaganda line which could attract the masses of ordinary Africans. Where the ANC argued that the struggle would fail unless its ends, a multiracial society and polity, and its means, multiracial cooperation, were consistent, the Africanists clung to their view that no ends at all would be achieved unless Africans were first mobilized through appeals to the only sentiments capable of arousing them to action: consciousness of their identity and unity as the oppressed, and hatred of their white oppressors.

The Issue of Communism

From what has been said so far about the political views of the Africanists, it should be clear that their most fundamental differences with the ANC did not hinge on the issue of communist influence in African politics, in spite of the frequent attacks on the left in Africanist propaganda. Just how anti-communist was the Africanist movement?

The second half of the 1950s had brought a new intensity in the cold war, and a country as economically important to the West as South Africa could hardly remain untouched by the strains of international conflict. Suppression of South Africa's tiny but resilient indigenous communist movement was a cardinal objective of the ruling National party, and African leaders were well aware that beleaguered white South African Marxists, banned from openly promoting their views, were reaching out to black organizations as their most potentially powerful ally. How Africans reacted to unity moves from the left depended, as we have seen, on a variety of considerations, most of which had nothing to do with the substantive content of communist ideology, but a great deal to do with the fact that its proponents were, by and large, white, while their prospective allies were black. That a small number of influential

Africans in the ANC were recruited to a pro-socialist and anti-western perspective over the course of the 1950s is certain; but if there was any significant deflection of the ANC as a whole from its earlier course, that deflection, away from orthodox nationalism and back toward a more militant version of traditional liberalism, came as a result of the ANC's association with non-Africans, not its cooperation with communists as such.

The Africanists knew this, and accordingly directed their attack primarily along racial lines. But they also knew that to have a political impact on the mass mind, they had to take popular perceptions and prejudices into account as well. To most ordinary unschooled Africans, the abstraction of "communism" meant nothing when discussed from public platforms or in house-to-house political recruiting. However, most literate or mission-trained Africans, or Africans with some higher education, had absorbed the unambiguous message transmitted to all South Africans by church, school, press, and government: communism was an evil and sinister force. Prejudice against communism was thus strong among a politically significant segment of urban Africans, and even the Africanists themselves were not untouched by it. Under these circumstances it is not surprising that anti-communism became an auxilliary theme of the Africanist attack on the Congress Alliance, with white and Indian designs to "capture" and "dominate" the ANC portrayed as part of a sinister offensive directed from Moscow and carried out through African "functionaries."

The ANC had found that a strong public stand against racialism brought support from elements as politically inimical to one another as white communists and members of the Liberal party. The Africanists too found support in unusual quarters once their dispute with the ANC became openly associated with the issue of communism. Anti-communists in the Liberal party, most notably Jordan Ngubane through his columns in the journal *Opinion* in Natal, and later Patrick Duncan through his editorship of *Contact,* did much to spread an "East versus West" image of the dispute within the Transvaal ANC. *The*

World (previously *The Bantu World*), a major Johannesburg paper, written by and for Africans but owned and controlled by whites, likewise took up the cold war theme and gave the Africanist critics of Congress more coverage in the mid-1950s than their numbers or influence initially warranted. Lacking a press of their own apart from the ephemeral mimeographed issues of *The Africanist,* Leballo and his colleagues found themselves subject through these largely self-appointed allies to the same kind of distorted image-building which had troubled the ANC in its relationship with the leftwing paper, *New Age*.[49]

ANC tempers often flared over these efforts to taint Congress with the communist label or to portray it as controlled by sinister behind-the-scenes forces. It was insulting that critics of Congress should assume that respected ANC leaders were incapable of holding their own, politically and intellectually, in multiracial circles. "This theory of 'Domination' is a product of inferiority whereby some people look at Europeans and Indians as superior beings," wrote Robert Resha, a member of the Congress National Executive, in a press counterattack on the Africanists in 1958.

> This complex flows from the slave mentality that "An African is incapable of standing on his own in the presence of men of other nationalities. . . ." It is . . . significant that the leaders who are being accused of having sold out Congress to Europeans and Indians, are tried and tested leaders who suffered imprisonment, bannings and banishments. Surely, such men as Chief A. J. Luthuli, O. R. Tambo, Professor Z. K. Matthews, to cite a few, can only be thought of as being stooges by people who are either deliberately malicious or completely naive.[50]

It was not communists who were out to sow seeds of dissension and confusion as the Africanists charged, Resha argued; the disrupters were the anti-communists. There were African

49. Leballo's critics have also pointed to the fact that he was employed for a brief period in the late 1950s by the United States Information Service in Johannesburg, raising the suspicion that he may have received funds in return for his efforts to smear the ANC as communist-led.

50. Robert Resha, "Is the ANC Dominated By Communists? No!" *Golden City Post,* 21 December 1958.

communists who had done yeoman service for Congress over many years; Congress had welcomed their contributions, and would continue to welcome assistance from anyone dedicated to the same goals as the ANC. "Our fight in South Africa is not an ideological one," Resha wrote. "It is a natural struggle of a people who demand the end of color-bar and fight for economic and social changes, equal opportunities for all irrespective of race, color or ideology."[51]

From the Suppression of Communism Act in 1950 through the massive Treason Trial beginning in 1956, the government had made clear its intention to smash the ANC "legally" by linking it with alleged communist designs to overthrow the state. In light of the government's strategy, the Africanists' stand against communist influences laid them open to the charge that they were assisting the government, or at least trying to buy its protection. When only a handful of Africanists appeared among the 156 treason suspects, reinforcement was lent to ANC propaganda portraying the Africanists as unwitting allies of Prime Minister Verwoerd. What more could the government ask than to have vocal African politicians giving credibility to its own wild allegations about the "red threat"?

The charge that they were doing the government's dirty work was not an easy one for the Africanists to argue down. The same dilemma would arise for the "Black Consciousness" generation of the early 1970s once they had singled out white liberals for attack. Politics made strange bedfellows. The most that any individual or movement could do was weigh carefully the dictates of both conscience and political intuition and then set a course of action that did the minimum of violence to either.

The Africanists and the Mass Mood of the Late 1950s

As the 1950s drew toward a close and South Africa marked its first decade under Afrikaner Nationalist rule, the mood of urban Africans grew discernibly darker and the nerves of

51. Ibid.

whites correspondingly more tense. National party politicians continued, in tones of sanguine self-congratulation, to assure white voters that, with the exception of a few malcontents and communist "agitators," the country's native population was satisfied, loyal and law-abiding. Evidence to the contrary abounded. "White men knew little about the Africans they worked next to," one foreign white journalist observed.

> I used to hear from my window Africans lifting heavy machinery in the street to the rhythm of traditional chants. One day the Johannesburg municipality announced that they were installing loudspeakers to relay the songs to the workers.
> "What they don't realize," one of our staff explained, "is that they're mostly songs of hate against the white man. The most popular one begins 'abelungu goddamn,' which means 'god-damn the white man.' "[52]

Africans who had grown to maturity in the pre-Nationalist era remained set, to a considerable extent, in habits of political expectation and reaction carried over from the days of Smuts. If the Nationalists seemed oppressive and callous, it nevertheless was possible for older Africans to view them with a certain long-term perspective: the Nationalists had defeated the more moderate United party of the English; was it not possible that in time the English would come to power again and institute reforms which would ease the African's lot? In the meantime, a fatalistic attitude prevailed; the black man, it seemed, was always the passive object of policies made and actions taken somewhere else, by other people. Implicit in this outlook was a limitation on the possibilities for political action: if the African stated his grievances in no uncertain terms, and looked to wise and able leaders to put his case before the authorities, he had done the most that could be done.

The African generations which had grown to adolescence and adulthood since the advent of the Nationalists likewise included their share of individuals resigned to sullen acceptance or passive complaint. The temper of younger Africans in

52. Anthony Sampson, *Drum: A Venture into the New Africa* (London, 1956), p. 60.

general, however, was hardening, and each year saw more grievances added to a list which had already stretched the goodwill of older Africans nearly to breaking point. "Our children have been born, with the whole of their generation, into the midst of the triumph of prejudice," wrote Lutuli later, comparing the world view of youth with that of his own generation. "Young Africans know from infancy upwards—and the point here is that they know nothing else—that their strivings after civilized values will not, in the present order, ever earn for them recognition as sane and responsible civilized beings."[53]

As far as younger Africans were concerned, it was no longer possible to read the slightest shred of benevolent intention into any piece of government legislation regarding Africans. The National party's goal was total control over every aspect of African life and labor, and the truth of this ominous new dispensation was brought home daily to the hundreds of Africans—their numbers mounting by thousands annually— arrested under the Kafkaesque system of passes and permits known collectively as urban "influx control."[54] For younger Africans, whose increasing levels of education qualified them in theory for more rewarding and remunerative jobs than those held by their elders, the heavy hand of influx control often meant opportunities lost and expectations thwarted, for the laws were designed to minimize the African's ability to sell his labor in a free market.

Africans who found their existence in the city defined as "illegal" in terms of apartheid regulations usually resigned themselves to living outside the law and depending on their wits to avoid jail or deportation to the rural reserves. The point at which honesty ended and criminality began was difficult for most urban Africans to specify. In the cities of the Witwatersrand, people stretched meager incomes by buying black-market goods, stolen out the "back door" from white-owned shops and businesses. The schoolboys of today became the

53. Luthuli, *Let My People Go*, pp. 42–43. On the generation gap in the 1950s, also see Nkosi, *Home and Exile*, pp. 3–9.
54. See above, p. 24.

pickpockets and gangsters of tomorrow, driven to crime by disintegrating family life, deteriorating education, and the prospect of nothing but dead-end employment. Measured by any index of social pathology known to industrial societies, the African population of South Africa's cities ranked among the world's most troubled masses of humanity.[55]

Who was to blame? Older Africans might equivocate or avoid the question of guilt; after all, they could remember when times were in some ways worse, when housing and schooling were even harder to come by; and in any case, criticism of the African's condition implied a criticism of themselves for failing to make improvements in that condition. If anyone was to blame, it was the government—Strijdom, Verwoerd, the cabinet, the National party, perhaps the Afrikaners as a whole.

Such cautious judgments and reactions from the middle-aged and the elderly tended to evoke an impatient and even scornful response from the young. How could the blame be laid merely on Verwoerd or a few Afrikaners? It was clear from the way the system worked that *all* whites were out to enslave the black man, exploit his labor, and check his social, cultural and educational advance. If pass and job restrictions failed to accomplish this, the new scheme for "Bantu Education" was designed to relegate Africans to a permanently inferior status. Why should Africans bother to think of reforming this system or of pressing whites to reach some kind of compromise? Why not just take over the country and use force to get justice for the black man? Africa for the Africans. Ghana and Guinea were becoming free, and Kenyans were using force to drive whites out of East Africa. Why not South Africa? It was not a widely articulated set of sentiments, let alone a plan. It was just a mood, an undercurrent of anger and hostility, brewing in the

55. The best substantiation for this characterization can be found in the short stories and novels of black South African writers like Can Themba, Lewis Nkosi, Nat Nakasa, Alex La Guma, Dugmore Boetie, Ezekiel Mphahlele, Bloke Modisane, Arthur Maimane, Tod Matshikiza, Casey Motsisi and others.

spirit of the young and spilling over, little by little, into the consciousness of the wider society.[56]

Sniffing this new mood in the air, the Africanists took heart. Here was the raw material of African nationalism and ultimately of revolution. The African's urge to become master of his own destiny was in fact, the Africanists argued, an urge to nationhood. Far from being a product of new circumstances, this "urge" was a primordial sentiment, dating from the first contact of conquered and conqueror; social conditions were only now drawing out the African's long-latent consciousness of his condition. Soon, the Africanists believed, the full force of the pent-up revolutionary energies of the masses would be unleashed. Lembede had proceeded from a somewhat similar assumption in 1947, when he compared the latent revolutionary potential of the African to the power of atomic energy. Mda had echoed the same idea in references to Africans as a "sleeping giant," powerful, but as yet not fully conscious of their own strength.[57] Men of "rebel" temperament, it seemed, usually being young themselves and sensitive to the

56. Extensive statistical evidence on African opinion in this period does not exist, but impressionistic evidence is abundant. One list of detailed African grievances collected during the campaign for the Congress of the People was preserved among the Treason Trial documents. Compiled in a section of Alexandra township in Johannesburg, it shows influx control and low wages as the predominant African problems, with poor quality education being a grievance of lesser intensity (Treason Trial documents presented in evidence). Also see Edward Feit's analysis of this data in *South Africa: The Dynamics of the African National Congress* (London, 1962), pp. 70–73. Brett's 1961 survey of a sample of 150 middle class, predominantly young, Africans found Bantu Education to be the chief grievance, with influx control and pass laws a close second (*African Attitudes*, pp. 51–53). Brett found a strong awareness of independent Africa in his sample (pp. 69–72). Seventy percent felt change in South Africa could come only through violence, passive resistance, or other forms of active struggle (p. 64). Crijns, in a survey of African university students and recent graduates in the late 1950s, found that 77 percent felt violence was the likeliest solution to the South African conflict (*Race Relations and Race Attitudes*, p. 134).

57. Mda, "The Analysis" (Treason Trial transcript, p. 9888).

heightened tensions of youth around them, never hesitated to project onto all of African society the same sentiments and urges they associated with the prevailing mood of their own generation. Neither this tendency in their own thinking, nor the prospect that the anger and zeal of their own age-group would eventually mellow into the apathy of middle-age, were factors which ever counted heavily in their political calculations. The Africanists were no exception to this pattern. The militant spirit of youth was proof to them that "the masses" were prepared for action. The people were ready, they felt; it was their overly cautious leaders who were holding back. There was, of course, a measure of truth in this conviction, but also a point where truth left off and the ambitions of a new and more daring would-be leadership began.

6

The Pan Africanist
Congress, 1959–1960

The Africanists Break Away

By the late 1950s, the government's campaign against the Congress movement had taken a heavy toll.[1] With nearly all its most able leaders subject to bans which limited their mobility and even prohibited some of them from legally belonging to the ANC, Congress faced serious organizational strains. In the Transvaal, these strains threatened to wreck the movement from within, even if the government declined to implement its threat of outright proscription. In Pretoria the marathon Treason Trial dragged on, sapping the energies and destroying the livelihood of the accused. Substituting for the accused—and for the real Congress decision-makers who, though banned, nevertheless continued from behind the scenes to guide the ANC as best they could—were a second- and third-string group of office bearers whose political talent was not always equal to the task of leadership which they had inherited. As normal democratic procedures increasingly conflicted with the need to coordinate a nominal and a "shadow" leadership, and as disaffection and factionalism spread, the ANC began to take on some of the characteristics of a political machine; elections were prearranged, decisions were steam-

1. Portions of this chapter and the next have previously appeared in altered form in Karis and Carter, vol. 3.

rollered through conferences, and criticism from the general membership was stifled.

The treason arrests in December 1956 had provoked a defiant African response which was summed up in the Congress slogan, "We Stand By Our Leaders!" In the Transvaal Congress, however, the spirit of unity expressed in the slogan proved short-lived. At a provincial conference in October 1957 the incumbent Transvaal executive, many of whom were among the treason defendants, invoked the call to stand by the leaders and prevailed upon the assembled delegates to return them to office en bloc as a show of unity and loyalty in the face of government persecution. This turned out to be an artificial display of solidarity, however, and by the time the annual ANC national conference met in December 1957 it was clear that there was serious rank-and-file dissatisfaction with the running of Transvaal affairs. A group of branches calling themselves the "petitioners" filed complaints alleging that the elections had been unconstitutional, and that outlying branches had not been invited to the provincial conference. The African press chided the Transvaal leadership for treating ordinary members like "babies" and mere "voting cattle."[2] Similar disputes plagued areas of the Cape. Instead of uniting under the pressure of government harassment, the ANC appeared to be slipping into a morass of squabbles and petty rivalries.

The Orlando Africanists, swept by the general anti-government mood in the opening months of the Treason Trial, at first refrained from pressing their attack on the Transvaal Congress. But as 1957 wore on and dissension and impatience spread among the rank and file, Leballo and his group began to step up their criticism of the Congress Alliance in the hope that popular dissatisfaction could be molded into a movement to oust the "multiracialists." An Africanist call for a vote of no confidence in the Transvaal executive failed to carry at the annual national conference in December 1957, but the petitioning branches were assured that a new conference would soon be convened to consider their grievances. When this special conference met in the Orlando Communal Hall on

2. *The World,* 7 December 1957, and *Golden City Post,* 2 March 1958.

23 February 1958, a showdown appeared inevitable. The Africanists, few in number but adept at manipulating their less ideological fellow dissidents, had by this time closed ranks with the "petitioners." Their combined strength posed a credible threat to the provincial office-bearers and their unpopular stand-ins. Wrangling and fist-fighting broke out as "volunteers" loyal to the executive attempted to screen out hostile would-be "delegates." The mood of the meeting, once proceedings got underway, was antagonistic towards the inept provincial executive committee, and, taking advantage of the temper of the delegates, Leballo moved that new elections be held immediately. Enthusiastic applause welcomed the motion. But just as it seemed that the dissidents would prevail—opening the possibility that the Africanists might gain a bridgehead in the Transvaal provincial executive—the chairman declared the meeting closed because time had expired for use of the hall. Loyal delegates rose and broke into strains of "Nkosi Sikelel i-Afrika," the ANC anthem, but most people present remained seated in confusion and protest.[3] The Transvaal had reached a new organizational low, bordering on complete collapse. Following renewed haggling behind the scenes, the disputed executive was eventually removed and the National Executive Committee assumed emergency powers to direct the affairs of the Transvaal.

Poor popular response to an election-day stay-at-home in April 1958 drove the stocks of the Transvaal Congress leadership still lower, and the Africanists, who had opposed the calling of the strike, did not hesitate to exploit this new evidence that the ANC was out of touch with mass sentiment. Hoping to isolate and deflate Leballo's supporters, and perhaps also hoping to turn the Africanist "disrupters" into scapegoats for the failure of the stay-at-home, a top-level Congress caucus, consisting mostly of banned leaders, decided in May to expel Leballo from the ANC for the second time. Josias Madzunya of Alexandra township in Johannesburg was likewise expelled.

3. Descriptions of this conference appear in *The World,* 1 and 8 March 1958; *Rand Daily Mail,* 25 February 1959; *Golden City Post,* 2 March 1958; and *Contact,* 8 March 1958.

Madzunya, a street peddler with a flamboyant personality and an elementary school education, had been portrayed by *The World* and *Golden City Post* as a leading Africanist, but he was in fact only on the periphery of the Africanist movement. A former brief association with the Communist party had left him strongly critical of white radicals, and like the Africanists he was opposed to any cooperation between the ANC and the Congress of Democrats. His distinctive appearance (he was heavily bearded and always wore a black overcoat) and his knack for calling a spade a spade from the public platform made him good copy for journalists seeking sensational news. The Africanists at this stage were not particularly concerned with projecting a highbrow image, and they felt that they could use Madzunya's popularity to augment their own limited support, without suffering unduly from being identified with his admittedly crude "anti-white" style. The more the press built Madzunya up as a spokesman of Africanist opinion, the more convenient it became for the Orlando Africanists to use him to publicize their case against the Congress Alliance. Madzunya on his part played the role of fire-eating nationalist with enthusiasm, largely unaware that the Africanists considered him a politically dispensable stalking-horse.

A few days before the white general election of April 1958, the government placed a ban on all political meetings of over ten Africans in Transvaal urban centers. When this restriction was lifted in late August 1958, disputes which had been simmering under the surface again came into the open. The issue of incompetence and irregularities in the Congress provincial administration had died down somewhat with the take-over of provincial affairs by the National Executive Committee. When the clash between loyalists and Africanists surfaced again, the ground had shifted back to ideology and strategy, with the Africanists reasserting their attack on the Alliance with new fervor.

Within the ANC, the Africanists could call on the support of some of the former petitioning branches, factions of varying sizes within other Transvaal branches, Madzunya's followers from Alexandra, and on an assortment of individual nationalists in Congress who opposed the Alliance on the grounds that it was divisive and harmful to the ANC's popular image. Under the manipulating guidance of Peter Raboroko, an early Youth Leaguer and member of the Africanist inner circle, an ad hoc grouping called the "Anti-Charterist Council" was formed to coordinate these forces as the November Transvaal provincial conference approached. To test the strength of anti-Alliance sentiment in the ANC, the "Council" proposed to run its own candidate for Transvaal President: Josias Madzunya. Madzunya, who was contesting his expulsion and hoped to have it overruled at the conference, agreed to run and to publish an Africanist election manifesto ghost-written by Raboroko.[4]

The two-day conference opened on the afternoon of 1 November, 1958 with an address by Lutuli denouncing the National party and blaming the government for injecting "the virus of prejudice and sectionalism" into the African community.[5] White "panderings to racialism," he said, were causing some Africans to try to "emulate the [Afrikaner] Nationalists in claiming exclusive control of South Africa. . . . We have seen developing—even though it is in its embryonic stage—a dangerously narrow African nationalism, which itself tends to encourage us to go back to a tribalism mentality."[6] In the fierce debate which followed the address, Africanist spokesmen held forth on their theory that Africans would have to fight alone if they were to achieve maximum strength in the struggle. A crowd of tough Africanist camp followers who were clustered at the back of the hall heckled the speakers who rose to support Lutuli, and expressed their support for Africanist speakers by stamping their feet and shouting "Afrika!" As tensions rose and the test of voting strength approached, the inevitable dispute over credentials ensued. Africanist branches and branch-factions had sent representatives, but their credentials

4. *The World,* 27 September and 4 October 1958; *Contact,* 1 November 1958; and interviews with Raboroko and Molete.
5. Descriptions of this conference appear in *The World,* 1 and 8 November 1958; *Rand Daily Mail,* 3 November 1958; *Cape Times,* 3 November 1958; and *Drum,* December 1958.
6. Quoted in *Contact,* 15 November 1958.

were challenged by loyalist representatives from the same areas. The Africanists refused to recognize the credentials committee on the grounds that it was biased. Oliver Tambo, the ANC Secretary General, who was attempting to chair the meeting, remained calm, but the hall seemed ready to explode into violence at any moment. When the first day's session closed, it was ruled that the conference would be open the next day only to accredited delegates.

The next morning it became clear that the loyalists were prepared to back up their "delegates only" ruling with force if necessary. A crowd of ANC volunteers assembled behind the conference hall, armed with sticks and lengths of iron. A crowd of Africanist supporters, some similarly armed, gathered in front. Each group numbered at least a hundred men. The loyalists were posted to the doors of the conference hall, and the screening of delegates began. Police and security branch detectives watched from a distance, anticipating an explosion if the Africanists tried to enter the conference.

But no explosion came. Realizing that they had been out maneuvered, the Africanists held a quick caucus outside the hall. Some argued for an attempt to enter the conference, but a majority felt that the time had come instead for a parting of the ways. A letter declaring an Africanist breakaway was drawn up and delivered to the door of the hall as elections were proceeding inside among the loyalists. The Africanists, declared the letter, were not a "para-military clique" and were not prepared to settle their quarrel with the ANC by violence; nor were they prepared to remain tied any longer to an organization which had adopted the Freedom Charter in defiance of the principles of African nationalism embodied in the 1949 *Programme of Action*. They were therefore launching out, they said, "as the custodians of the ANC policy as it was formulated in 1912 and pursued up to the time of the Congress Alliances."[7]

7. "Copy of a Letter Sent to Mr. Speaker, A.N.C. Conference Held at Orlando on the 1st to the 2nd November, 1958," signed S. T. Ngendane, *The Africanist*, January 1959, reproduced in Karis and Carter, vol. 3, pp. 505–6.

The break was neither wholly spontaneous nor wholly pre-meditated. A few individuals in the Africanist inner circle had been pressing for an independent organization for several years. The majority, however, had clung to the hope that Congress would eventually reject multiracialism of its own accord. Mda had always opposed the establishment of any rival organization to the ANC, and his consistent advice to the Africanists had been to work within Congress, building support for "un-adulterated" African nationalism, so that the organization might eventually be brought back to the doctrines of the early Youth League. Whatever its failures or successes, its weakness or wisdom, the ANC was an African tradition, an institution enshrined in African hearts, as even its bitterest critics were compelled to admit. The Industrial and Commercial Workers' Union, the African Democratic party, and Selope Thema's National-Minded Bloc, had all come and gone while the ANC remained, surviving every political storm. It was therefore with some trepidation that the Africanists began to launch out on an independent course, for they too had a strong faith in the durability of the ANC.

Predictions varied as to how strong the new movement might become. From the vantage point of the ANC's national leadership, the Africanists appeared to constitute just one more ephemeral "mushroom" grouping, closest in form and motivation to the short-lived National-Minded Bloc of the early 1950s. In interpreting the conflict to their more un-sophisticated followers, Congress leaders could easily dismiss the Africanist walkout as the action of a clique of disappointed position seekers. It was clear to any unbiased observer that both the African and white press had consistently exaggerated the actual strength of Leballo and Madzunya. As a result, when newspapers referred to a "Big-Scale ANC Split," there was a tendency among many ANC leaders and loyalists to react with scorn and to dismiss such journalistic pronouncements as mere sensationalism or malicious anti-ANC propaganda.[8]

8. Headline in the *Rand Daily Mail*, 3 November 1958. The *Golden City Post*, 9 November 1958, proclaimed: "Now There Are Two ANCs."

Among older Africans of the liberal school who were sincerely apprehensive about the growth of an aggressive black nationalism, there was a tendency to take the Africanist threat more seriously, but at the same time to feel a sense of relief that the Congress had at last shed its extremist or "racialistic" wing. Caught between the Africanists and the old guard liberals were those Congressites who were opposed to both the disruptive tactics of the Africanists and to the basic trend of ANC policies regarding cooperation with non-Africans. This element, which was not a cohesive group but was sometimes referred to as the "nationalists," remained for the most part within the ANC, awaiting further developments.

In spite of the Africanists' acute sense of being a distinct group within the ANC, their movement lacked any systematic structure. At the time of their breakaway they had only the rudiments of an internal organization of their own, consisting mainly of an informal network of contacts between Leballo's circle in Johannesburg and small groups of like-minded Congress members in other centers. During the Treason Trial, some opportunity was afforded for direct contact between the Transvaal Africanists and Africanists from Natal and the Cape who were defendants in the trial. Communication was otherwise confined to occasional letters and visits. Africanists outside the Transvaal were therefore taken by surprise by the events of 2 November 1958, and a number of weeks passed before formal secessions took place in Natal and the Cape. In the Free State, always the most politically lethargic province, there was little Africanist activity until after March 1960. In neither Natal nor the Cape had the divisions within the ANC become so severe and near-violent as in the Transvaal; but once the Transvaal Africanists had broken off, their sympathizers elsewhere were confronted with a fait accompli and had little choice but to follow suit. In Natal, A. B. Ngcobo, a Youth League Africanist, announced the secession of the Natal faction without fanfare at the annual national conference of the ANC held in Durban in mid-December. In spite of strong anti-Indian antagonism among Africans, Africanist sentiment was not widespread in Natal, in part because Chief Albert

Lutuli, the ANC President General, was highly popular among his fellow Zulus. In the Cape, where nationalist-minded Africans had long resented attempts by white radicals to use the ANC in their campaigns for election to Parliament as Native Representatives, two rival provincial executives, one loyalist and one Africanist, had coexisted throughout most of 1958. In spite of efforts by the National Executive to bring about a reconciliation, the split deepened and in the early months of 1959 a number of Cape branches and branch factions began to defect from the ANC to the Africanist side.[9]

Over the Van Riebeeck Day holiday weekend in April 1959, the Africanist movement formally transformed itself into the Pan Africanist Congress at a three-day conference held at the Orlando Communal Hall. Among the three to four hundred people who attended, Transvaal representation was the heaviest, but delegates were also present from Natal and the Cape, along with a small number from the Orange Free State. Placards carrying nationalist and pan-Africanist slogans lined the walls of the hall: "Africa for Africans, Cape to Cairo, Morocco to Madagascar," "Imperialists Quit Africa," and "Izwe Lethu i-Afrika" ("Africa, Our Land"). Following tradition, the conference opened with prayers and sermons by prominent clergymen, but in keeping with the inclinations of the Africanists, the principal clergyman invited to speak was the Reverend Walter M. Dimba, leader of what was then the country's largest federation of African independent churches. Cabled greetings from Kwame Nkrumah and Sekou Toure were triumphantly read out, underscoring the Africanists' determination to identify their cause with the continent-wide progress of anti-colonial struggles. "Today, three hundred and seven years ago," proclaimed the conference agenda for 6 April, Van Riebeeck Day, "began the act of Aggression against

9. "Report on Cape Dispute," *Annual Report of the National Executive Committee of the 46th Annual General Conference of the African National Congress,* December 1958 (Carter-Karis collection). Also see *The World,* 6 and 20 September and 25 October 1958; *Rand Daily Mail,* 10 February 1959. Information on Cape disputes is also drawn from interviews with Elliot Magwentshu and from an interview with Peter Hjul by Gwendolen Carter.

the Sons and Daughters of Afrika, by which the African people were dispossessed of their land, and subjected to white domination. As it was here, and on this day that it began, it is imperative that it should be here, and on this day that it should be buried."[10]

Newsmen covering the conference reported being impressed with the serious and orderly atmosphere now prevailing among the Africanists, in contrast to their disruptive and frustrated conduct over the preceding years. A further surprise for the press was Madzunya's failure to win so much as a seat on the National Executive Committee of the new organization, even though some papers had suggested earlier that he might be elected president. Instead, the movement's leading back-room theoretician, Robert Mangaliso Sobukwe, emerged as president in a unanimous vote, and Leballo was chosen national secretary.

Robert Sobukwe

Sobukwe's employment, first by the Transvaal Department of Education and then by the white University of the Witwatersrand, had been a constant constraint on his overt political participation and he had never actively sought any position of leadership. Yet he was not a political dark horse at the time he assumed direction of the PAC. To people who had known him as an outspoken Youth Leaguer ten years earlier, his re-emergence came as no particular surprise. Though he was more an academic than a politician by calling, his eloquence on the public platform and his passionate commitment to political change had marked him out from his college days as a natural leader.

Sobukwe was born in the predominantly Afrikaner town of Graaff Reinet in the Cape in 1924, the last of six children. His father, who worked as a laborer for about $4.40 a month, had

10. Agenda for the Africanist Inaugural Convention (Hoover microfilms), and interviews with 'Molotsi and A. B. Ngcobo. Descriptions of the PAC Inaugural Convention appear in *The World*, 11 April 1959; *Star*, 4 April 1959; *Times*, London, 7 April 1959; *Contact*, 18 April 1959; *Drum*, May 1959; and *Africa South*, July–September 1959.

an elementary school education, but his mother was without formal schooling.[11] Father and sons chopped wood at the end of each day to supplement the family's income. Both parents were active in the local Methodist church, and like Lembede and Mda, Sobukwe grew up with Christianity as his earliest ideological frame of reference.[12] Precocious in his early school years, he won a scholarship to Healdtown, a Methodist boarding school, where he studied for seven years. With financial help from Healdtown's missionary headmaster and other scholarship money, he entered Fort Hare in 1947.

The quiet college town of Alice in the Cape was not the political maelstrom of Johannesburg, but Fort Hare's faculty did boast one African politician of national standing in Professor Z. K. Matthews, a leading Congress light and a member of the Natives' Representative Council. As the critical election of 1948 approached and white politicians debated their respective solutions to the "Native problem," the fate of the NRC became a focal point of concern to politically conscious Africans. Smuts proposed enlarging the NRC and increasing its functions, and this had renewed the boycott dilemma. Sobukwe's interest in poetry and literature began to be overshadowed by a new concern with politics, and in his second year he and two fellow students started producing a handwritten commentary which they posted on college bulletin boards, attacking the NRC and all manifestations of African collaboration. When Pitje, under Mda's prodding, brought the Youth League to Fort Hare after the election, Sobukwe became one of

11. Facts on Sobukwe's early years are drawn from information given by himself to Benjamin Pogrund and Gwendolen Carter, and from the following: C. and M. Legum, *The Bitter Choice: Eight South Africans' Resistance to Tyranny* (Cleveland, 1968); M. Nkoana, "Political Tough-Talker," *Drum*, May 1959; L. Nkosi, "Robert Sobukwe: An Assessment," *Africa Report*, April 1962; A. B. Ngcobo, "'This Side of Eternity': An Appeal to the United Nations Special Committee on Apartheid on Behalf of Mangaliso Robert Sobukwe," *The New African*, November 1965; and R. Leshoai, "The Man Who Will Win," *Azania News*, February 1972 and July 1973.

12. Sobukwe became a Methodist lay preacher, authorized to preach in the absence of an ordained minister. One of his two surviving brothers became an Anglican bishop.

the League's most active and articulate members. College and Youth League politics intermingled. To the student mind there was scant difference between paternalistic authoritarianism in the mission school microcosm and Malan's promise of white *baasskap*. A strike of student nurses at nearby Lovedale brought the Fort Hare League out in force in 1949, and for Sobukwe, head of the Students' Representative Council in his final year, it was the first real taste of confrontation politics.[13] In a speech to the graduating class in October 1949, he sounded many of the themes of his later career as a political "rebel":

> You have seen by now what education means to us; the identification of ourselves with the masses. . . . We must be the embodiment of our people's aspirations. *And all we are required to do is to show the light and the masses will find the way.* Watch our movements keenly and if you see any signs of "broadmindedness" or "reasonableness" in us, or if you hear us talk of practical experience as a modifier of man's views, denounce us as traitors to Africa. . . . I wish to make it clear again that we are antinobody. We are pro-Africa. We breathe, we dream, we live Africa; because Africa and humanity are inseparable. It is only by doing the same that the minorities in this land, the European, Coloured, and Indian, can secure mental and spiritual freedom. . . . We have been accused of blood-thirstiness because we preach "non-collaboration." I wish to state here tonight that that is the only course open to us. History has taught us that a group in power has never voluntarily relinquished its position. It has

13. Sobukwe submitted an article on the strike to *Inkundla ya Bantu,* then edited by Ngubane in Natal. Ngubane felt the article might be libelous, and wrote to Pitje for advice. Pitje supported Ngubane's decision, but commented: "I must endorse what Mr. Mda told you about Mr. Sobukwe. He is by far the most brilliant fellow we have at College at the moment, and it is doubtful if Fort Hare will get the like of him within the foreseeable future. The boy is a thinker, and a scholar and has full command of the English language. That is why his attacks, whether on the College or on the Conventionists [the AAC], never fail to get their mark. Were it not that he was handicapped by events here at College—the Nurses' Strike, Youth League affairs, etc.—we would be sure that he will get a double first class [degree]. But now we cannot expect it" (letter from Pitje to Ngubane, 9 November 1949, Carter-Karis collection).

always been forced to do so. And we do not expect miracles to happen in Africa.

We want to build a new Africa, and only we can build it. . . . Talks of co-operation are not new to us. Every time our people have shown signs of uniting against oppression, their "friends" have come along and broken that unity. . . . Between 1900 and 1946 it has been the professional Liberal. Today it is again the Missionary who fulfills this role. . . . I am afraid these gentlemen are dealing with a new generation which cannot be bamboozled. "What you are thunders so loudly that what you say cannot be heard."

Let me plead with you, lovers of my Africa, to carry with you into the world the vision of a new Africa, an Africa re-born, an Africa rejuvenated, an Africa re-created, young AFRICA. We are the first glimmers of a new dawn. And if we are persecuted for our views, we should remember, as the African saying goes . . . that the dying beast kicks most violently when it is giving up the ghost so to speak. The fellows who clamped Nehru into jail are today his servants. And we have it from the Bible that those who crucified Christ will appear before Him on the judgment day. We are what we are because the God of Africa made us so. We dare not compromise, nor dare we use moderate language in the [cause] of freedom.[14]

Two months later the annual national conference of the ANC met in Bloemfontein, and Sobukwe was present with the Fort Hare Youth League delegation to press for passage of a strong program of action. Working from a preliminary program drawn up for the 1948 annual conference by Mda and others, Sobukwe and Pitje had drafted their own version of a program for submission to the Cape provincial conference held at Queenstown in June 1949. This version had been endorsed by the Cape, and some of its ideas were subsequently included in the final program that emerged at Bloemfontein.

Like all younger militants, Sobukwe applauded the decision at Bloemfontein to adopt new methods of civil disobedience. But if the relative emphasis in the Cape draft can be taken as a guide, his primary concern was that the ANC adopt and

14. Speech at the "Completers' Social," 21 October 1949, reproduced in Karis and Carter, vol. 2, pp. 331–36. Emphasis added.

adhere to a strategy of political boycotts. "We claim the right of direct representation in all the governing bodies of the country (National, provincial and local) on a democratic basis," declared the Cape program in a passage carried over nearly verbatim into the final Bloemfontein version.

> And we resolve to work for the abolition of all differential institutions or bodies specially created for Africans, e.g. Local or District Councils, Advisory Boards, NRC and the present form of Parliamentary representation. This means the adoption for active application of the policy of boycotting.[15]

The boycott question had always been more salient in the Cape than elsewhere because of the greater range of token representation of Cape Africans in "white" political institutions. The All African Convention, a nationwide organization at its founding in 1935–36, eventually found its only substantial backing in the Cape, in part because it championed the idea of boycott. Some of Sobukwe's enthusiasm for boycotts no doubt resulted from his immersion in the Cape political environment, and his exposure to the ideas of the AAC. But faith in the potential efficacy of boycott was not confined entirely to the Cape. As we have already seen, it had also been a feature of Lembede's thinking, and was a common element in the "rebel" outlook of most Youth Leaguers in the 1940s. To the rebel's way of thinking—and Sobukwe in his college years was to become set in the nonconformist psychological mold—nothing was more contemptible than the "realist's" willingness to accept the compromise of half a loaf.

Approval of a boycott policy by the 1949 national conference thus fulfilled one of the most cherished goals of Lembede and the early Youth League, and Africanists loyal to Lembede's

15. The Cape program, reproduced in *Inkundla ya Bantu*, 30 July 1949. This version closely resembles both the December 1948 draft (Carter-Karis collection) and the final draft, which is reproduced in Karis and Carter, vol. 2, pp. 337–39. A long report on the Cape provincial conference appears in *Inkundla ya Bantu*, 23 July 1949. Sobukwe's role in the passage of the Cape program is the basis for later claims that he was one of the authors of the *Programme of Action* of 1949.

principles continued to defend non-participation in "dummy institutions" after the ANC had again reverted by the mid-1950s to a laissez faire "realist" stance. To many people, the issue seemed a sterile one; the government would continue to maintain such institutions, and Africans would continue to man them, whether the ANC boycotted them or not. To radical intellectuals, however, the issue could never be reduced to one of pure practicality. The principles involved were too compelling. Ten years later, Sobukwe was still arguing the case in the same terms in which Lembede had argued it in the 1940s and that SASO intellectuals would argue it in the 1970s. "The white minority," Sobukwe wrote in 1959,

> can maintain its continued domination only by perfecting the techniques of control in such a way as to enlist the active co-operation and goodwill of the oppressed. These techniques include the creation of bodies calculated to maintain and develop the relations of dominating and dominated, as well as to condition the minds of the dominated for the unquestioning acceptance of their role as collaborators in the perpetuation of their own domination.[16]

For Sobukwe as for Lembede, this process of mental conditioning was at the root of race relationships in South Africa. It was the secret of the whites' continuing control, and it was the key to African liberation. If Africans could only be brought to mentally reject their subject status, Sobukwe believed, it would not then be difficult for them to find means of ending white domination. Seen in this light, a policy of non-collaboration was an essential part of the strategy of conditioning African political reflexes. "We are not so much concerned with the complete negative abstention of the people [from voting] as with the creation of a state of mind," Sobukwe told the Cape provincial conference of the ANC in June 1949. "The boycott is an appropriate weapon of the moment; . . . [it] will work tremendously on the mental state of the people."[17]

16. "Sobukwe Outlines Africanists' Case," *Contact*, 30 May 1959.
17. Quoted in "The Annual Provincial Conference," *Inkundla ya Bantu*, 23 July 1949.

More vital still to this process of political education, Sobukwe believed, was the propagation of orthodox nationalism, for only through nationalist thinking could the masses eventually be aroused to the necessary pitch of revolutionary fervor. Organizational structures, tactics, and techniques of struggle, all were secondary compared to the problem of getting the masses to "think nationalist." In Sobukwe's conception of the situation, the achievement of this mental transformation was the most important responsibility of African leaders; their task was to "show the light," and the masses, in their own time and using their own methods, would thereafter somehow "find the way."

Following his graduation from Fort Hare in 1949 Sobukwe began a period of relative isolation from the mainstream of ANC politics. He had been elected national secretary of the Youth League at the December 1949 conference, but with the overthrow of the Congress old guard and under Pitje's uncertain leadership as president, the League declined and lost much of its former zeal. Sobukwe moved to Standerton in the eastern Transvaal where he took up employment as a high school teacher. After speaking publicly in support of the Defiance Campaign in 1952, he was fired from his position and made a brief attempt to go into business as a coal dealer. His school reinstated him, however, and he returned to teaching, a profession better suited to his interests and personality. In 1954, he was hired as a language instructor by the University of the Witwatersrand, and in June of that year he moved from Standerton to Johannesburg.

When Sobukwe arrived at the geographical center of African politics, the ANC had already passed through its transformations of the early 1950s; the Defiance Campaign had left it greatly enhanced in membership and prestige, and its affiliations with the SAIC and the COD had already been cemented. The day-to-day exigencies of organization and finance, and the new climate of multiracial camaraderie in Congress leadership circles, were things that Sobukwe had not personally experienced during his four years in the eastern Transvaal. Instead, living in the predominantly Afrikaner town of Standerton, his concept of race oppression as primarily an attitudinal problem on the part of Africans had been reinforced; Africans in "tough" towns like Standerton deferred to whites, lacked confidence in themselves, and shied away from politics.

Arriving in Johannesburg, Sobukwe found preparations underway for the Congress of the People. The ANC was addressing itself to the need for much higher African political consciousness, but what had happened to the ideology of nationalism, the only creed that could maximize that consciousness? The warnings issued by Mda's Bureau of African Nationalism had, in Sobukwe's view, proven accurate: the ANC had rejected the insights of Lembede and allowed its organization in the Transvaal to be captured by a congeries of liberal-leftist "multiracialists."

When ANC loyalists later attacked the PAC's perspective as unrealistic, they sometimes referred to Sobukwe's isolation from the national scene in the critical years 1950–54 and to his "country" background. Elaborating on the contrast between Sobukwe and the more experienced leaders of the ANC, Joe Matthews commented in later years that

> some of us like [Duma] Nokwe and others, and myself, . . . had come to Fort Hare from [St. Peter's School in] Johannesburg. . . . We had spent five years in Johannesburg, and had been in the Johannesburg political whirlpool. . . . And it was a very, very exciting time to be in Johannesburg, during and just after the war. . . . By the time we got to the college, we had ideas. . . . We were members of the movement; we had been in that movement for some time, and we knew all the ins and outs of the ANC. And we found . . . chaps like Sobukwe and others, had just come straight from Healdtown, spent some years at Healdtown, and from Healdtown six miles across to Fort Hare. And this was their life . . . the quiet sort of life of that part of the country. . . . And from there into teaching at Standerton, another little town. . . . He might have been able to adjust if he had been participating [in 1950–4] but being out of the sort of practical day-to-day thing, he then came with what he considered was an idea which he had and which had not been fulfilled. . . . [He was a] sincere sort of chap. And sincere in a way which unfortunately politicians are not. By that I mean that he had a sincerity of a starry-eyed type.[18]

18. Interview with Joe Matthews.

There was unquestionably an inflexibility in Sobukwe's thinking, expressed so pointedly in his graduation address, and an unwillingness to allow experience—his own or anyone else's—to modify the original conception of politics which he had formed in his youthful years. The experience of multiracial cooperation which had caused Sisulu, Mandela, Matthews and others to temper their earlier mistrust of non-Africans was something which never impinged on Sobukwe's world view, partly because of circumstances perhaps, but also by conscious choice on his own part. The other side of his transparent sincerity was a streak of militant egalitarianism which caused him to shun any manifestation of elitism. The mixed gatherings so popular with Johannesburg's political "in crowd" aroused his instinctive aversion, as did the airs of sophistication assumed by Africans who spoke of the "immaturity" of orthodox nationalism. Whether or not multiracialism had proven practical in the short run, Sobukwe, like Mda, held that liberation in the end could only be achieved by a leadership which represented the aspirations of the common African. Multiracialism, Sobukwe felt, merely represented the aspirations of a cosmopolitan upper stratum.[19] "It must be confessed," he wrote in a sharp attack on his ANC critics in 1959, "that the Africanist view of democracy must be startling and upsetting to all those who have been bred and fed on the liberal idea of an African elite being gradually trained, brain-washed, fathered and absorbed into a so-called South African Multiracial Nationhood, whilst the vast masses of Africans are being exploited and denied democratic rights on the grounds of their unreadiness, backwardness and illiteracy."[20] The charge was an unfair one if applied to the conscious intentions of the ANC's national leadership as a whole, but it revealed a sensitivity on Sobukwe's part to the elitist tendencies inherent in the day-to-day dynamics of multiracial politics.

Sobukwe did not immediately identify himself openly with

19. See especially Lewis Nkosi, "Robert Sobukwe: An Assessment," *Africa Report*, April 1962, p. 7.
20. R. Sobukwe ["Pan Afrika"], "Pan Africanist Congress on Guard in Defence of P.A.C. Policy and Programme," *The Africanist*, December 1959, p. 13 (Carter-Karis collection).

Leballo's group on his arrival in Johannesburg, but when *The Africanist* began publication in late 1954 he contributed a short theoretical piece on "The Essentials of Democracy," which was printed under a pseudonym. Leballo and his circle were on the right track, Sobukwe felt; what they needed was less emotion and more intellectual discipline. Mda had tried to provide this as best he could, but he was engaged in his legal studies in the Cape and was in touch with the Orlando Africanists only by letters and on occasional visits to the Transvaal. In any case, Mda had proved reluctant to take the field openly against his friends and former colleagues in the Youth League, Mandela, Tambo and Sisulu, who were now defenders of the Congress Alliance. Sobukwe felt no such restraints, however, and his talent for excoriating the Congress leadership on paper or from the public platform rapidly became apparent to his fellow "rebels."

Only after Sobukwe had gone to prison and become a martyr of the 1960 Sharpeville emergency did his charismatic qualities become recognized widely. Within the Africanist movement and the PAC, however, he was regarded almost from the beginning as a man of extraordinary gifts. Expressing typical feelings about Sobukwe, one of the Orlando Africanists wrote in later years:

> About . . . 1955, our numbers were swelled by the arrival of . . . Robert Sobukwe. . . . I was impressed by Sobukwe, in particular by his clear, incisive mind, his ability to bring himself to the level of anyone he talks to, his glowing honesty portrayed in his eyes, his earnest desire to know and his concern for the welfare of each one of us; his willingness to assist in whatever capacity; his sternness that is so subtly couched in that visible human touch. These characteristics and many others particularly enhanced when delivering a speech, did make me feel that there was that attribute in him which is so visibly lacking in many of his contemporaries. His approach on various subjects on which I have been privileged to hear him was so simple and yet so revealing; no one could fail to appreciate that Sobukwe was an intellectual—vastly read and apparently knowing the solutions to many of our problems, yet not at all keen to impose himself upon those whom he found at the helm of things at the time.[21]

21. Charles Lakaje, untitled MS, 1970, p. 22.

Sobukwe was reluctant from the beginning to thrust himself forward as a leader within the Africanist movement, and even on the eve of the PAC's inaugural conference, outsiders to the movement were not certain whether he would become the president of the new organization.[22] In private his manner was self-effacing almost to the point of diffidence; only before audiences did he become the impassioned politician, striving for an emotional impact. In a group with many thwarted would-be leaders, he was almost the only man for whom politics was wholly the product of a sense of duty and never an outlet for frustrated ambition.

Polite and good-natured in the presence of whites, Sobukwe in front of Africans could be more cynical and cutting on the subject of race relations than any politician ever charged with incitement. Whites who denounced Leballo as a "race hater" often praised Sobukwe as a "non-racialist," and some outsiders to the movement purported to see two "wings" in the PAC: the "racialistic" Leballo wing, and the "nonracialist" Sobukwe wing.[23] Yet the views of the two men on the subject of race were scarcely distinguishable. Their differences were simply a matter of personality and sophistication. Leballo saw an enemy in every individual white South African, and exhorted his audiences to do the same. Sobukwe likewise rejected that in political terms there could be any such thing as "good" whites in South Africa, but, unlike Leballo, he did not feel compelled to demonstrate this conviction to every white he encountered. Leballo, while never regarding Sobukwe with quite the same admiration he reserved for Mda, nevertheless drew strength from Sobukwe's reflected intellectual luminance. Sobukwe on his part stood in awe of Leballo's boundless stamina and physical courage, finding in it a spur to his own sometimes reluctant involvement. In short, for two men whose styles were so oppo-

22. See, for example, the *Golden City Post* of 9 November 1958, which mentions three possible presidents for the new movement: Sobukwe, Raboroko, and Zephania Mothopeng.
23. See, for example, Jordan Ngubane, "Pan-Africanism and the ANC," *Opinion*, 17 April 1959.

site, Leballo and Sobukwe in fact enjoyed a robust mutual respect.

Ideological Refinements

The major initial task facing the PAC was the recruitment of followers, and this in turn required the Africanists to project a more widely acceptable formulation of their ideology. Press coverage given to bellicose statements by Leballo and Madzunya had led to an association in many people's minds between the Africanists and the extremist slogan "Drive the white man into the sea." Strong Africanist rhetoric that referred, for example, to white South Africans as "foreigners" and to cooperation between Africans and Indians as "banana politics," had inevitably contributed to an image of African nationalism as xenophobic and bigoted.[24] This image had to be dispelled, or at least tempered, if the PAC was to attract broad support from educated Africans. While many Africans in their individual lives might speak or think in ways no less "extreme" than the Africanists, it still seemed morally unacceptable to many people for an organization to indulge openly in threats of violence or racial slurs. Leaders were expected to behave more nobly than individuals acting in their private capacities. If the PAC was to succeed in forging an effective partnership between ordinary working class Africans and more sophisticated "school people," it had to fashion an ideological line which retained an emotional appeal but at the same time laid to rest lingering uncertainties about the moral respectability of orthodox nationalism. "Racialism," "black domination," and "Africanism" were all value-laden terms which had acquired a distinctly negative connotation in the prevailing liberal mores of black middle class society. The task of the PAC's leaders as propagandists was to foster an understanding of nationalism as a positive creed of democratic majority rule rather than a "racialistic" or "anti-white" doctrine of vengeance. "For a long

24. See Can Themba, "Politics Gone Crazy!" *Drum*, February 1958.

time," wrote Sobukwe in *Contact* shortly after the founding of the PAC,

> the impression has persisted . . . that the Africanists are a wild "cowboy" crew, undisciplined and confused. The South African Press has created this picture in most cases, out of sheer malice. The Press set about creating an effigy that it christened "African Nationalism" or "Africanist" and then systematically and methodically destroyed that effigy.[25]

The ANC, as we have seen, had preserved its positive moral image by bending over backwards to avoid "racialistic" statements or definitions of the struggle which suggested that the conflict was strictly one of all blacks against all whites. Consistently observing the taboo on discussions of "black domination," Congress had advocated universal suffrage but had never tried openly appealing to Africans by promising them control of a post-liberation government. No such inhibitions had ever affected the Africanists, however, and the PAC's new executive took no pains to avoid the question of how they wanted political power distributed after freedom: Africans would rule.

Africans would rule, the PAC declared, because they were the majority and because freedom by definition would mean the return of power to the indigenous "sons of the soil." But, as Sobukwe hastened to clarify on every possible occasion after April 1959, freedom would not mean that whites and Indians would be driven from the country or excluded from political rights; once pigmentocracy had been destroyed in South Africa, people of all colors would be equal citizens and an individual's color would become as irrelevant as the shape of his ears.[26] South Africa would become an "African" country because it was part of Africa geographically and its major cultural heritage was the same as that of the rest of the continent. Immigrant minorities would be welcome to stay and become

25. "Sobukwe Outlines Africanists' Case."
26. R. Sobukwe, "The State of the Nation," an address on "National Heroes' Day," 2 August 1959, reproduced in Karis and Carter, vol. 3, pp. 542–48.

"Africans" if their only loyalty was to Africa and if they unconditionally dropped all arrogant attitudes of superiority. There was no reason, said Sobukwe, "why, in a free, democratic Africa, a predominantly black electorate should not return a white man to parliament, for color will count for nothing in a free Africa."[27] Once exploitative relations between man and man were eliminated, South Africans would recognize only one race: the human race.

Proposals for political reform in South Africa have often taken for granted a need for an electoral or constitutional system that would somehow guarantee the rights of minorities. The ANC had lent its support to this concept in general terms. The PAC, however, rejected the idea of minority guarantees as contrary to the goal of a nonracial society. The policies of an African nationalist government, it said, would aim not at the protection of minorities but at their ultimate assimilation into the single national identity of "African." Outlining this view to the PAC's Inaugural Convention, Sobukwe declared:

> To us the term "multiracialism" implies that there are such basic insuperable differences between the various national groups here that the best course is to keep them permanently distinctive in a kind of democratic apartheid. That to us is racialism multiplied, which probably is what the term truly connotes.
>
> We aim, politically, at government of the Africans by the Africans for Africans, with everybody who owes his only loyalty to Africa and who is prepared to accept the democratic rule of an African majority being regarded as an African. We guarantee no minority rights, because we think in terms of individuals, not groups.[28]

Before racial equality had been achieved, according to the PAC's official doctrine, no whites could fully identify with the African cause because, as Sobukwe often repeated, groups in privileged positions never voluntarily relinquished their

27. "Sobukwe Outlines Africanists' Case." Sobukwe had earlier made the same comment to a white newsman following the Inaugural Convention; see the *Star*, 7 April 1959.
28. Sobukwe's opening address to the PAC Inaugural Convention, in Karis and Carter, vol. 3.

privileges.[29] "Our contention," he wrote in May 1959,

> is that the Africans are the only people who, because of their
> material position, can be interested in the complete overhaul of
> the present structure of society. We have admitted that there are
> Europeans who are intellectual converts to the African's cause,
> but, because they benefit materially from the present set-up, they
> cannot completely identify themselves with that cause.[30]

If some members of the privileged class appeared sympathetic
to African demands, he had written earlier,

> it is only in so far as those demands do not threaten the privileges
> of the favored group. If they (the privileged) offer assistance, it is
> for the purpose of "directing" and "controlling" the struggle of
> the under-privileged and making sure that it does not become
> "dangerous."[31]

The political behavior of individuals, in other words, could
never be independent of the economic forces shaping the
broader conflicts in society. The argument was Marxist in
spirit: Africans were as historically and morally justified in
being "anti-white" as members of the proletariat were justified
in being opposed to all members of the ruling or owning classes. Was it true, Sobukwe wrote in January 1959, that the
Africanists were "anti-white"?

> What is meant by anti-whiteism? Is it not merely an emotional
> term without a precise signification? Let me put it this way: In
> every struggle, whether national or class, the masses do not fight
> an abstraction. They do not hate oppression or capitalism. They
> concretize these and hate the oppressor, be he the Governor-
> General or a colonial power, the landlord or the factory-owner,
> or, in South Africa, the white man. But they hate these groups
> because they associate them with their oppression! Remove the
> association and you remove the hatred. In South Africa then,
> once white domination has been overthrown and the white man
> is no longer "white-man boss" but is an individual member of
> society, there will be no reason to hate him and he will not be

29. R. Sobukwe, "Future of the Africanist Movement," *The Africanist*,
January 1959, in Karis and Carter, vol. 3, pp. 506–10.
30. "Sobukwe Outlines Africanists' Case."
31. "Future of the Africanist Movement," in Karis and Carter, vol. 3.

hated even by the masses. We are not anti-white, therefore. We do not hate the European because he is white! We hate him because he is an oppressor. And it is plain dishonesty to say I hate the *sjambok* [whip] and not the one who wields it.[32]

Not surprisingly, in the politically charged atmosphere of 1959, these explanations of the PAC's position evoked a heavy round of attacks, with critics of all shades denouncing the new organization's line as contradictory, vague and threatening to the spirit of democracy and reconciliation. Spokesmen for the PAC, including Sobukwe himself, were often not able to satisfy critics who demanded less ambiguous explanations of the PAC line. How did the PAC really define an "African"? What was the actual difference between "nonracialism" and "multiracialism"? "Sometimes one feels sheer anarchy is loosed upon the world of language," wrote a white reporter following the PAC's Inaugural Convention.

> The Africanists import the derogatory connotations of the term "multi-racialism" from other parts of Africa, where British colonial practice has turned it into a swear-word, and use them against the Congress Movement. So to them the term means "racialism multiplied," while to white supremacists it means miscegenation rampant. And herein perhaps lies the Africanists' greatest responsibility: to resist the temptation to manipulate language and encourage words like "African" to mean all things to all men. . . . The Africanist line implies somehow first and second-class Africans, with skin color being a factor in classification. In other words: "All who give their allegiance to Africa are Africans, but some Africans are more African than others."[33]

Other critics attacked the Africanist position that guaranteeing individual rights could provide adequate protection for minority races. "In countries where the population is not homogeneous," wrote Joe Matthews in *Liberation* in July 1959,

> . . . it becomes necessary to go further than merely to recognize the right of each individual citizen of the state. It becomes essen-

32. Ibid.
33. P. Rodda, "The Africanists Cut Loose," *Africa South*, July–September 1959.

tial to create conditions under which those who do not belong to the numerically superior national groups are able to develop their languages, culture and customs without let or hindrance.[34]

Giving rise to the most skepticism among critics, however, was the PAC's contention that Africans could organize a revolution admittedly fuelled by hatred of whites but could then establish a political order into which whites would be accepted without bitterness as fellow "Africans." Was this not ascribing a quality of virtue to South Africa's blacks which no similar group in any society had ever demonstrated?

Jordan Ngubane once observed that leaders of oppressed groups tend to assume that the downtrodden have a monopoly of virtue and that all immoral motives lie on the side of the oppressors.[35] Even if the PAC's leadership shared this tendency, however, it would still not fully account for their blasé optimism in predicting a future of social harmony and happiness for South Africa beyond what Sobukwe often euphemistically called "the stormy sea of struggle." A fuller explanation of their attitude must acknowledge the obvious element of cynicism in the rosy prognostications of post-revolutionary reconciliation. Clearly, the Africanists, on launching what they hoped and believed would soon become the most formidable political organization in the country, felt compelled to state their long-range goals in a way which would be as attractive as possible to their potential following. Whether or not these goals were actually realistic, or appealing to non-Africans, was hence of no immediate consequence. The real concern of Sobukwe and his colleagues was not with the ultimate goals of change but with change itself, not with ends but with means. They were prepared to use any means necessary to achieve political change, and they believed, rightly or wrongly, that orthodox African nationalism was an historical necessity given South African circumstances.

34. J. Matthews, "'Africanism' Under the Microscope," *Liberation*, no. 37, July 1959.
35. Interview of Carter team with Ngubane. PAC documents sometimes referred to Africans being "purified in the crucible of oppression."

To Sobukwe personally, and to some if not all of those around him, nationalism had a strong positive quality of patriotism; it meant love for Africans and Africa, and a striving for the fulfillment of human potential. For most ordinary Africans, however, the most potent emotions of nationalism were the negative ones of hatred and anger. Rather than deny this or attempt to work against what they saw as the compulsions of historical necessity, the leaders of the PAC chose instead to accept the moral ambiguities of nationalism as part of the price of change. Africans, they believed, had to be fired to a point where they would offer total opposition to white rule—through non-cooperation, the withdrawal of labor, and ultimately perhaps even violence. Only consciousness of their oppression as a race could draw them together and inspire them to the necessary heights of sacrifice and suffering; only the preaching of a blacks-only nationalism could in turn inspire this necessary level of consciousness. Africans could not be expected to worry about the creation of a future nonracial utopia, any more than they could be expected to embrace in the present the "broad humanism" of racial cooperation being preached by the ANC. The ANC, in the Africanists' view, had failed to confront historical necessity head-on; it wanted freedom but was not willing to pay the price or take the steps required to create a successful black revolution.

We have seen how in the early days of the Youth League Lembede had attempted, with only limited success, to pose African nationalism as an alternative value system for an African intelligentsia trained to think in a moral frame of reference inherited from the Christian-liberal tradition. By the 1950s the foundations of this older perspective had begun to crumble. The authority and prestige of Christian missionaries had declined as a factor in shaping the world view of urban Africans. Growing secularism was accompanied by new cynicism toward the much-acclaimed benefits of "Western Christian civilization," which had for so long served white South Africa as its rationale for race domination. More numerous, more educated, and more sure of themselves, urban Africans were increasingly inclined to speak their own minds instead of looking to African notables to mediate on their behalf with white authority. Out along with the notables went the polite and restrained tone of public discourse which had for so long been a hallmark of the African political style. Tougher language was accompanied by tougher, more cynical and pessimistic evaluations of the African situation. The old optimism of liberals, white and black, that Afrikaner nationalism could be modified by "logic" or defeated at the polls, had faded away. Afrikaner politicians were following a logic of their own design and it had swept them back to power with an increased majority in the general election of April 1958. Africans were losing ground as whites busied themselves with perfecting the mechanisms of apartheid. New directions in the African struggle were urgently needed, and changing conditions were shaking loose the intellectual conventions which had circumscribed the vision of older political generations. African assessments of political "reality" were shifting. The way was now prepared for acceptance of ideas which had earlier fallen on infertile ground.

The PAC and African Cultural Reassertion

The early Youth Leaguers had all shared Lembede's emotional patriotism to one degree or another, and his determination to restore dignity and respect to Africans; but they had proved less enthusiastic about his emphasis on the cultural aspects of nationalism. Following Lembede's death, lip service was paid to the need for African cultural assertion, and when the *Programme of Action* was formulated in final form in December 1949 it called on the ANC to "unite the cultural with the educational and national struggle," and to this end to establish an African Academy of Arts and Science.[36] These declarations of

36. Writing to the *Inkundla* in 1946 (exact date not available), Mda had endorsed the idea of an African Academy: "So important is this idea that I feel it must be taken up soon. We all know how much the Afrikaans Academy has done for the Afrikaans language and culture. There is no reason why an African Academy should not do the same for our language and culture."

intent notwithstanding, no plans for a cultural offensive ever
got off the ground. The principal obstacle was an obvious one:
Africans attracted to political activity were among those striving to attain a modern life style; such people, by and large,
wanted to put the greatest possible distance between themselves and traditional tribal life. The whole idea of "African
culture" smacked to them of the tribal past, of beads and blan-
kets and primitivism, and they wanted to have nothing to do
with it. If cultural nationalism was to have the desired impact, it
could not rest on a search for ethnic authenticity or a rejection
of European material culture; its thrust had to be far more
subjective, emphasizing the spiritual side of "Africanness" or
what Nkrumah in West Africa was trying to define as the
"African personality." It had to exorcise the African's image of
himself as the perpetual underling and imitator, the "non-
white" in a white world. It had to help Africans find a new sense
of cultural identity which placed their own history, achievements, and standards of beauty and worth at the center of the
psychological universe. Defined in such terms, cultural
nationalism meant a reorientation towards the present, rather
than a backward-looking longing for the quaint customs of
some idealized past.

The idea of such a cultural thrust in African nationalism,
dormant for the most part since Lembede's day, began within
the PAC to reemerge as a political force. Never well articulated
by PAC leaders, and finding no direct forms of expression in
political action, it did not assume the proportions of a full-
fledged movement. Nevertheless, as an indicator of the shifting intellectual climate of the late 1950s and as a foreshadow-
ing of the much more fully articulated Black Consciousness
movement of the 1970s, it stands out as an important aspect of
PAC ideology.

Much of the PAC's effort to introduce a cultural reorientation into African politics centered on its attempts to revive and
popularize as a nationalist rallying point the memory of eigh-
teenth- and nineteenth-century African heroes. As we have
seen, the point was not to return to the past, but rather to rein-

terpret the present as an extension of an heroic ongoing African struggle against conquest. Commemoration of African heroes, Sobukwe declared in regard to the PAC's "Lembede memorial service"—rechristened National Heroes' Day— in August 1959,

> is in line with the general trend in Afrika towards an African orientation, the attempt to recreate a set of values that will give meaning to the lives of our people because . . . values serve as the lodestar to life. . . . [This memorial] service is significant because it indicates our determination no longer to swallow the white man's propaganda. In deciding who are national heroes, we set up our own criteria which needs must be different from those of the oppressor, so that his scoundrels are our heroes, and his "heroes" are our renegades.[37]

Less direct than the PAC's appeal for new attitudes toward history was its tacit bid for support on the religious front from the country's separatist churches. There was a clear affinity between the PAC's "go it alone" spirit and the anti-white mood of independent churches; they were a natural recruiting ground, and had the PAC not brought about its own demise as an organization so prematurely, it might eventually have succeeded in redirecting some of the energies of religious separatism into political channels. That it was the intention of the Africanists to do this can be inferred from their invitation to Bishop Walter M. Dimba to deliver the principal opening sermon and prayers at the PAC Inaugural Convention. The impressive Dimba was a leading separatist and head of the then prominent Federation of Bantu Churches in South Africa.[38] He was accompanied in performing the customary religious preliminaries at the conference by two other ministers, including the Reverend Nimrod B. Tantsi, a prominent leader of the African Methodist Episcopal Church, another African-run denomination. According to one white observer present, these men of the cloth conveyed the message of "an emotional and sometimes eccentric and exclusive Christianity," referring to

37. R. Sobukwe, "The Editor Speaks," *The Africanist,* July–August 1959 (Carter-Karis collection).
38. See Sundkler *Bantu Prophets,* pp. 306–7.

"the hooligans of Europe who killed our God and have never been convicted," and "the legend of Christ's education in Africa." Cheers, said the observer, "greeted the salute to 'a black man, Simon of Arabia, who carried Jesus from the Cross.' "[39] All this was standard rhetorical fare in independent churches, but seldom had such a direct move been made to link the theology of separatism so overtly with political ends. Later in the conference, in a speech that was loudly applauded, Madzunya called for the establishment of an African national church. Why should there be a host of "foreign" religions, like the Anglicans, Catholics and Lutherans, if this was not to divide and confuse the mind of the African, he said. Africans needed to practice their own religion in their own united church.[40]

The idea of an African national church was not a new one among nationalists, nor was it one likely to be readily implemented, but it was a clue to the strong current of cultural reassertion flowing beneath the surface of political revolt in the PAC. There were other religious manifestations of this current as well. In Cape Town, speakers at PAC meetings made frequent references to the hypocrisy of the white man's Christianity,[41] and a handful of Africanist adherents split off from Christian churches altogether and converted to Islam.[42] In Cape Town and elsewhere where PAC made a play for support among less sophisticated semi-urbanized Africans, speakers

39. Rodda, "The Africanists Cut Loose," p. 23. Nkoana challenges Rodda's account, and claims the rhetoric noted was characteristic only of Dimba and not the other two ministers. See M. Nkoana, "On Counter-Revolution," *The New African* no. 51 (1968), p. 31.

40. Recorded observations of Benjamin Pogrund, who was present. Sundkler, pp. 50–53, gives background on the idea of an African national church.

41. See extensive police records of PAC public meetings at Langa and Nyanga locations in Cape Town *(Reg. vs. Synod Madlebe and others,* 1960, documents presented in evidence).

42. Interview with Elliot Magwentshu, a Cape Town PAC activist. He did not recall the timing of their conversion, but it probably preceded the founding of PAC. There are a substantial number of Moslems in Cape Town, but virtually all are Coloureds of Malay origin. There is no African Moslem community in South Africa.

sometimes invoked the sanction of African ancestors or the "gods of Africa" in exhorting their audiences to join PAC.[43] Later, after 1960, when PAC made a fitful comeback in the Cape in the form of the terrorist movement called Poqo, there were reports of quasi-religious oathings during which Poqo members were assured that they were being made immune to the white man's bullets.[44] It was the ultimate attempt to identify strength with a return to the indigenous "African way."

Reverberations from Africa to the North

Just at the time the Africanist movement was transforming itself into the Pan Africanist Congress, a dramatic transfer of political power was under way across the entire face of Africa. Earlier predictions by the imperial powers that Africans would need decades or even centuries to prepare themselves for self-rule fell rapidly out of fashion as nationalist leaders persisted in demanding the right of Africans, in Nkrumah's words, to "manage or mismanage" every inch of Africa. In a political environment where the hopes of generations seemed to be coming true nearly overnight, optimists naturally turned anew to the vision of W. E. B. DuBois, George Padmore, Nkrumah and the other ideological fathers of pan-Africanism who had spent years dreaming of a time when Africans would come together to form an independent United States of Africa.

43. Interview with Magwentshu, who recollected: "At times we would say this struggle of ours is entirely depending on the trust we have to our gods. . . . We didn't actually mean God; we meant the gods. . . . We knew this had terrible appeal to the Africans. They still believe . . . that the ancestors are watching, standing somewhere watching. . . . That had a meaning [to me myself]. . . . The African people believed in the god that was represented by the ancestors. I think I used to appeal, satisfied within myself sincerely, for instance, that people like Makana who died in Robben Island, were somewhere, looking at us. I used to believe this." Phillip Kgosana twice invoked the "Gods of Africa" in his speech launching PAC's anti-pass campaign in Cape Town in March 1960. *Report of the Langa Commission of Enquiry* (Diemont Commission), 1963, Annexure "A", p. 137. Also see M. Wilson and A. Mafeje, *Langa* (Cape Town, 1963), p. 112.
44. *Report of the Paarl Commission of Enquiry* (Snyman Commission), 1963, p. 10. On Poqo, see below, pp. 225–26, 252–53.

South Africans looked on from the side lines, reading their own hopes and fears into events in the rest of the continent as European governments retreated and international prestige and legitimacy were bestowed on the black leaders of new African states. For whites, the expansion of African power and the world's recognition of the principle of African self-determination seemed a grim harbinger of future discord within South Africa's own domestic colonial system. For many politically conscious and idealistic Africans, on the other hand, independent Africa took on the quality of a New Jerusalem and its leaders the appearance of infallible prophets of free-dom. To the Africanists, it seemed that Lembede's predictions about the destiny of Africa might at last be coming true. It is easy with hindsight to conclude that these African hopes were unrealistic, but in 1959 the honeymoon period of indepen-dence was barely underway. Without taking into account the euphoria of *uhuru* and its profound impact on the aspirations of black South Africans, some of the optimism of the PAC's pan-Africanism might seem inexplicable; yet seen in the con-text of the times, it was not as utopian as it appears today.

The ANC had a long background of association with pan-Africanism, but there was a strain of ambivalence in its attitude towards the rest of Africa.[45] Older Congress leaders were par-ticularly conscious of South Africa's unique situation. "South Africa," wrote Professor Matthews in late 1957,

> differs from other territories in Africa such as Ghana or Nigeria or even Uganda where the black man outnumbers the white man to such an extent that it is ridiculous to talk about the country being anything other than a black man's country. In South Africa in addition to the African we have *settled* here significant num-bers of other groups—Europeans, Asians, and Colored—and therefore the country must frankly be recognized as a multi-racial country with all that that implies.[46]

Thus South Africa's large population of non-Africans made

45. See Benson, *The African Patriots,* pp. 49, 56–57, 117, and Walshe, *The Rise of African Nationalism,* p. 566ff.
46. Z. K. Matthews, "Non-White Political Organizations," *Africa To-day,* November–December 1957, p. 21.

it an exception, in the view of Matthews and others in the ANC, to the pattern of politics taking shape in the rest of Africa. While Africans in South Africa might draw pride and inspiration from the political progress of Africans elsewhere, it was inappropriate in South Africa and inconsistent with the policies of the ANC to give to the terms "self-determination" or "independence" the same meaning attributed to them in the rest of the continent.

The leaders of the PAC, whose thinking was shaped by a different set of assumptions about South Africa's past and future, perceived developments in Africa in a radically different light. In keeping with their tendency to ignore practical obstacles and complexities and to reduce the terms of the struggle to a set of absolutes, Africanist leaders put heavy emphasis on what they asserted to be the identical situation of Africans in South Africa and in the rest of the continent. As the number of soon-to-be independent African states continued to multiply in the late 1950s, the Africanists, with a ring of drama and triumph, began to make the claim that their movement was marching in step with the continent. "The Africanists do not at all subscribe to the fashionable doctrine of South African exceptionalism," Sobukwe told the PAC inaugural conference.

> Our contention is that South Africa is an integral part of the indivisible whole that is Afrika. She cannot solve her problems in isolation from and with utter disregard of the rest of the continent. . . . We take our stand on the principle that Afrika is one and desires to be one and nobody, I repeat, nobody has the right to balkanize our land.[47]

Lembede's precedent, sincere conviction, and a large measure of political expediency all combined to lead the Africanists into an espousal of pan-Africanism. Lembede had preached a pan-Africanist doctrine, looking forward to a time when Africa would emerge and take its place as one united country among the nations of the world. The appeal of this idea had been revived among the Africanists by George Padmore's book, *Pan-Africanism or Communism?*, which was published in 1956

47. Opening address to the PAC Inaugural Convention.

and had become compulsory reading in Africanist circles by the time of the PAC's founding.[48] In November 1958, just when the Africanists were launching out on their independent course, Ghana announced its "union" with Guinea, and it could have appeared to African optimists that a United States of Africa, along the lines proposed by Padmore, was already in the making: regional federations were forming which would ultimately give way to a giant monolithic state.

In December 1958, the historic All-African Peoples Conference met in Accra and brought together the continent's most prestigious leaders in a highly impressive show of pan-African unity and purposefulness. No part of Africa could consider itself truly free, the conference proclaimed, until every part of the continent had been liberated. The year 1963 was set as the projected deadline for total liberation. The Africanists, always pan-Africanists at heart but now swept by the intense enthusiasm generated at Accra, decided to adopt the doctrines of the All-African Peoples Conference in toto. By the time the Africanist inaugural conference had met in April 1959, not only had pan-Africanism been incorporated into the name of the new movement, but virtually every tenet of pan-Africanist doctrine had been incorporated as an article of faith into PAC ideology. "The African people of South Africa," declared the PAC *Manifesto*, "recognize themselves as part of one African nation, stretching from Cape to Cairo, Madagascar to Morocco, and pledge themselves to strive and work ceaselessly to find organizational expression for this nation in a merger of free independent African states into a United States of Africa."[49] The PAC, said its Constitution, pledged itself to

48. Interviews with Leballo, Mda, and Mfaxa. Sobukwe cites Padmore's book in his inaugural address.
49. *Manifesto of the Africanist Movement*, reproduced in Karis and Carter, vol. 3, pp. 517–24. Among the other names considered for the PAC were the Africanist Liberation Congress, the All African National Congress, the Africanist Congress, and the Africanist Revolutionary Party. It was felt by the conference that the word "Congress" should be retained for sentimental reasons, and that the word "Africanist" should be carried over with a new and more positive connotation.

promote the concept of a "Federation of Southern Africa," along the lines of Padmore's blueprint. "Positive neutrality" as endorsed by Nkrumah would be the PAC's position in foreign relations, and the organization would strive to project the "African Personality" as its social and cultural goal. The PAC's flag, the inaugural conference decided, would show a green field with a black map of Africa and a gold star in the northwest, beaming its light southward from Ghana.

The formulations of Accra came as an inspiration to the PAC's leaders at exactly the stage when they were seeking ways to reinforce and justify nationalist ideology. If other African nations were freeing themselves without the assistance of "foreigners," why could Africans in South Africa not do the same? If African nationalist heroes like Nkrumah and Mboya were warning against the "imperialism of the East," was PAC not also justified in warning against the activities of communists in South Africa? If other nations were committing themselves to the goal of a united Africa, why should Africans in South Africa not do the same? Expediency complemented idealism in the adoption of this line. If all of Africa could be viewed as a single nation, it became far easier to dismiss South Africa's few million whites as an insignificant minority within the larger population. "We are not isolated," Sobukwe told a PAC conference in December 1959. "We are many. We are not fourteen million. We are two hundred thirty-two million. And we all say Afrika will be free by 1963!"[50] "The crucial issue today," wrote Peter Raboroko several months later,

> is whether the interests of the five million Europeans *throughout* Africa must continue to dominate over those of the two hundred and eighty million Africans, or whether the reverse process should obtain. This is an issue that no social philosophy pretending to have a solution for *Africa's* social problem can afford to gloss over.[51]

50. Sobukwe's address to the first annual national conference of the PAC, 19–20 December 1959 (Hoover microfilms).
51. P. N. Raboroko, "Congress and the Africanists," *Africa South*, April–June 1960 (emphasis added). That Raboroko had a long-standing pan-Africanist perspective is evident from his numerous

Such geographical arithmetic, denying the uniqueness of South Africa's race problem, made it possible to deny that South Africa deserved any unique political solution. If "Independence" and "Africa for the Africans" were the correct nationalist line elsewhere, they could also be the correct line for South Africa. In time, a United States of Africa would render insignificant the whole question of minorities, predicted Sobukwe in an article for *Drum* in late 1959. "In a United States of Africa," he wrote, "there will be no 'racial' groups and I am certain that with the freedom of movement from Cape to Cairo, Morocco to Madagascar the concentration of so-called 'minority groups' will disappear."[52]

If such blithe expressions of optimism seem simplistic or even cynical in retrospect, it is still important to set such sentiments against the background of independence euphoria which had so strongly affected the thinking of most African intellectuals at that time. Being the furthest of all Africans from the actual realization of their hopes, South Africans were perhaps the most susceptible to idealistic flights of fancy regarding the "New Africa." Having taken into consideration the time-bound quality of PAC perspectives, however, it is also necessary to recognize the more opportunistic side of the pan-Africanist line. Independent Africa symbolized success and strength, and the efforts of the PAC to identify itself with the nationalist movements of tropical Africa and with the aspirations of pan-Africanism were clearly part of its attempt to upstage the ANC in appealing for mass support. The demonstrable weakness of the ANC was one of the trump cards in

---

articles in the early 1950s dealing with the question of a "national" language for all of Africa. He proposed the use of Swahili, or alternately the development of a synthetic all-inclusive Bantu language called "Siafurika." These pieces appear in *The Bantu World*, 29 September 1951, 12 January and 15 March 1952; *Liberation*, no. 5, September 1953; and *African Lodestar*, January 1954 (Carter-Karis collection).

52. R. Sobukwe, "My Idea of Africa in 1973," *Drum*, November 1959, p. 49, reproduced as "One Central Government in Africa," in Karis and Carter, vol. 3, pp. 562–63.

the PAC's hand; in all its forty-seven year history, the ANC could not point to a single significant victory over the forces of white supremacy, and by 1959 its record of failure was severely limiting its ability to attract mass backing. Yet beyond the borders of South Africa to the north, other Africans were achieving startling and rapid victories, and these victories were being won under the banner of orthodox African nationalism. Here was a model of success and achievement from which Africans could draw confidence. Here too were leaders who seemed to have the answers to Africa's problems. Measured beside prestigious elders of the ANC like Chief Lutuli, Z. K. Matthews and J. B. Marks, the officials of the new PAC lacked standing in the African community. Adoption of a pan-Africanist line allowed them in some measure to compensate for this disadvantage through an association with "higher authorities" on the subject of liberation—men like Nkrumah, Toure, Mboya and Kenyatta, whose ability to vanquish the Europeans had already been demonstrated. A would-be follower of the PAC might be skeptical about taking orders from just any untried leader, but could he doubt the authority of one who had received the blessing of Nkrumah?

Branch level leaders and local PAC activists lost no time in seeing the appeal of pan-Africanist themes, and policemen present at street-corner PAC meetings have left notes replete with references to African rule "from Cape to Cairo" and the imminent coming of a United States of Africa. The example of free Africa was a favorite theme of PAC speakers:

> Ghana is free now. Dr. Nkrumah said that he will not be pleased unless he sees that other African territories are also free. That's why you see Mboya and others making such a noise. Dr. Banda is in jail on account of the same trouble of freedom. We have hope that when he comes out of jail he will be a Prime Minister.
>
> Africans, open your eyes and ears so that you may hear and see what is happening at other countries.
>
> Ghana's free and it will soon get a republic; then all other countries will get it; but what about South Africa?
>
> You might think that Madzunya is speaking his own madness, but I am speaking the language of Dr. Banda, Julius Nyerere,

Tom Mboya and Mr. Nkomo. [Josias Madzunya, Alexandra township]
We are the majority, two hundred fifty million in Africa....
Look at the star [on our flag]. The star is Ghana's Nkrumah.[53]

As the PAC's "positive action" campaign of 1960 approached, national PAC leaders referred more and more often to the "avalanche force of African nationalism" sweeping the continent. Their hope, of course, was that such prophecies of an "avalanche" hitting South Africa might turn out to be self-fulfilling. The followers of any liberation movement, they reasoned, had to feel that if they followed the prescriptions advocated by their leaders, there was at least a reasonable chance of their efforts being crowned with success. The most that the ANC could do to inspire confidence and resolve in its followers by the late 1950s was to assure them that the entire civilized world condemned apartheid. This may have been comforting to some, but it could hardly convince most people that a greater effort on their part would actually bring the entire civilized world to their aid. The PAC, on the other hand, by evoking the parallel, however misleading, between its own program in South Africa and the successful nationalist movements of free Africa, hoped to inspire in people the belief that their efforts would actually succeed if they would only follow the same methods that were bringing victory elsewhere. Whether a reasonable chance for success really existed in any objective sense in South Africa was less important than creating in South Africa's oppressed the belief in victory which could inspire them to "do or die" in the revolutionary cause.

53. From police notes used in evidence at PAC trials in Johannesburg and Cape Town (*Reg. vs. Robert Sobukwe and twenty-two others*, 1960, and *Reg. vs. Synod Madlebe and others*, 1960). Although the accuracy of such notes in translation can often be questioned, they provide a general guide to the ideas expressed by speakers.

7

Sharpeville and Quiescence

Popular Responses to the PAC

At the time of their breakaway from the ANC in November 1958 the Africanists realized that their numbers were few. Those who consciously thought of themselves as orthodox Lembedists had never numbered more than a few dozen at most. Of these, only Leballo had any wide reputation outside the Transvaal. What influence the Africanist movement had enjoyed inside the ANC before the break had derived less from the development of orthodox nationalist thinking per se within Congress than from the ability of Africanist spokesmen to identify themselves with the more generalized sense of grievance and impatience among ordinary members and lower-ranking cadres. Once outside the ANC and unrestrained by its customary moderation, no one could foresee how far the Africanists might be able or inclined to go. Anyone could see that frustration and impatience were widespread in the general African population—but how could this discontent be harnessed to achieve political ends? No African organization in South Africa's history had yet found a satisfactory answer to this question.

The leaders of the PAC were so convinced of the appeal of orthodox nationalism that they confidently set themselves a high target for membership. Three months before the PAC Inaugural Convention of April 1959, an editorial in *The*

Africanist predicted that the movement would report a paid-up enrollment of one hundred thousand by July, a number equal to the peak membership of the ANC at the time of the Defiance Campaign.[1] At the celebration of PAC's "National Heroes' Day" on August 2, the National Executive Committee announced that membership had in fact reached 24,664—a figure far short of the target, but nevertheless an impressive showing for a newly formed organization and a total almost certainly larger than the ANC's formal membership. The provincial breakdown of membership was given as[2]

Transvaal	47 branches	13,324 members
Cape	34	7,427
Natal	15	3,612
O.F.S.	5	301
	101	24,664

The PAC's failure to reach its initial goal, Leballo explained, was due to inexperience in methods of organization and lack of funds; but in spite of these setbacks, the Africanists could still say *Sikifile!* (We have arrived!) Membership figures did not tell the whole story of an organization's support, as any political organizer knew. The ANC had always commanded much more grass roots support than its meager membership figures revealed, and for all its failures and shortcomings it still ranked as the premier mass organization of Africans. Nevertheless, PAC seemed to be capturing the initiative in some areas of the country, making inroads into the membership of the ANC, and winning over people previously uncommitted to political activism.

There was a strong contrast between the loyalties commanded by the ANC and those now being inspired by PAC. While PAC sought to ride the ground swell of mass discontent

1. *The Africanist*, January 1959.
2. *The Africanist*, November 1959. Membership figures for the ANC in the late 1950s are not available, but total formal membership may have been in the range of 10,000.

and to identify itself with the most embittered and impatient elements of popular opinion, the ANC maintained its habitual avoidance of extremes. The ANC's aim, as always, was more to educate and guide than to follow public opinion, an approach inherited from earlier days when levels of popular political consciousness and knowledge had been much lower. Demagoguery and cheap plays for popularity were not only frowned upon as dangerous and irresponsible by the ANC's top leadership; they were also seen as unnecessary, since the ANC had never in its history come up against a rival organization that it had not been able to outlast. As one partisan once put it, the ANC was a "mansion" while other organizations were "shanties."[3] Its President General was automatically known and revered. There was an atmosphere of pageantry at its conferences and demonstrations. It had the aura of tradition and permanence. "For some it was the only black organization that they knew," Mahomo later observed. "For others it was the organization in which they were brought up. It was traditional . . . to belong to the ANC—not because of its accomplishments but because it was there. . . . Some likened it to going to church."[4] As in churches, men occupied the positions of leadership, but the most steadfast members were women. Decisions and policies made at the top found much blindly loyal support, especially among women, older men, and others of a relatively low educational standard whose inclination was often to accept the judgments of the organization on faith rather than to reach their own independent conclusions regarding political questions.

The new leaders of the PAC could rely on no such unquestioning loyalty, nor could they look to any established constituency of habitual supporters. With no money, no press of their own, and no "big name" leaders, they were starting from political scratch with little to sustain themselves initially

3. Typed statement (n.d., early 1950s) signed by P. Mnguni, G. Mabokoule and S. Mhlambi of Albertensville (Treason Trial, documents presented in evidence).
4. Mahomo, "The Rise of the Pan Africanist Congress," p. 43.

except an overweening sense of ideological amour propre.[5] Like the leaders of the ANC, they had no spoils to dispense, and no honors to confer other than the intangible rewards of public service. With characteristic brashness, they conferred elaborate ministerial titles upon themselves (Secretary for Education, Secretary for Labor, and so on), suggesting to their prospective following that support for PAC was support for a hypothetical alternative government. It was an appealing symbolic gesture, but not one quite likely to recruit hungry packs of political patronage-seekers.

The principal reward the PAC offered to its prospective adherents was something the ANC could not, or would not, offer: an opportunity to give full and unrestrained vent to political emotion. Few in the ANC were prepared to admit to any ideological shortcomings, but it was evident by the late 1950s that the ANC was taking a line which no longer adequately reflected the mood of the urban African, or in particular the impatience of urban youth. The ANC's record for courage and outspokenness was good, but as an organization it had now begun to lag behind the times, a captive of its traditions, its allies, and of the world view of its prestigious older leaders. Younger Africans needed an organization which could more readily "speak their language," and it was this need which the PAC now intended to satisfy, hoping that somehow in the process a spark might be struck that could ignite the fires of mass rebellion. It was a risky strategy, many said a foolhardy one, but to the PAC's leaders it seemed to be the one course open, the only approach which could tap what they felt were the masses' unexploited reserves of latent energy. The country had reached what many sensed was an emotional crossroads. The choices being made by African leaders were

5. Johannesburg's two newspapers for Africans, *The World* (formerly *The Bantu World*), and *Golden City Post,* both white-owned, gave considerable coverage to PAC, primarily playing up the controversy over the ANC's alliance policy. The Liberal party-oriented periodical, *Contact,* owned and edited by Patrick Duncan, which came out every two weeks, was firmly pro-PAC by 1960, but focused its support primarily around the issue of alleged communist control of the ANC.

pivotal ones, for it was the leaders, not the inarticulate masses, who could decide in which direction to steer the struggle. Should African anger be stirred up on the chance that the time was ripe for a successful confrontation with white power, or cooled down in order to buy time until conditions were more favorable? The ANC, intentionally or otherwise, gave the appearance of having chosen the latter course. The PAC without hesitation chose the path of confrontation.

When the Africanists set out to refashion their public image after their November 1958 breakaway from the ANC, they hoped to neutralize criticism which had been leveled at nationalist "extremism" by certain journalists, white liberals and members of the educated African elite. For the sake of winning approval from "respectable" middle class Africans— teachers, white collar workers, nurses, clergymen and the like—it was important for the PAC to project an image of moral respectability, and it was with this object in view that Sobukwe and his colleagues formulated their ambiguous and controversial doctrine of a nonracial future society in which people of all colors would be "Africans." Some of the conflicting pressures at work on the PAC's national leaders in this period came through in the later recollections of 'Molotsi, discussing the PAC's decision to avŏid the slogan "Drive the white man into the sea!"

> [People] liked it, privately! But we didn't want to go down on paper. . . . In fact Dr. Xuma told us that it would damage us with our friends overseas. Dr. Xuma was a widely travelled man who was aware of world opinion. . . . Privately, we said the world can go to hell; we don't care for the world; it also doesn't care for us, otherwise we would not be in this condition. However, we did not want to go down on paper as having said "back to the sea" . . . [because] the police would come in. . . . We would have been destroyed within a day. We wanted a lease of life to continue—to get the bloody bastards, that's all![6]

New problems of organizational survival and public image-making had become mixed with the old stark hatred of the

6. Interview.

enemy—with the latter always threatening to overwhelm all other considerations.

Whatever official doctrinal refinements the PAC's national leaders chose to make, the fundamental premise behind nationalist ideology remained unchanged: ordinary Africans needed to be guided by political principles which were in tune with their "deep, undefined yearning for self-realization, self-expression, and nationhood," as *The Africanist* put it in December 1959.[7] The African was viewed as basically an emotional and psychological being, driven by spiritual strivings. In the African's pursuit of his own destiny, as the PAC interpreted it, paralleling Fanon's description of colonized peoples, the desires, yearnings and interests of whites counted for nothing; whites were in fact regarded by virtually all Africans as the foremost obstacle to the achievement of the African's destiny, which was to regain possession of his stolen fatherland. Translated into the parlance of the ordinary African—the van driver, the office tea boy, the factory worker, the shop assistant, the street sweeper—nationalism had less to do with moral niceties than with rough and ready justice, little to do with constitutional rearrangements but much to do with the bald realities of power. If, therefore, in spite of the Africanists' image-mending efforts, the white press or African moderates continued to call the PAC an "anti-white" movement, this was not an altogether unwelcome label as far as national PAC leaders were concerned. The ordinary African was nothing if he was not anti-white, and the PAC was determined to mirror the emotions of the common man.

It is not surprising therefore that when we turn again to the public speeches of local PAC stalwarts and branch leaders we find almost no discussion of any hypothetical nonracial future. Instead the message is an unvarnished "Africa for the Africans," with African understood as "black." Such comments as these occur many times over:[8]

7. "Zwelinzima" [unidentified], "Has PAC Come to Stay?" *The Africanist,* December 1959 (Carter-Karis collection).
8. Quotations are taken from notes made by African policemen attending PAC public meetings in Johannesburg and the Western Cape.

This country is for Africans. There is no room for Europeans in Africa. The Europeans in this country must give the reins to the Africans. We are going to rule this country. [Nyanga]

Africans, I want to tell you about African nationalism from Cape to Cairo and all those places belong to us; we will not share any of those places with white people. We will rule them, and if they do not want that they will pack and go. . . . If a white man will not obey an African he must pack and go. Africa is for Africans alone. [Nyanga]

They don't demand passes from Indians and Chinese. Why? Because they got their own countries. England is for English people, America for Americans, Africa must be for Africans. [Alexandra]

As can be seen today the whites are making a big exodus from Nyasaland and Kenya into Rhodesia and into South Africa. We must tell them that things are worse here because we are going to send them to Australia. [Alexandra]

Occasionally there is a more temperate acknowledgment that whites and blacks might eventually reach an accommodation:

The Europeans must adopt themselves as children of this country. [Instead] they write that they are "Europeans." [Nyanga]

We say Africa for Africans, Africans for humanity, humanity for God. Let those here in Africa divorce his own land and adopt the African democracy of the majority. [Langa]

We do not hate white people, but we hate their deeds. [Nyanga]

Proposals for reconciliation are rare, however. Much more

Places are given in parentheses. Punctuation and spelling have been edited to clarify the meaning. Usually the speaker used an African language and the policeman made his own translation into English. In intertribal areas like Johannesburg, political speakers using one vernacular would often be aided by a second speaker giving a running translation into a second vernacular. In cases where the policeman was not fluent in the language of the first speaker, he made his notes from the translation of the second speaker. The quotations thus only approximate the idea of the speaker, and do not represent his exact words. The comments quoted are taken from police notes presented as evidence before the Sharpeville Commission of Inquiry, and the 1960 trials of PAC leaders noted above, p. 211.

common are remarks that suggest a desire for revenge or a
hope that all whites will quit South Africa:

> I do not want to be equal with Europeans. I want the white people
> to fall under the African people. [Langa, Cape Western regional
> chairman of PAC]
>
> We want the Dutch people to call us *baas* [boss]. [Alexandra]
>
> I want the Europeans to become our boys, and they will be our
> boys from next year. [Naledi, Johannesburg]
>
> White foreign dogs in our continent! . . . The Europeans must
> leave us alone. Indians, Europeans and Italians must go from
> South Africa. . . . The white people must surrender to the rule of
> Africa by Africans. [Naledi, P. K. Leballo]
>
> I wish I can live till we rule. I will do the same to them. You see
> Dr. Nkrumah is deporting them. I will demand to be the Minis-
> ter of Justice. I will send all the police to demand the permits
> from the whites for about two months. [Alexandra, Josias Mad-
> zunya]
>
> We do not want [to] chase them away. If we chase them from
> here, we'll have no servants. Their wives are going to work for
> our wives. [Langa]

African solidarity is applauded, and hostility directed at all
non-African minorities:

> The Indians do not fight for Africans. They want to rule the
> Africans. . . . Look, here they have business, e.g. Queens Dairy.
> They hire Africans for £6 per month. Do you look at this as
> justice? We Africans hate such things. [Nyanga]
>
> If a Coloured should say that they are not an African, we will
> throw them away. [Langa]
>
> We still say no bail, no fine, no defence. We do not want to make
> the government rich, or the Jews [i.e. lawyers]. We fight for free-
> dom. We must not be deceived. How long have we been misled by
> these Jews. [Windermere]

When the ANC is attacked, the most frequent point of criticism is that it has allied itself with the enemy, whites:

> Our leaders are Africans, not Europeans in Parktown.
> [Alexandra]

> We will tell you why we do not wish to mix with other races. Since 1912 when the ANC was established it was never successful. . . . For forty-seven years we were under their campaign. We got angry because we saw Europeans amongst us. . . . We are fighting for the full rights of Africans. We do not fight to dance and sit with Europeans. [Nyanga]

> We have come to preach to you to leave all the organizations where you are led by Europeans who call you good boys because you sell *New Age* for them. [Langa]

> Some say that a white person is good, but we say that a rabbit never made friends with hounds. [Alexandra]

> There is no liberty while you are still with Europeans. Since 1912 South Africa was on the battlefield without any progress. Why? It is because of the Europeans. We do not hate ANC. We hate their mixing up with Europeans. There can be no cooperation with non-Africans. Let the cow of sacrifice be pure. If you join with Europeans the Europeans will come and demand the blood of those Europeans who died. The same with the Indians who might die in the struggle. [Nyanga]

Speakers sometimes alluded to fighting and death, although it was most often the African who was seen as dying or heroically sacrificing himself for the cause of freedom. Occasionally there was an official eschewal of violence, but more often there seemed to be an assumption that violence was inevitable, or even desirable. Unlike the ANC, for which nonviolence was a recognized policy, the PAC pointedly left its options open regarding methods of struggle. This, together with the propensity of many PAC members for bravado and threatening language, was enough to make many Africans assume that PAC was an organization committed to violence.[9] Whether or not this was in fact the case is a question which will be considered in due course. As far as the PAC's recruitment of followers was concerned, however, the ambiguity was useful; it allowed the

9. Brett in his study, *African Attitudes* (Johannesburg, 1963), which is based on interviews with 150 middle class Africans around January 1961, concludes on p. 63 that "the willingness to accept violence was found to be positively correlated with support for the P. A. C. and lack of support for the A. N. C. . . . This suggests that the P. A. C. is tending to attract the more violent and aggressive members of the African elite."

action-hungry to imagine themselves marching in the midst of vast throngs of armed insurgents—but at the same time permitted the more intellectual adherent to defer the problem of action and to see PAC merely as a champion of unsentimental truth, an organization not afraid to face the seriousness of the black man's situation.

Even the most general socio-economic information on the rank-and-file membership of the ANC and PAC has never been compiled, and hence only a few impressionistic observations on the PAC's supporters can be offered, with the hope that future research may cast more light on this important aspect of social and political history. First it must be noted that, without any doubt, age and not class was the most distinguishing characteristic of the PAC's following. At every level of organization, from the national leadership down to the least regimented non-card-carrying supporter, the people associated with the PAC were at least a decade younger on average than those in the ANC. The PAC, it was sometimes said, needed no youth league because it was itself an organization of youth from top to bottom. Also cutting across class lines was a distinction between ANC and PAC based on sex: it was claimed that the PAC needed no women's league, because its membership was almost entirely male. The characteristics of age and sex were related. Older Africans, older women in particular—and African women in general—were inclined to give a wide berth to any organization associated with violence, and to see threatening talk and heroic posturing on the part of the young as wild and irresponsible behavior. Conservative-minded people tended to perceive the PAC in just such a light, especially when nationalist ideology was shorn of its intellectual language and transmitted to the untutored man in the street.

For certain types of younger Africans, however—high school boys, the unemployed and underemployed young men overflowing the African locations of industrial cities—the strongest attraction of the PAC was its promise of tough "action." What actual form the action would eventually take, what would happen in the event of a full-scale white-black confrontation, what chance there was that Africans would persevere under pressure or rally to a single unifying leadership—these were not questions which impinged on the consciousness of impatient younger militants to any great extent. To their way of thinking, it was merely necessary to strike the first match; the fire would then somehow take care of itself. The PAC was a new organization with an untried leadership, but at least it shared the same sense of urgency and frustration, the same explosive anger as the younger generation. What the PAC was actually saying, or not saying, was less important than the "language" it was speaking, a language attuned to the mood of youth, in contrast to the more restrained accents of the ANC, "an organization," as one PAC man put it, "of our fathers and mothers."[10]

Like the ANC, the PAC succeeded in attracting some degree of support, formal or informal, from every stratum of African urban society, from the professional elite down to the most marginal semi-rural migrant workers. Within this wide class spectrum, however, certain broad contrasts can be drawn. Among working class Africans, for example, organized labor had stronger ties to ANC than to PAC, in part because of the ANC's alliance with the leftwing South African Congress of Trade Unions (SACTU), the largest labor federation to include unregistered (i.e. African) unions. The PAC's efforts to organize a rival federation of anti-communist unions, the Federation of Free African Trade Unions of South Africa (FOFATUSA), had barely gotten underway by the time of the 1960 emergency, and, for the most part, industrial workers who joined or supported the PAC did so as individuals rather than through trade union ties. In the industrial centers of Durban and Port Elizabeth, the latter an ANC stronghold, the PAC failed to make significant inroads. In Cape Town, and in the Vaal complex around Vereeniging—areas where ANC organization was weak—worker support for PAC was substantial; nevertheless, on balance, ANC could justly claim a stronger hold than PAC over the South African proletariat proper.

10. Interview with 'Molotsi.

Turning to the non-industrial proletariat—unskilled service workers, domestics, messengers, waiters and the like—no clear pattern of affiliation is apparent; nor is it possible to document any significant differences in organizational support among the more affluent petty bourgeois stratum of clerks, salesmen, artisans and shopkeepers. Each organization had followers drawn from all these groups, although it is possible that representatives of the middle classes made up a larger proportion of the PAC's support, particularly if high school students, who were important in PAC, can be counted as predominantly or at least prospectively middle class. Teachers in the Transvaal, while perhaps not constituting a numerically significant proportion of PAC support, seem to have been important in bringing students in, and also in lending weight to the claim of PAC leaders that their movement was the one backed by "intellectuals."[11] Insofar as the expansion of educational facilities had permitted younger people everywhere to achieve a higher educational level than their elders, it seems likely that the PAC represented a constituency which was, on the whole, better educated than that of the ANC.[12]

If any single group could be identified as distinctively PAC in orientation, it would be the broad category of Africans known in some contexts as "location boys" and in others as *tsotsis*. While these terms are far from precise and their particu-

11. This claim has been made by former PAC leaders, a large number of whom are or were teachers themselves. Peter Raboroko and Z. L. Mothopeng, both members of the PAC National Executive, were former Presidents of the Transvaal African Teachers Association, indicating perhaps that their views were similar to those of many teachers.

12. See Appendix, "Composition of ANC and PAC Leadership by Age and Class," p. 317–319. Benjamin Pogrund, a journalist with the *Rand Daily Mail* who was present at several PAC conferences in Johannesburg in 1959–60, observed that compared to ANC gatherings, PAC audiences appeared relatively well dressed and also showed greater concern for punctuality and brevity of speeches. These indications of comparatively greater concern with "Europeanized" appearance and behavior among PAC members may be primarily a reflection of younger age and higher educational level, or it could also indicate occupational upward mobility relative to their elders in the ANC.

lar connotations vary from city to city, they describe a type of young, urbanized African who falls outside and somewhere in between the proletariat proper and the respectable middle class. Usually more educated than lower class workers, yet unable to break into the ranks of the petty bourgeoisie, they are scornful of the low status and low paid employment available to them, and engage in rackets, con games and thefts of every description. Those who are unemployed may group into gangs of juvenile delinquents (referred to as *tsotsis*) and participate in crimes of violence. But unlike the more violent type of criminals, who tend to come from the semi-urbanized lumpenproletariat, most "location boys" support an essentially middle class life style by specializing, as Kuper observes, in sophisticated crimes that require "operational skills" rather than violence.[13] They are "embittered, frustrated, aggressive, non-comformist, suggestible, and prone to violence," he notes, and "they reject the polished behavior of the educated elite," the so-called "excuse me" type of respectable older urban African.[14] With little to lose materially and much to gain from the removal of job and wage discrimination, they are a politically volatile element and one which was drawn strongly toward the PAC.[15]

13. Kuper, *An African Bourgeoisie*, p. 425.
14. Ibid., p. 164. Kuper bases these characterizations on the observations of Anthony Ngubo.
15. The preference of *tsotsis* for the PAC was frequently mentioned in interviews. Ngubane was the only person to use the term "location boys," identifying this group as the younger, more educated element. Kuper (p. 425) notes that by the early 1960s, *tsotsi* and "location boy" had become virtually interchangeable terms, with *tsotsi*, at least in Durban, losing its connotations of violence. "The tendency," Kuper (and Ngubo) suggest, "is to reserve the word '*tsotsi*' for the smart 'location boys' who tend to avoid violence because this would expose them to the police, thus interfering with their sly ways of making a living. *Tsotsis* tend to identify with the younger members of the African bourgeoisie [e.g. the PAC national leadership group], whom they consider not 'starchy' and therefore 'non-'scuse me'. . . .'Scuse me' people are those members of the African bourgeoisie who are particularly concerned with the rules of etiquette and correct behavior, that is, imitators of White middle-class behavior." Wilson and Mafeje cite many more or less interchangeable terms for young, urban lower and

Lacking money to buy supplies or pay organizers, the PAC depended to a considerable extent on the resourcefulness of youthful "task forces" made up of *tsotsis* and students. Ordered to distribute leaflets, members of a task force might steal a car to do the job. "The morality of the task force," 'Molotsi later observed, was "efficiency."

> I mean . . . if we said this *Africanist* must be produced; we want ink, paper, . . . roneo machine, . . . these things would be in our offices. . . . Our fellows [would] come in . . . the big vans of Croxley stationaries and Transvaal Paper, day time with the police standing there, I being there to see to the stuff, our fellows coming off and working, delivering the goods, and I sign [for them] . . . And *The Africanist* would come out in the weekend from us. We were not a rich organization, and only the task force could deliver these things.[16]

In Cape Town, where PAC task forces were used with great effectiveness in mobilizing an African work stoppage after Sharpeville, youthful PAC supporters later revived the idea of executing political "jobs." Banding into the amorphous reconstruction of the PAC known as Poqo (a shortened version of the Xhosa name for PAC, *UmAfrika Poqo,* or "Africans alone," i.e. no Europeans), they had, by mid-1963, murdered a handful of whites, some dozen or more African policemen and police informers, and—in a futile effort to stop the implementation of the unpopular government plan for rural "Bantu Authorities"—a number of Transkeian chiefs and headmen.[17] Many of the men responsible for these acts were caught, and

---

lower middle-class Africans: townees, "location boys," *tsotsis, ooclever,* "bright boys," and "spoilers," *Langa,* p. 22. Lewis Nkosi offers interesting speculations on the political future of the *tsotsis* in "On South Africa [The Fire Some Time]," *Transition,* no. 38 (1971), pp. 30–34. For a description of *tsotsi* life, see Dugmore Boetie, *Familiarity Is the Kingdom of the Lost* (New York, 1970).

16. Interview with 'Molotsi.

17. Also see below, p. 298–300. A listing of Poqo murders, attempted murders, and other acts is given in the *Report of the Paarl Commission of Enquiry,* pp. 7–8. Most Africans in the Western Cape are Xhosas originating from the Transkei.

some were executed. Poqo throughout made no attempt to project any defined set of objectives or ideological principles; it spoke only the language of action. Police were initially baffled when witnesses and suspects referred to the Poqo "t.f.'s" but this was simply the terminology of the PAC task forces brought back to life. The PAC had been reincarnated minus its top level of more sophisticated leadership, allowing the urge toward a Fanonesque apocalypse to overwhelm all other considerations of ideology, strategy, or even organizational survival.

Moving Towards Confrontation

By late 1959 a long overdue lesson had come home to the men at the helm of the PAC: a "correct" ideology was not going to be enough to insure political success for their movement. In analyzing the African's political situation, they had been accurate in some aspects of their diagnosis and inaccurate in others. As the intellectual heirs of Lembede, they had inherited his sensitivity to the psychological dimensions of the African struggle. Like Lembede, who had predicted that Africans could wreck the NRC overnight if a few ANC leaders would only declare themselves for a policy of boycott, the PAC's leadership tended seriously to underestimate the organizational strength necessary to translate any ideology into effective action. "We think people will automatically respond to us because we give them the correct lead. But so much more is needed," an ANC report had admonished a few years earlier.[18] This was a basic truth which the PAC had to rediscover for itself. Given time and dedication to grass roots organization, it might have eventually been able to improve on the uneven and unprofessional organizing efforts of the ANC. But by the time serious organizational work had actually gotten underway in the PAC, its national leaders had already set themselves on an overambitious course of action.

18. *Report of the 44th Annual Conference of the African National Congress (Transvaal), Held in the Bantu Hall, Lady Selbourne, Pretoria, on the 3rd and 4th November, 1956*, p. 3 (Carter-Karis collection).

Had the PAC remained true to its own intellectual tradition, it would have mapped out a long-term psychological "nation-building" plan. The alleged inability of the ANC to implement any such strategy or program had been a favorite Africanist theme throughout the 1950s. The idea of a long-range building and conditioning process, an unremitting campaign to destroy the African's sense of inferiority, was a grand conception of the type that appealed to Sobukwe's idealism and intellect, and after years of thinking in such terms, it was not easy for him to accept that the idea had some practical disadvantages. Most importantly, any plan of action directed primarily at raising the political consciousness of the most demoralized and unassertive members of African society was, under the circumstances, a plan which by-passed the people who were in practice most attracted to the PAC, namely the relatively politicized and aggressive elements among urban youth. No African organization could hope to implement a country-wide program of political education without a large number of dedicated party cadres, but the activists who came forward to join the PAC from the time of its founding were almost all attracted by the prospect of militant action; the notion of merely spreading propaganda among the unawakened masses did not hold much appeal for them. With more time and the development of a disciplined organization, the PAC might perhaps have succeeded in training its initial recruits for the waging of a protracted and complex struggle. In practice, in the short period of twelve months during which the PAC was free to operate legally, this proved to be much beyond the capability of Sobukwe and his lieutenants.

That Sobukwe initially hoped to guide the PAC through a phased program of political consciousness-raising was clear from his plan for a PAC "status campaign." Addressing the National Heroes' Day conference on 2 August 1959, he called on PAC members to support a program of boycotts designed to exorcise all traces of "slave mentality" and to teach the people to assert their "African personality." The immediate target was to be shops and businesses which failed to give courteous service to African customers or persisted in addressing Africans as "native," "Kaffir," "boy," "girl," "Jane," or "John." Such businesses would be picketed and boycotted, Sobukwe warned, unless their differential treatment of Africans was stopped forthwith. "It must be clearly understood," he said, "that we are not begging the foreign minorities to treat our people courteously. We are calling on our people to assert their personality," and to be mindful "that acceptance of any indignity, any insult, any humiliation, is acceptance of inferiority."[19]

The idea of such a campaign was not a new one. Sobukwe had publicly urged the adoption of economic boycotts of this type on a number of occasions in 1957.[20] But explaining the principle behind the campaign was not the same thing as mobilizing party cadres for its implementation, and it was an inescapable fact that patient, disciplined and relatively "safe" action of the boycott type was not the kind of defiant political activity for which the PAC's militant young recruits were itching. As a result, although general plans for launching the status campaign were not abandoned following Sobukwe's August announcement, implementation was postponed to the indefinite future. Eventually, in early 1960, the PAC National Executive Committee did send out letters to large numbers of firms threatening pickets and boycotts.[21] There were ripples of reaction, but no wide-scale response or mass action to back the threats, in part because the energies of PAC members were by this time being directed into a new channel—the organization of a campaign to defy the pass laws.

19. "The State of the Nation." Also see "Statement on the Status Campaign," signed by Molete and Leballo, *The Africanist*, July–August 1959 (Carter-Karis collection).
20. Sobukwe had put forward the idea of a similar campaign in *The Africanist* of December 1957, and had also raised the idea early in 1957 in a speech to the Basutoland Congress Party, "Facing Fearful Odds," reproduced in *The Commentator* (Lesotho), August 1968. The ANC had itself made an abortive attempt to launch a courtesy campaign in 1953–54.
21. Letter "To All Public and Private Institutions, Commercial and Industrial Enterprises," signed by P. K. Leballo, 25 January 1960 (Hoover microfilms). Also see "PAC Ready to Picket Shops," *Golden City Post*, 7 February 1960.

The idea of a campaign against passes began to take shape in the latter part of 1959, when membership was still below expectations and it was becoming clear to the PAC's leadership that the movement would have to produce some concrete results if it wanted to hold and increase its following. When the National Executive Committee convened in Bloemfontein in September, it decided to propose a pass campaign for ratification by the organization's first annual conference, which was to meet in December.

The December conference met in an atmosphere of anticipation. PAC headquarters had announced that plans for "positive action" would be drawn up, and the *Golden City Post* had mooted that the PAC was preparing to unveil a master plan for liberation. The Executive Committee's report to the conference betrayed a certain pessimism about the movement's organizational efforts, but echoing Leballo's characteristic optimism, it assured the delegates that they had come together with "one aim in view—to take positive steps to crush, once and for all, White colonialism and imperialism in our Fatherland."[22] When delegates complained that the organization had been taking too soft a position, Sobukwe called for the conference to give the executive a mandate to launch a campaign against the pass laws. The response was unanimously favorable. The movement, Sobukwe declared, was about to "cross its historical Rubicon."[23]

Why did the PAC rush into a campaign of confrontation with the government when its forces were still undisciplined and its organizational structure still feeble? Pressure from an action-hungry following was clearly an important force in PAC decision-making; so was the strong sense of rivalry with the ANC and the desire to woo away its following with a demonstration of PAC strength. Having spent years trying to analyze the defects of the ANC, PAC leaders only naturally felt an urge to try out their own theories of action and leader-

22. Karis and Carter, vol. 3, p. 549.
23. Address by Sobukwe to the PAC national conference of 19–20 December 1959 (Hoover microfilms).

ship, and to prove that they could find the successful liberation formula which had always eluded Congress. Sobukwe and some of those around him, for example, shared a strong belief that heroic leadership was an essential factor missing in the conduct of past ANC campaigns. Top Congress leaders, they felt, had too often been ready to choose safety over danger, to hire lawyers and put up bail when arrested, and to shirk the need to set an example for the masses of sacrifice and solidarity. There was a portion of African opinion which had always felt that the Defiance Campaign of 1952–53 had been prematurely called off, not because violence had erupted, but because Congress leadership had developed cold feet. Most often cited was the example of Dr. Moroka, who, wary of being dealt with harshly by the courts as a leader of the campaign, had hired separate counsel, dissociated himself from his more radical fellow-accused, and made an obsequious plea in mitigation at the trial of the Defiance Campaign leadership.

"No bail, no defence, no fine," Sobukwe told a regional conference in Johannesburg in May 1959, would be the slogan under which PAC's leaders would go into action; leaders would always be in front to inspire the masses with an heroic spirit.[24] The principle seemed a sound one, and the willingness, even eagerness, of Sobukwe, Leballo and others to court martyrdom was genuine. The ANC was planning its own pass campaign for early 1960. If PAC was to seize the initiative, it had to be the first to go into action.

None of these reasons for the PAC's rush to confrontation really probes to the heart of the matter, however. A more searching explanation must take into account the entire framework of perceptions and beliefs shaping the decision-making process at the top level of Africanist leadership, for it was here that concepts of ideology and action met and merged into what was to become the PAC's political death wish. The relatively poor response to the PAC call for mass civil disobedi-

24. Address by Sobukwe to the Witwatersrand Regional conference of the PAC, 31 May 1959 (Hoover microfilms).

ence on 21 March 1960 indicated that the vast majority of
Africans were unready to participate in a showdown with white
power; yet the PAC's leadership cherished visions of launching
a massive campaign of defiance which would ultimately erupt
into a full-scale popular uprising. Africans, Sobukwe promised, would be free by 1963. What had led the Africanists to
become such willing victims of their own propaganda?

From the time of Lembede onward, African leaders of "rebel" temperament had talked of the masses' deep aspirations
for nationhood, aspirations which were sometimes described
as actual and sometimes as latent or buried beneath the surface
of an aberrant slave mentality. But how literally, in fact, did
orthodox nationalists take these theories about the African
mass mind? We have seen how Lembede's original formulation
of Africanism took shape out of his readings in world history
and philosophy, woven together with emotional strands from
Zulu tradition and his own peasant background. Modified in
the course of long arguments with his Youth League colleagues, Lembede's nationalist credo was a set of beliefs consciously devised with a particular end in view. However much
Lembede or any of his contemporaries may have identified
their own idealistic aspirations with the inchoate strivings of
the masses, the fact remained that nationalist doctrine was still
fundamentally an intellectual contrivance, and its Youth
League originators by and large recognized it as such. Only in
his wildest flights of philosophical fancy could Lembede claim
that in nationalism he had discovered a God-given law of nature rather than a time-tested—but man-made—political re-
cipe for mass mobilization. On the public platform, he or Mda
might speak of Africans yearning for their "divine destiny of
nationhood," but privately they recognized that popular
yearnings were in fact very amorphous—and eminently susceptible to molding ideological influences. An orthodox
nationalist ideological framework, they believed, held more
promise than any other for rousing and consolidating mass
energies; but this did not mean that nationalism was ultimately

anything other than a political device, or as Mda later called it, with typical detachment, a "great intellectual discipline."

By the second generation of Africanists, however, nationalist ideas had begun to take on a life of their own, like doctrines of a religious faith. It was a cardinal tenet of Africanist philosophy that Africans were striving, unconsciously if not consciously, to be a nation. For the orthodox nationalist who believed in the goal of an African-run state, it was only a short leap of faith to the idea that the masses too were "by nature" yearning for this goal. This was a comforting belief, moreover, for it allowed the nationalist to perceive all the anti-white passions of ordinary Africans in a positive light, thus making them seem more morally and intellectually respectable. Furthermore, a belief in the "natural nationalism" of the masses introduced a heartening note of optimism into what cold realists might otherwise have found an intolerably hopeless political situation: if the dynamic force of nationalistic emotion was latent beneath the surface of African docility, surely it was just a matter of time until that energy would be unleashed in all its power.

The literal-minded nationalist was, in other words, predisposed to a faith in mass spontaneity, that bane of serious revolutionaries the world over since the days of Lenin. Since the literal-minded nationalist saw the *aspirations* of the masses as having a natural coherence of their own, a kind of inner logic growing out of the related desires for dignity, self-determination, and repossession of the stolen fatherland, it was again an easy leap to the assumption that any *action* by the masses would also have coherence and would proceed to victory by the inherent logic of some natural law. The crucial challenge then became not so much guiding the masses through the heat of battle, but rather touching off the initial spark, giving a tottering and explosive situation one well-placed shove. Violence was probably inevitable, and it could certainly not be ruled out because of some sentimental belief in pacifism; but violence was not an eventuality that Africans could be expected to plan for, and the PAC accordingly had no blueprint for violent rebellion.

Ideological convictions can seldom if ever dictate what action a political leader ought to take in any given situation. They can, however, profoundly affect action by creating in political actors the psychological predisposition to interpret a situation in some way that is less than totally objective. When the leaders of the PAC, and in particular Leballo, sized up the mass mood and the prospects of the PAC, their perspective on the situation had already been powerfully conditioned by a belief in the possibility of a spontaneous mass uprising. Evidence, of course, could be cited to reinforce this belief: spontaneous bus boycotts in Evaton and Alexandra in the years 1955–57 had demonstrated popular discipline and determination, for example; in January 1960, African women in Cato Manor in Durban, protesting against police raids for illegal liquor, had sparked a riot in which nine policemen had been murdered by an angry mob; the revolutionary energy of thousands of young Africans seemed coiled tight like a spring, ready to be released. It was immaterial that other evidence could be marshaled to show that African political consciousness was not in fact particularly high countrywide, and that the limits of African tolerance had been far from reached. The optimism born of an ideological "true religion" easily won out. Even Sobukwe, who was much less prone than some of his colleagues to take the tenets of nationalism literally, was swept along by a conviction that the time was ripe, and that all that was required was for bold leaders to show the light and the masses would find the way.

In February 1960 Sobukwe, Leballo, and Howard Ngcobo, an executive committee member from Durban, drove through the Cape to assess the state of the PAC's organization there and to lay plans for the pass campaign. Selby Ngendane, another executive member, joined the group in Cape Town, and Elliot Mfaxa, the movement's national organizer, accompanied them as they touched centers of PAC activity in the eastern Cape. In

Port Elizabeth and other urban areas where support for the ANC was strong, popular interest in the touring Africanist delegation was meager. In Cape Town, however, where the ANC was relatively weak and had made little effort in the 1950s to address itself to the grievances of the city's many migrant and semi-urbanized workers, the PAC leaders were enthusiastically received. A crowd of about 2,000 assembled to hear Sobukwe speak at Langa township on February 14. Speaking in his native Xhosa, Sobukwe told his audience that the PAC was guiding Africans toward the creation of a New Africa. The first targets in its unfolding program were abolition of the pass laws and the achievement of a guaranteed minimum wage of £35 ($98) a month for all Africans. African men were to prepare themselves, he said, to receive the call from national headquarters. When the call came, all were to leave their passes at home and surrender for arrest at their local police stations; no one was to resort to violence or to let himself be provoked by police or provocateurs.[25]

In this speech and in propaganda issued in the period leading up to the launching of the campaign in March, there was an air of uncertainty about the final aims of the PAC campaign. On the one hand, passes and low wages were singled out as the target grievances. On the other hand, there was a strong suggestion in all PAC pronouncements that the campaign would not actually confine itself to these issues alone; rather, it would be the first stop in a rapid march to total freedom. The PAC opposed every piece of the government's apartheid legislation, Sobukwe told his audiences, but when a man's house was flooding the solution was not to try to throw the water outside; the PAC aimed, he said, at "closing the tap from which all this vile legislation flows," and it would not rest until all white rule was overthrown. Privately, PAC leaders believed that defiance of the pass laws would snowball, that defiers would obey the PAC's call to stay away from work, and that eventually there would be chaos in both the economy and the internal security system.

25. See *The World*, 27 February 1960, and Sobukwe's speech as transcribed by the police, reproduced in Karis and Carter, vol. 3, pp. 559–60.

The problems the PAC might face once it had been decapitated by arrests were the cause of some concern to the organization's leaders, but they did not allow doubts on this score to dissuade them from the course they had set. Plans were laid to choose and train subordinate layers of leadership within each region, men who could come forward when top leaders were jailed. In practice, however, implementation of this plan had not progressed very far by the time of the 1960 launching.

Over the doubts of some of the PAC's most influential supporters including Jordan Ngubane and A. P. Mda, Sobukwe and Leballo pressed forward with plans for launching the campaign in early 1960. The ANC at its annual national conference in December 1959 had resolved to launch a pass campaign of its own and had set 31 March 1960 as the date for its initial action. Its campaign was to begin with the sending of deputations to local authorities and Bantu Affairs commissioners throughout the country to demand abolition of the pass laws. It was clear that the PAC would have to launch its campaign before the thirty-first if it hoped to take the lead. The choice of an exact date was left to Sobukwe.

On March 4 Sobukwe sent his final instructions for the campaign to all branches and regional executives of the PAC. The people were to be instructed to observe the rules of strict nonviolence; no one was to resort to violence and emotionalism in the belief that the PAC was trying to engage in "revolutionary warfare." In a somewhat different vein, a party flyer issued at about the same time declared that the pass laws had to be "blown to oblivion this year, now and forever."[26] On March 16, Sobukwe wrote to Major-General Rademeyer, the commissioner of police, to inform him that the PAC would begin "a sustained, disciplined, nonviolent campaign" and its members would surrender themselves for arrest on Monday, March 21. He warned of "trigger-happy, African-hating" police, and assured Rademeyer that the people would disperse if given clear orders and adequate time to do so.[27]

26. Karis and Carter, vol. 3, p. 561.
27. Ibid., p. 565–66.

On Friday, March 18, Sobukwe announced at a press conference in Johannesburg that the campaign would begin the following Monday. PAC circulars announcing the launching date were already in the streets. "I have appealed to the African people," Sobukwe told the press, "to make sure that this campaign is conducted in a spirit of absolute nonviolence, and I am quite certain they will heed my call. . . . If the other side so desires," he went on, sounding a prophetic note, "we will provide them with an opportunity to demonstrate to the world how brutal they can be. We are ready to die for our cause."[28]

Emergency

If police had not shot into the crowd of demonstrators that gathered at Sharpeville location outside Vereeniging on 21 March 1960, the day might have marked merely another abortive campaign in the history of African protest. Contrary to the expectations of its leadership, response to the PAC's call was almost negligible in Johannesburg. Publicity for the campaign had been inadequate, opposition from the ANC had been appreciable, Madzunya had decided to oppose the campaign in Alexandra township, and the relatively materialistic and sophisticated population of the southwestern townships showed itself to be little disposed towards risky political protest. Sobukwe, Leballo, and other members of the PAC executive presented themselves for arrest at the Orlando police station followed only by some 150 volunteers. In Durban, Port Elizabeth and East London, no demonstrations took place.

Thirty-five miles south of Johannesburg, however, in the industrial complex around Vereeniging, PAC militants had organized well and had faced little or no competition from the ANC, which had never been strong in that area. A long bus boycott at nearby Evaton in 1955–56 had impressed political organizers with the strategic importance of the transport systems carrying Africans to their jobs in the white cities of Ver-

28. Ibid., p. 566–67.

eeniging, Vanderbijlpark, Meyerton and Johannesburg. Local activists were adept at coercing and cajoling African bus drivers into cooperation, and in the hours before dawn on March 21 they brought transport out of Sharpeville to a near standstill.

At Evaton, a predominantly African town, thousands of people gathered on Monday morning and were addressed by PAC organizers. Several hundred men presented themselves for arrest, but police refused to imprison them, claiming that jail facilities were inadequate. Military aircraft were sent to swoop low over the assembled crowds, and by nightfall no violent incidents had occurred. At Vanderbijlpark, a large industrial town about twelve miles from Evaton, several thousand protesters gathered at the police station and refused to disperse either when the aircraft dived at them or when police threw tear gas. Police fired at protesters who were throwing stones, and two men were killed. A police baton charge eventually scattered the crowd, and by midday police reinforcements began shifting from Vanderbijlpark to Sharpeville a few miles away, where the demonstration appeared to be getting out of control.

Eye-witness accounts of the Sharpeville massacre vary considerably in their assessment of the mood of the large crowd which surrounded the location police station there on March 21. Witnesses sympathetic towards the demonstrators testified, both at the official commission of inquiry and at the trial of the Sharpeville PAC leaders, that the crowd was unarmed, amiable, and well-mannered. They estimated that at the time the shooting occurred in the early afternoon, the size of the crowd was between three and ten thousand. Police witnesses testified that the number of people was much larger (official reports placed it at twenty thousand), that many were armed with sticks and other weapons, and that the crowd's mood was hostile, aggressive, and volatile. Tear gas had failed to halt demonstrators marching through the town earlier in the day, and some witnesses estimated that diving aircraft had only attracted more people to the site of the demonstration. Moreover, apparently unknown to the police, a rumor had spread in the township that a high-ranking white official was coming to address the crowd at the police station.

The size of the crowd, the insults and threats (including cries of "Cato Manor") shouted by individuals in the throng, and the natural anxiety of whites surrounded and outnumbered by people whom they regarded as the enemy, brought police nerves after several hours to a snapping point. No order was given to shoot, and no warning shots were fired to frighten the crowd back from the fence surrounding the station. In a moment of panic, a line of white police opened fire on the crowd and continued to fire (for from ten to thirty seconds, according to the finding of the commission of inquiry) as the demonstrators fled.[29] Sixty-seven Africans were shot dead, the great majority being hit in the back as they ran. One hundred eighty-six others were wounded, including forty women and eight children. White press reporters on the scene recorded the carnage in a series of grisly photographs that were to appear in newspapers all over the world in the days that followed.

In the principal African locations of Cape Town—Langa and Nyanga—large crowds also gathered the morning of the twenty-first, and many workers did not report to their jobs in the city. In the early morning, a large throng marched from Nyanga to Philippi police station, and about 1,500 men gave themselves up for arrest. Their names were taken and they were told to go home and appear in court at a later date. At Langa, large crowds gathered and were ordered by police to disperse. PAC organizers told people to assemble again in the late afternoon, and despite a government order banning further meetings, a crowd estimated at about 10,000 people gathered at Langa by 5:30 p.m. As at Sharpeville, rumors had spread that a high official would make an announcement, and the crowd became confused and angry when police arrived in force and, instead of making the anticipated announcement, launched a baton charge. When some people resisted this at-

29. *Summary of the Report of the Commission Appointed to Enquire into and to Report on the Events which Occurred in the Districts of Vereeniging and Vanderbijl Park on the 21st Day of March, 1960*, p. 25.

tempt to disperse the crowd, police used firearms and two demonstrators were killed. As people scattered, rioting erupted, lasting several hours. Whites on the scene were attacked, public buildings were set afire, African policemen were stoned and assaulted, and a Coloured driver employed by the *Cape Times* was murdered. By late evening the rioting had subsided, but there was more tension and violence to come.

The PAC's leadership had taken to heart the experience of the Defiance Campaign, when outbreaks of violence in the eastern Cape had provided government authorities with an opportunity to "restore law and order" by means of force. It was on this practical consideration and not on any philosophical commitment to passive resistance as such that the PAC based its call for nonviolence in 1960. Sobukwe had realized, as his terse letter to Rademeyer indicated, that there was considerable potential for violence in the situation which PAC was trying to create; but if police acted in such a way as to provoke violence from Africans, Sobukwe's letter implied, it would not be the responsibility of PAC, because the organization was issuing "strict instructions," not just to its own members "but also to the African people in general," that they should be nonviolent.

PAC leaders optimistically hoped that the campaign would unfold into widespread disciplined acts of civil disobedience. Realistically, however, they had scant grounds for supposing that the campaign would actually develop in this way. The number of people who felt bound by PAC instructions was small, as the thin popular response on March 21 showed. Even within the organization's membership there were some, like Madzunya, who did not consider orders from national headquarters to be binding. In contrast to the small number of Africans prepared to respond in a disciplined way to the PAC's initial call, there stood a much larger number of unruly action-oriented youths yearning to strike out at symbols of white authority in any possible way and on any pretext. Predictably, once a tense crisis situation had developed, this violence-prone element became uncontrollable, eventually providing the police with all the necessary justification for massive counterviolence. The pattern was to recur in 1976.

Crowd at Sharpeville flees police bullets, 21 March 1960. Policeman on vehicle in background reloads a sten-gun. *Ian Berry/Magnum.*

Africans burn passes after Sharpeville, March 1960. Crowd makes "thumbs up" sign of the ANC. *Terrence Spencer.*

Students from the University of the Witwatersrand demonstrate on Jan Smuts Avenue, Johannesburg, in protest against Sharpeville shooting, March 1960. *Terrence Spencer*.

Philip Kgosana of the PAC leaves Caledon Square, Cape Town, on the shoulders of demonstrators, 25 March 1960, after police had refused to arrest a crowd of anti-pass protestors from Langa. *Wide World Photos*.

The widely publicized shooting at Sharpeville confronted the South African government with a political crisis of unprecedented magnitude. All efforts by Verwoerd and National party leaders to make light of the incident proved futile as the waves of reaction mounted in South Africa and abroad. In Cape Town and the Transvaal gun shops sold out their stocks within days to panicky whites, and inquiries about emigration inundated Canadian and Australian embassies. Political uncertainty brought immediate economic repercussions. Massive selling plagued the Johannesburg Stock Exchange, and speculation grew that the crisis would retard or halt the flow of outside investment so vital to white South Africa's prosperity. International condemnation and isolation, merely a worrisome threat to whites before March 1960, now seemed an imminent reality as protests against apartheid poured in from every corner of the world. To many whites it looked as though South Africa had reached a point where basic change might be unavoidable.

Pleas from the United party, liberals, and businessmen calling for the government to restore stability by making concessions to Africans at first met with intransigence from Verwoerd, who took the view that concessions would only cause Africans to make further and bolder demands. Subsequently, government orders went out on March 26 that pass arrests should temporarily be suspended. This proved to be a purely tactical move, however, and was accompanied by strong measures to counter the African challenge and suppress all threats to white control. Armored vehicles patrolled location trouble spots around the clock, all police leaves were cancelled, and white citizen reserve units were called up to supplement police and military forces. Public meetings were outlawed in main centers throughout the country, while raids and arrests systematically battered anti-government organizations.

Although the specter of violence and disorder hung heavily over the African residential areas of Johannesburg and the Reef as the crisis matured, it was in Cape Town that the security of whites appeared to be most directly threatened by African defiance. There the African stay-at-home which had begun on Monday the twenty-first continued until by the end of the week it was nearly total, bringing to a standstill those businesses and industries which relied on African labor. After police had jailed about one hundred anti-pass volunteers surrendering at Caledon Square police headquarters in downtown Cape Town on March 24, a crowd of two thousand men from Langa location gathered at the same place the next day to court arrest. Police refused to jail them, and they marched without incident back to the township—but not before many whites had become thoroughly alarmed at the sight of a large black crowd massed in the city center. On Monday, March 28, a crowd estimated at fifty thousand jammed Langa township for the burial of the riot dead and heard PAC funeral orators call for Africans to continue striking until three demands were met. These demands, repeatedly stated since the twenty-first, were the abolition of passes, a £35-a-month minimum wage, and no victimization of strikers. Elsewhere on the same day several hundred thousand Africans across the country observed a call by Lutuli to stay at home in mourning for the dead. Thousands burned their pass books, and in Johannesburg serious rioting erupted. In Parliament, the National party introduced a bill calling for emergency powers to ban the ANC and the PAC and to raise the legal punishments for political acts of defiance.

On Wednesday, March 30, the government declared a state of emergency and assumed broad powers to act against all forms of alleged subversion, including the power to arrest and detain indefinitely any person suspected of anti-government activity. Early that morning police had begun conducting nationwide swoops to arrest leaders and supporters of the African cause. In Cape Town they entered Langa and Nyanga, beat up striking workers, and began a systematic round-up of known PAC leaders. As word of the arrests and beatings spread, people began to congregate, and by mid-morning a broad column of Africans began to move out of Langa along the ten-mile route towards the city center. A white journalist who witnessed the march expressed the tension of Cape Town's whites:

There were about 5,000 when the march began. By the time I saw them, coming along the curved dual carriage-way that leads around the side of the mountain to the heart of Cape Town, there must have been at least 15,000. They were marching about twelve abreast, dressed in their workingmen's shirts, trousers and coats, and looking exactly like some sentimental Leftist painting, "The Peasants' Revolt." But this was real.[30]

Philip Kgosana, the PAC's regional secretary for the western Cape, was at the head of the marching column as it entered the city. He intended to lead the crowd to the Houses of Parliament and to demand an interview with the minister of justice, but was persuaded by police to divert the march into Caledon Square. As Saracen tanks and troops barricaded the approaches to Parliament and an air force helicopter circled overhead, Africans poured into the square and the surrounding streets. Press reporters estimated the crowd by then at about thirty thousand.

The spontaneous massing of such a large crowd of Africans in the center of a "white" city was an unprecedented situation, and neither the marchers nor the police were prepared with any plan of action. The marchers were unarmed, but had they became violent, perhaps in response to a police show of force, the toll in lives and property could have been immense. The outcome rested in the hands of Kgosana, a 23-year-old University of Cape Town student with a flair for leadership who had dropped his studies a few months earlier to devote himself full-time to politics. Negotiating on behalf of the demonstrators, Kgosana asked for the release of the arrested leaders, an interview with the minister of justice, and an assurance that police would stop using force to break the African stay-at-home. After consultations among high-ranking police, Kgosana was informed that his last two demands would be met if he would request the crowd to disperse. The gullible Kgosana, not realizing that his only bargaining power lay in his ability to keep the crowd behind him, took a police microphone and directed the people to return to Langa, telling them that

30. Kenneth Mackenzie, *The Spectator* (London), 8 April 1960, quoted by Myrna Blumberg, *White Madam* (London, 1962), p. 27.

the police had agreed to make concessions. The marchers returned home. That evening when Kgosana and several colleagues returned to the city for their promised "interview," they were arrested and jailed under the terms of the new emergency regulations. A decisive historical moment had come and passed by, leaving whites shaken but still firmly in control.[31]

From March 31 onwards police throughout the country spared no efforts in crushing all manifestations of revolt and silencing prospective troublemakers. Severe new penalties for publications deemed guilty of incitement or subversion curtailed press freedom. Thousands of Africans were arrested and charged with minor infractions, and nearly two thousand political activists, including many prominent non-Africans, were detained under emergency regulations which waived the right of habeas corpus.[32]

On April 1 in downtown Durban, police opened fire at thousands of African demonstrators, killing three. Outbreaks of violence and pass-burning in Port Elizabeth, Bloemfontein and other scattered centers met with swift police retaliation. In Cape Town, residents of Langa and Nyanga awoke the morning after their massive march to find the townships cordoned off by police and units of the army and navy. During the week

31. See *Cape Argus* and *The Star,* 30 March 1960, *Cape Times* and *Rand Daily Mail,* 31 March 1960, and *Contact,* 16 April 1960. Inaccurate accounts of the Cape Town march of 30 March are given by Roux in *Time Longer Than Rope* (p. 410) and by the Legums in *The Bitter Choice* (p. 106). These attribute a role in the negotiations between Kgosana and the police to Patrick Duncan, the editor of *Contact* and a leading member of the Liberal party. Duncan's diary (Hoover microfilms) shows clearly that he was not present on the 30th, but instead played a role as advisor to Kgosana on 25 March, when a smaller crowd of Africans, estimated at 2000, courted arrest at Caledon Square (see above, p. 243). Duncan's role on the 25th is mentioned in *New Age,* 31 March 1960. Duncan later formed a close friendship with Leballo and was the only white ever to become a member of the PAC. At the time of his death in 1967 he was PAC representative in Algiers.
32. The minister of justice told Parliament on May 6 that 18,011 arrests had been made since the beginning of the emergency, not counting political suspects. M. Horrell, comp., *A Survey of Race Relations in South Africa* [1959–1960] (Johannesburg, 1960), p. 84.

that followed, strike-breakers were permitted to pass out through the cordon in the early morning hours, following which police staged house-to-house raids, seizing anything resembling a weapon and assaulting workers with clubs and whips. By the second week of April, with the strike broken and their mopping-up operations complete, police ended their blitzkrieg in the sullen Cape Town locations. Enforcement of the pass laws was resumed throughout the country, and on April 8 the government announced in Parliament the banning of the ANC and the PAC under the terms of the newly enacted Unlawful Organisations Act.

Aftermath

The Unlawful Organisations Act empowered the government to proscribe the ANC, PAC and any other organizations attempting to further their aims. It also provided that persons found guilty of intimidating others to strike or to commit any offense by way of protest against a law, would be liable to a maximum penalty of five years imprisonment, a £500 fine, or ten strokes, or a combination of any two of these. This represented a tenfold increase in the penalties for such offenses prescribed under the Criminal Law Amendment Act of 1953, passed during the Defiance Campaign, which had set maximum sentences at six months or a £50 fine, or both. Clearly, whites were prepared to match any demonstration of black defiance with a show of force majeure.

The parliamentary debate on the Unlawful Organisations Bill afforded white politicians an opportunity to set forth their views on the proper limits and functions of black politics, and also revealed the extent of their understanding of black political history, personalities, and opinion. In support of the banning of the ANC and the PAC, National party spokesmen took a position which was essentially the same as the prosecution line of argument in the Treason Trial, then stretching into its fourth year in Pretoria: these organizations had far exceeded the limits of legality because their fundamental aim was violent overthrow of the government. Their actions bordered on revolution, the minister of justice, Francois Erasmus, told Parliament during the second reading of the bill on March 29. "Their aim is to bring to its knees any White Government in South Africa which stands for White supremacy and for White leadership . . . [They] do not want peace and order; what they want is not £1 a day for all the Bantu in South Africa; what they want is our country!"[33] Furthermore, maintained De Wet Nel, the minister of Bantu administration and development, the force being employed by these organizations to intimidate peace-loving Africans revealed their violent intentions. "Lutuli and these agitators," he said,

> are playing the diabolical role of inciting these people to revolt and then they issue pious statements in which they say that they are not in favor of violence, but behind the scenes the "spoilers" [hoodlums] and similar people are encouraged to commit violence. The tragic part of it all is that there are actually people who believe that Lutuli and his associates are honest when they say that they do not want bloodshed and violence. . . . Having inspired such mass psychology, particularly on the part of the Bantu who has not yet reached the standard of civilization of the White man, it is then very easy [for agitators] to strike the match, in which case the law-abiding Bantu become the victims of what is happening in the country today.[34]

Armed with the new legislation, Erasmus argued, the government would be able to protect innocent Africans and call a halt to the ANC-PAC "reign of terror." "The combined membership of these two organizations," he hastened to point out to Parliament, was "only about 70,000. . . . These two organizations are not at all representative of the Bantu in South Africa. They represent less than 1 per cent of the Bantu population. . . . They are just a small coterie of terrorists."[35] Given that the ANC and the PAC were extremist fringe groups with openly subversive aims, what could possibly be achieved by consultations or negotiations with them? What reason did they even have to exist? One member of Parliament, G. F. Frone-

33. *House of Assembly Debates,* 29 March 1960, columns 4302–3.
34. Ibid., column 4328.
35. Ibid., column 4302.

men, expressed a prevailing National party view when he stated in the debate on March 30 that "The Government has responsible, sound bridges with the Bantu by way of the tribal authorities. . . . It is only the 1 per cent, which is represented by the PAC and the ANC, with which it has no link. . . . 99 per cent of the Bantu people support the apartheid policy of the Government."[36]

In criticizing the government's position, opposition members from the United and Progressive parties argued that while the ANC and PAC had undesirable aims, their organizations did not pose a serious threat to the status quo. Far more serious, the Progressives argued, was the possibility that leadership among Africans would pass into even more extreme hands if the relatively moderate legal organizations were driven underground. This pattern was already apparent from the fact that the PAC had emerged after more moderate leaders in the ANC had been silenced by bans. Stability could only be insured, both opposition parties maintained, if urban Africans were allowed some channels for expressing their views. Their political organizations, particularly the ANC with its preponderance of middle class leaders, were just such a safety valve and therefore served a positive function in spite of the unconscionable nature of their stated goals.

The current crisis had arisen in part, said the leader of the United party, Sir De Villiers Graaff, because of the government's failure to

> recognize the emergent class of Native in our urban areas, a responsible class, a middle class . . . which could be a stabilizing influence and which could co-operate in the maintenance of law and order . . . a class entitled to own their own property in their own areas set aside for them, who have an interest, a stake . . . and who will accept with us the responsibility of maintaining Western standards in our South African community.[37]

The pass laws, Graaff said, could have a part to play in the process of encouraging this buffer class; if returned to power,

36. Ibid., column 4368.
37. Ibid., 29 March 1960, columns 4317 and 4321.

the United party would restore pass exemption certificates for qualified Africans, a provision of the pass laws which the National party had short-sightedly done away with.[38]

But faced with the most threatening challenge to their dominance up to that time in the history of modern South Africa, most whites were not prepared to reject the strong-arm tactics of the Nationalists in favor of the more subtle strategy of the United party. Sensing strong white public opinion in support of the government, the United party in the end defied the logic of its own arguments and voted in favor of the banning bill, leaving only the Progressives and the three Native Representatives voting "no."[39] In spite of the distinctions between the ANC and the PAC which were pointed out by a few better informed members of Parliament, there was no sentiment in support of banning the PAC while permitting the less extreme ANC to remain legal.

Even before bans officially terminated the legal existence of the two Congresses their operations had been drastically curtailed by arrests and police raids. Although leaders of both organizations had long foreseen a stepping up of government pressure, neither Congress was adequately prepared for an underground existence. In a statement issued on April 1, the ANC boldly declared that it would not submit to a ban and would continue to "give leadership and organization" to the people until freedom had been won.[40] Yet realistically, action other than the issuing of occasional clandestine bulletins had already become more than the ANC could effect; mere survival in the face of the police onslaught had become as much as either Congress could hope for.

The PAC was even less prepared than the ANC for illegality. The arrest of Sobukwe, Leballo, and other national PAC

38. Ibid., column 4322.
39. Following the formation of the Progressive party in November 1959 there were twelve Progressive members of Parliament. In the general election of October 1961, all but one, Helen Suzman, were defeated. The three MPs representing Africans were eliminated by law in 1959, but the incumbents remained in Parliament until the 1961 election.
40. Karis and Carter, vol. 3, p. 572.

leaders in Johannesburg on March 21 had left the PAC virtually leaderless overnight. In areas where men had been appointed to understudy the top officebearers, police swoops
netted activists down to the third and fourth layers of con-
tingency leadership. PAC headquarters in Johannesburg was
left in the hands of William Jolobe, a student who had previously been the organization's office manager. The "no bail, no
defence, no fine" slogan, effective as it may have been in building an image of the PAC as a resolute movement whose leaders
were prepared for sacrifice and suffering, became a handicap
once the campaign against passes had collapsed and the PAC
was forced to struggle for its very survival. With Sobukwe jailed
for three years on a charge of incitement and other top Pan
Africanists in the Transvaal also removed from the scene for
long periods, the PAC fell rapidly into a state of total disarray.

In reaction to the shock of the Sharpeville shooting and the
deepening crisis of the emergency, African political attitudes
readjusted somewhat to take new realities into account. Whatever disappointments the crisis period eventually held in store
for blacks, there was nevertheless a realization that the historical record of unmitigated failure had at least been broken.
African action had forced a brief suspension of the pass laws
and had threatened for a short time to paralyze the nation's
industries. Many Africans had at least glimpsed the potential
power of civil disobedience and economic disruption and had
begun to sense the important new influence of international
opinion. The reality of fear and moral uncertainty had temporarily broken through white South Africa's veneer of smug
self-confidence. On April 9, a white Transvaal farmer, apparently deranged by the crisis, narrowly failed in an attempt
to assassinate Verwoerd. Ten days later, Paul O. Sauer, the
minister of lands and senior member of the cabinet, delivered a
speech in which he said that the "old book" of South African
history had been closed at Sharpeville and that there was a
need for the country "in earnest and honestly" to reconsider its
whole approach to race relations.[41] Some employers raised the
wages of their black workers.

41. *Cape Times*, 20 April 1960.

All these developments were cause for measured optimism among Africans. On the negative side, however, stood the obvious determination of whites to maintain their position by any means at their disposal, including open violence and the suppression of all expressions of dissent. The myth that the African masses were a volcano on the verge of an explosion had itself been exploded. The PAC had invited Africans to pit themselves against the full might of white South Africa, and most had declined the invitation. By mid-April when workers began to queue at government offices to get replacements for their burned passes, it was evident that African demoralization was nationwide. A well-publicized call from the underground ANC for Africans to stage a week-long stay-at-home beginning on April 19 received no popular support. Efforts of African leaders to regroup and rally mass resistance later in 1960 and early in 1961 likewise proved abortive.

The Hiatus of the 1960s

In spite of banning and harassment, the PAC continued to enjoy wide prestige after 1960, both as a symbol of defiance and as a focus for political identification, especially among younger Africans. Nor could a mere ban obliterate loyalties to the ANC which had built up over generations. For the government permanently to stamp out allegiance to these organizations, a long campaign of intimidation and harrassment was necessary, together with renewed attempts to offer the diversionary political spoils of "separate development" under tribal authorities.

In rallying the support of Parliament and the white public for tougher measures to deal with African dissent, the National party was eventually aided indirectly by developments within the remnants of the ANC and PAC themselves. Both organizations, being unable to carry on as mass movements, turned instead to violent methods in the early 1960s—which in turn provided whites with renewed justification for wholesale repression. Leadership remnants of the ANC and the Congress Alliance, centering around Nelson Mandela and Walter Sisulu, having concluded that nonviolent tactics were no longer viable, undertook in 1961–62 to build a sabotage organization called Umkonto we Sizwe (the Spear of the Nation). Umkonto staged a number of successful bombings, but in July 1963, police raided its secret headquarters at Rivonia near Johannesburg and arrested the core of its leadership. There followed the much-publicized Rivonia trial which ended in May 1964 with the passing of life sentences on Mandela, Sisulu, and six other Umkonto leaders.

In the PAC, things took a different turn. With Sobukwe removed from the scene, and various other members of the PAC executive, including Leballo, imprisoned for two years, there was a long lull in activity. Then in late 1962, after Leballo had completed his sentence and had transferred PAC head-quarters to Maseru in Basutoland, a crudely organized PAC underground began to operate, leading to minor acts of violence, many committed by school-age youths. In the western Cape, and centered on Langa location in Cape Town, an offshoot of the PAC with no apparent links to Maseru also began in late 1962 to organize Africans into groups for the purpose of attacking whites and African agents of the govern-ment. This Cape-based movement, known as Poqo, managed, with a minimum of formal leadership and organization, to create widespread fear among whites, who saw it as a local version of the dreaded Kenyan Mau Mau. Police were able to infiltrate Poqo and curb its activities by 1963, however, and in this they were greatly aided by Leballo himself, who turned out, predictably, to be a poor substitute for Sobukwe at the helm of the PAC. Unable to control an urge to boast about his grandiose plans for revolution, Leballo announced at a press conference in Maseru on 24 March 1963 that the PAC (which he claimed was one and the same with Poqo) was on the verge of a violent "launching" throughout South Africa.[42] A few days later, newly-alerted police arrested two of Leballo's agents crossing the border with a large number of letters to be sent to PAC contacts. On April 1, Basutoland police raided PAC of-

42. *Star*, 25 March 1963.

fices in Maseru and seized lists reported to contain thousands of names of PAC members.

Between public alarm over Poqo incidents in the Cape and Leballo's boasts from Maseru, the government needed no further pretext to launch a massive new assault on its enemies. While wide-scale raids and arrests netted thousands of PAC and Poqo adherents, the Nationalists, with full support from the United party, put through Parliament the General Laws Amendment Act of 1963 giving the government unprecedented power to deal with its foes. Most notable of the new powers granted under the act was the provision for detention, without trial or charges being laid, for repeated periods of ninety days, of anyone deemed subversive by the minister of justice. Also notable was a provision making it legal for the government to imprison Sobukwe beyond the end of his three-year sentence, which was due to expire within days after the passage of the Act. In the second week of June 1963, the minister of justice, B. J. Vorster, told Parliament that 3,246 suspected members of Poqo or PAC (the two were treated as synonymous) had been arrested, and that 1,162 had already been convicted and sentenced.[43] The government, it was claimed with considerable accuracy, had stamped out "Poqo terrorism."

With the government firm in its resolve, and white public opinion running strongly against "terrorism," "communism," and other real and imagined threats to the status quo, opposition politics became increasingly hazardous for blacks and whites alike. Police spies and informers were at work everywhere, and for the average African it became wise to regard politics as a taboo subject even in casual conversation. White radicals too found their ranks decimated. The African Resistance Movement (ARM), an amateurish underground sabotage organization of white university students and elements from the left wing of the Liberal party, was rapidly disposed of by government action in 1964, and in 1965–66

43. *House of Assembly Debates,* 12 June 1963, col. 7771, and 10 June 1963, cols. 7634 and 7636.

Abram Fischer, a distinguished Afrikaner lawyer, was tried and sentenced to life imprisonment for being the chairman of the central committee of the underground Communist party.

To the government's stick of legislative and judicial action was meanwhile added the carrot of "separate development," the Nationalist blueprint for partitioning South Africa into white and black spheres. Besides trying to divert politically-inclined Africans towards the innocuous channels of ethnic politics, the plan aimed at deflating pressure from the United Nations and from critics in Europe and America who charged that South Africa was denying political rights to its black majority. In the Transkei, the first showpiece bantustan, the rate of economic progress was negligible, but politically by the late 1960s things were going well for the apartheid planners; the pro-apartheid party of Prime Minister Kaiser Matanzima, after initial unpopularity with the Transkei electorate, had used its position of power to undermine its opposition and consolidate support for eventual "independence." Moves were underway to extend the bantustan plan to other tribal reserves. In Soweto (the name now applied to all Johannesburg's south-western townships, with their combined population of about three-quarters of a million Africans), a partly elected Urban Bantu Council was established in 1968, replacing the older system of advisory boards. Similar "UBCs" were set up in other large towns. In each case, council seats were apportioned on an ethnic basis, with Zulus voting for Zulu candidates, Tswanas voting for Tswanas, and so on. In the same year a Coloured Persons' Representative Council and a South African Indian Council were established on a nationwide basis, both, like the UBCs, having functions which were almost wholly advisory. Adding the final touch to its newly created institutions, the National party in the same year, 1968, pushed through Parliament, this time over the objections of the United party, the Prohibition of Political Interference Act, making it illegal for any political party to have a racially mixed membership. The government, claimed the defenders of the act, wanted to insure each racial group the right of "untrammelled" self-determination—within, of course, the limits set by the government-determined goal of segregation. Rather than comply with the terms of the act, the Liberal party, which had many black members, disbanded; bans on most of its leaders had already rendered it impotent. The Progressive party, reduced to one member of Parliament, decided to comply with the act and close its membership to blacks, who between the 1960 banning of the ANC and PAC and 1968 had joined Progressive ranks in considerable numbers. For the politically-minded African, the choice was rapidly becoming apartheid politics-within-the-system, or no politics at all.

Crucial to the National party's long-term plan for dividing Africans along ethnic lines was the Bantu Education system, introduced in 1953 and applied at the university level starting in 1959. Under this system, control of African schools was taken away from the church institutions and provincial departments and turned over to the national government, which had in most cases been financing the greater part of black education for some years. Gradually, in those areas where African school populations were ethnically mixed, the system provided for the segregation of schools by language group so that mother tongue instruction could replace English and Afrikaans-medium instruction at the primary level. Speaking in Parliament on behalf of the proposed system in 1953, Verwoerd, then the minister of native affairs, had noted that "good racial relations cannot exist when the education is given under the control of people who create wrong expectations on the part of the Native." Education had to train people "in accordance with their opportunities in life," he said. Under the National party's plan, there was no place for Africans in "white" South Africa "above the level of certain forms of labor." Within their own rural reserve areas, however, Africans would find that "all doors were open."[44] Curricula were thereafter redesigned with a view to eliminating "wrong expectations" and creating African support for policies of "separate development."

44. Quoted in M. Horrell, *A Decade of Bantu Education* (Johannesburg, 1964), p. 6.

The Extension of University Education Act of 1959 closed to African students the previously "open" white universities, and provided instead for the building of new universities for blacks on an ethnically segregated basis. Control of Fort Hare was transferred to the government, in spite of strong protests, and its admissions limited to students of Xhosa and Fingo origin. In 1960, two new African universities were opened, one at Ngoye in Natal for Zulus and Swazis, and the other at Turfloop, near Pietersburg in the northern Transvaal, for Sothos, Tswanas, Vendas, Tsongas and Transvaal Ndebeles (the University of the North). Separate universities for Coloureds and Indians were also later established, Coloureds being required to attend the University College of the Western Cape, and Indians the University College of Durban-Westville. In mid-1968, the total enrollment at these five institutions stood at 3,508.[45] In addition, 130 Africans, 209 Indians and 31 Coloureds were enrolled in the nonwhite division of the University of Natal Medical School, the only medical school open to blacks.[46] Control of students on all campuses was tight, and faculty and administrative positions were strictly limited to government-approved appointees, the great majority being whites and for the most part, except at the Natal Medical School, Afrikaners. By 1969, on the tenth anniversary of the Extension of University Education Act, it still remained to be seen whether or not success would crown the government's efforts to mold a more compliant generation of black leadership.

45. M. Horrell, comp., *A Survey of Race Relations in South Africa* [1968] (Johannesburg, 1969), p. 254.
46. M. Horrell, *Bantu Education to 1968* (Johannesburg, 1968), p. 117.

8

Black Consciousness in the 1970s

Origins of the Black Consciousness Movement

Silence pervaded African political life in the 1960s to an extent which had not been known since the years before 1912. Though Africans were free to join the Liberal and Progressive parties until 1968, it was whites in these organizations who for the most part took on the task of articulating African grievances and demands. Blacks who spoke out invited martyrdom. To liberal whites it seemed a matter of duty to shield politically-motivated blacks from government retaliation.

In the wake of Sharpeville, African students loyal to the ANC had formed the African Students' Association (ASA), PAC students had formed the African Students' Union of South Africa (ASUSA), and students loyal to the Non-European Unity Movement had formed other organizations in the Cape and Natal. None of these organizations, however, had survived for long, since identification with banned movements was hazardous, university authorities were hostile to student political groups, and the groups themselves were uncooperative with one another. For want of other political outlets, many African students by 1963–64 had begun focusing attention instead on NUSAS, the multiracial National Union of South African Students, an outspokenly anti-government organization with a membership drawn heavily from white English-speaking universities. Bolder at the verbal level than either the Liberals or the Progressives, the leaders of NUSAS tended to identify strongly with the black cause, and were in turn seen by many blacks as important spokesmen for that cause. Paying uninvited tribute to the national role which NUSAS had assumed by 1963, Vorster in a speech in May of that year condemned the organization as a "cancer in the life of the nation."[1]

Reflecting the same emotional pressures that were to draw several prominent NUSAS figures into the illegal African Resistance Movement, the leadership of NUSAS in 1963–64 bent itself away from the more middle-of-the-road liberalism of its white rank and file and began responding instead to the mood of the NUSAS black minority, a mood which was angry and impatient for meaningful action. In April 1964, addressing what he believed was a closed NUSAS seminar at Botha's Hill, NUSAS president Jonty Driver called for students to turn from protest politics to real action for liberation; in effect, his proposal was that NUSAS convert itself into an extra-legal revolutionary organization. Reports of the speech reached the press, and negative reactions from white students were strong; threats of disaffiliation followed, Driver was censured at the July 1964 NUSAS annual conference, and the organization began a firm swing toward the right, largely confining itself for several years to symbolic multiracial activities and protests after-the-fact against government infringements on academic freedom. The involvement of several NUSAS leaders in the African Resistance Movement, including Adrian Leftwich, a former NUSAS president, had also been revealed in mid-1964, contributing to the conservative backlash.

The late 1960s thus found Africans caught in an extremely frustrating political situation where virtually all channels for the expression of anti-apartheid sentiment were closed. Memories of the pre-1960 years faded, and parents tended to shield their children from what was widely regarded as the "dangerous" history of pre-Sharpeville political movements. Apathy and silence were all-pervasive, except among those few

1. *A Brief History of Student Action in South Africa,* p. 3 (NUSAS files).

Africans—a new breed of "realists"—who were willing to turn their energies to the system of bantustans, UBCs, and other government-created institutions of "separate development." Within these institutions a certain amount of anti-system criticism was tolerated, and to the new "realists" there seemed to be at least some advantage in taking whatever institutions were offered to the African, however meagre or inadequate these might be, and trying to use them as instruments with which to maneuver for something better. As in the past, it could always be argued that the politics of half a loaf was preferable to no politics at all. But for those Africans who were still attracted to the idea of militant opposition, government-created institutions seemed very inadequate vehicles for political activity. Among African university students in particular, a group which had historically produced many political activists of "rebel" temperament, dissatisfaction was intense. After futile years of trying to make NUSAS into a satisfying political home, it was clear that progress had been negligible.

This frustration among university students found little focus or articulation, however, until the years 1967–68, when a few blacks in NUSAS began seriously to analyze and reflect upon their political predicament. The most important of these new black critics within NUSAS was a Natal University medical student named Steve Biko. Born in 1946 in Kingwilliamstown in the eastern Cape, the son of a government-employed clerk, Biko's initiation into politics had come as a teenager in 1963 when his older brother, a student at Lovedale high school, was arrested as a suspected Poqo activist and jailed for nine months.[2] Interrogated by the police about his brother's activities, and expelled because of his brother from Lovedale where he himself had been a student for only three months, Biko developed a strong resentment toward white authority, an attitude he carried with him in 1964 when he entered St. Francis College at Mariannhill in Natal, a liberal Catholic boarding school and one of the few remaining private high

2. Biographical information on Biko is drawn primarily from his interview with the author in 1972.

schools for Africans in South Africa. Even in the relatively liberal atmosphere of Mariannhill, it seemed to Biko that thought-control was the norm. Christian principles impressed him, as did the ideal of an eventual common, integrated society; but he was not satisfied to have any white try to influence his thinking about the precise detail of either ends or means when it came to the future of Africans.

From Mariannhill, Biko in 1966 entered the Natal University nonwhite medical school, familiarly known as Wentworth. He soon was elected to the Students' Representative Council, and through the SRC was drawn into participation in NUSAS. In July 1966 he attended the NUSAS annual conference as an observer, and in 1967 he participated as a Wentworth delegate at the July annual conference which saw bitter reactions from black students when Rhodes University, the host institution, prohibited mixed accommodation or eating facilities at the conference site. Undogmatic but highly disciplined in his thinking, possessed with a rare insight into human and political situations, Biko increasingly began to question the value of what he saw as the artificial integration of student politics. As in South African politics generally, Africans were hanging back, resentful but reticent, hiding behind white spokesmen who had shouldered the job of defining black grievances and goals. For liberal whites, verbal protest and symbolic racial mixing were seen as the outer limit of action. Apartheid was defined as the enemy, and nonracialism prescribed as the antidote. Repeated over and over in words and symbols, this liberal approach, and in fact the entire liberal analysis, had to Biko's way of thinking become not an inspiration to constructive action but a sterile dogma disguising an unconscious attachment to the status quo.

At the NUSAS congress of July 1968, Biko and some of his fellow medical students began to draw black students into a candid discussion of their role as second class citizens within NUSAS. Moving from the NUSAS congress to a conference of the multiracial University Christian Movement (UCM) meeting nearby at Stutterheim, Biko began to canvass support for the idea of an all-black movement which would do away with the artificiality of symbolic integration and white liberal leadership. The University Christian Movement, led by Basil Moore, a Protestant minister, and Colin Collins, a Catholic priest, had attracted many black students to its ranks since its founding in 1966–67, and had begun to show a strong interest in "Black Theology," an American intellectual movement with obvious applicability in South African churches. A number of Africans within UCM reacted enthusiastically to Biko's soundings, and buoyed by this response, he decided to let his medical studies slide temporarily and to organize a formal meeting of black student leaders to discuss the launching of a new movement.

In December 1968 during Christmas recess this meeting took place at Mariannhill and was attended by about thirty members of black university Students' Representative Councils. Starting from scratch to analyze the NUSAS experience for this group, Biko found an encouraging receptiveness to his idea of an all-black organization. Except at Wentworth, university authorities on all African campuses had refused students permission to formally affiliate to NUSAS, and as a result the goal of "getting into NUSAS" had retained a certain appeal for many African student leaders. Asked to examine carefully the rationale for this attitude, however, the pro-NUSAS students present were quickly swayed by Biko's arguments for going it alone. From Turfloop a number of student leaders were present who had formerly been pro-PAC and ASUSA in their loyalties; their antipathies to NUSAS had always been strong, and they needed no persuasion to accept the idea of an exclusively black organization. The name of SASO, the South African Students' Organisation, was chosen, and plans were laid for a formal inaugural conference. When that conference met at Turfloop in July 1969, Biko was named president. Other leading figures from the beginning in SASO were Barney Pityana, an ex-Fort Hare student from Port Elizabeth, Harry Nengwekhulu, Hendrick Musi, Petrus Machaka, and Manana Kgware of Turfloop, Aubrey Mokoape, a medical student, and J. Goolam and Strini Moodley, Indian friends of Biko's, the former a medical student and the latter an ex-student at the University College of Durban-Westville.

Because of lingering loyalties to NUSAS among many black students, and the initial suspicions which some harbored about the motives and origins of SASO, Biko and his colleagues decided that an open break with NUSAS and a frontal attack on its ideology would be inadvisable until after SASO had begun to find its feet as an organization. The first constitution, adopted in July 1969, accordingly stated the purpose of SASO as promoting "contact and practical cooperation among students studying at the affiliated centers." SASO, it stated, would "represent the nonwhite students nationally," noting that "owing to circumstances beyond their control, students at some non-white centers are unable to participate in the national student organization of this country."[3]

By July of 1970, however, when SASO convened its first General Students' Council at the University of Natal, this somewhat apologetic stance was replaced by a bolder line. Contact between SASO and such multiracial organizations as UCM and the Institute of Race Relations was commended, but recognition of NUSAS as a "true" national union of students was withdrawn. SASO, declared a carefully worded resolution, was "aware that in the principles and make up of NUSAS the black students can never find expression for the aspirations foremost in their minds." Instead, the conference resolved, SASO would now act "in accordance with its belief that the emancipation of the black people in this country depends entirely on the role black people themselves are prepared to play."[4] Self-reliance was the new message. "Blacks are tired of standing at the touchlines to witness a game that they should be playing," Biko had written in a policy declaration earlier in 1970. "They want to do things for themselves and all by themselves."[5]

3. Constitution of SASO, adopted in July 1969 (SASO files). The focus of SASO at this stage on the limited goal of interstudent contact is also reflected in the Communique (As Drawn Up By the 1969 SASO Conference) (SASO files).
4. "Resolutions Adopted at the 1st SASO General Students' Council, July 4th–July 10th" [1970], p. 2 (NUSAS files).
5. S. Biko, Letter to "S. R. C. Presidents, National Student Organizations, Other Organizations, and Overseas Organizations, Re: South African Students' Organization," February 1970 (NUSAS files).

When the *SASO Newsletter* of August 1970 appeared, it carried a blistering critique of white liberals called "Black Souls in White Skins?," written by Biko. This piece must be quoted at some length, for although it offers no detailed solutions, it spells out SASO's definition and analysis of the race "problem." "Basically the South African white community is a homogenous community," the article begins. All whites enjoy privileges and have to try to justify their privileged positions to themselves. The National party ideologues offer the theories of "separate development" as a rationale. "But these are not the people we are concerned with," Biko continues.

> We are concerned with that curious bunch of nonconformists . . . that bunch of do-gooders that goes under all sorts of names—liberals, leftists, etc. These are the people who argue that they are not responsible for white racism. . . . These are the people who claim that they too feel the oppression just as acutely as the blacks and therefore should be jointly involved in the black man's struggle. . . . In short, these are the people who say that they have black souls wrapped up in white skins.[6]

These liberals, he writes, arrogantly presume that the country's problems require integration as a means as well as an end: "hence the multiracial political organizations and parties and the 'nonracial' student organizations." Because of the influence of whites over blacks, this prescription had come "to be taken in all seriousness as the modus operandi in South Africa by all those who claim they would like a change in the status quo." Yet

> the integration they talk about is . . . artificial . . . [because] the people forming the integrated complex have been extracted from various segregated societies with their in-built complexes of superiority and inferiority and these continue to manifest themselves even in the "nonracial" setup of the integrated complex. As a result the integration so achieved is a one-way course, with the whites doing all the talking and the blacks the listening.[7]

However sincere the whites in such situations imagine them-

6. S. Biko ["Frank Talk"], "Black Souls in White Skins?" *SASO Newsletter*, August 1970, p. 15 (SASO files).
7. Ibid., p. 16.

selves to be, they cannot escape the hypocrisy inherent in their position as privileged members of society.

> In adopting the line of a nonracial approach, the liberals are playing their old game. They are claiming a "monopoly on intelligence and moral judgment" and setting the pattern and pace for the realization of the black man's aspirations. They want to remain in good books with both the black and white worlds. . . . They vacillate between the two worlds, verbalizing all the complaints of the blacks beautifully while skillfully extracting what suits them from the exclusive pool of white privileges. . . . The black-white circles are almost always a creation of white liberals . . . [who] call a few "intelligent and articulate" blacks to "come around for tea at home.". . . The more such tea-parties one calls the more of a liberal he is and the freer he shall feel from the guilt that harnesses and binds his conscience. Hence he moves around his white circles—whites-only hotels, beaches, restaurants and cinemas—with a lighter load, feeling that he is not like . . . the others.[8]

On the other side of the color line in these situations, the article continues,

> one sees a perfect example of what oppression has done to the blacks. They have been made to feel inferior for so long that for them it is comforting to drink tea, wine or beer with whites who seem to treat them as equals. This serves to boost up their own ego to the extent of making them feel slightly superior to those blacks who do not get similar treatment from whites. These are the sort of blacks who are a danger to the community. Instead of directing themselves at their black brothers and looking at their common problems from a common platform they choose to sing out their lamentations to an apparently sympathetic audience that has become proficient in saying the chorus of "shame!"[9]

But when pretense and the search for ego gratification are stripped away, Biko writes, it turns out that the commitments of whites and blacks in the struggle are on very different planes. The white,

> although he does not vote for the Nats [Nationalists] (now that they are in the majority anyway), . . . feels quite secure under the

8. Ibid., p. 17.
9. Ibid., p. 19.

protection offered by the Nats and subconsciously shuns the idea
of a change. This is what demarcates the liberal from the black
world. The liberals view the oppression of blacks as a problem
that has to be solved, an eye-sore spoiling an otherwise beautiful
view. From time to time the liberals make themselves forget
about the problem or take their eyes off the eye-sore. On the
other hand, in oppression the blacks are experiencing a situation
from which they are unable to escape at any given moment.
Theirs is a struggle to get out of the situation and not merely to
solve a peripheral problem as in the case of the liberals. This is
why blacks speak with a greater sense of urgency than whites.[10]

Not only were liberals attacked for playing a diversionary
and confusing role among blacks and for not living up to their
professed ideals of colorblindness, but the very ideals of
liberalism as an ideology were called into question in the SASO
critique. Liberalism as an ideology had altered its emphasis
somewhat over the years, but its fundamental premise remained the same: nonwhites had to be permitted—at one pace
or another—to enter the white world and be accorded equality
with whites in a common society. This premise, rejected but
never publicly attacked in a well worked out analysis by the
PAC in the late 1950s, was now openly and emotionally repudiated by SASO. Does a rejection of artificial racial mixing
"mean that I am against integration?" wrote Biko in the same
piece in August 1970.

If by integration you understand a breakthrough into white society by blacks, an assimilation and acceptance of blacks into an
already established set of norms and code of behavior set up by
and maintained by whites, then YES I am against it. . . . I am
against the fact that a settler minority should impose an entire
system of values on an indigenous people. . . . For one cannot
escape the fact that the culture shared by the majority group in
any given society must ultimately determine the broad direction
taken by the joint culture of that society. This need not cramp the
style of those who feel differently but on the whole, a country in
Africa, in which the majority of the people are African, must
inevitably exhibit African values and be truly African in style.
. . . One does not need to plan for or actively encourage real
integration. Once the various groups . . . have asserted them-

10. Ibid., pp. 17–18.

selves to the point that mutual respect has to be shown then you have the ingredients for a true and meaningful integration . . . [and] a genuine fusion of the life style of the various groups.[11]

Another important premise of liberal ideology—that exclusive black political approaches were "racist" and just as deplorable as exclusive white approaches—was also repudiated by SASO. This was the "morality argument" which had succeeded in preventing blacks for so long from determining their own responses to white racism. "Not only have the whites been guilty of being on the offensive," noted Biko in a later article,

> but, by some skillful maneuvers, they have managed to control the responses of the blacks to the provocation. Not only have they kicked the black but they have also told him how to react to the kick. For a long time the black has been listening with patience to the advice he has been receiving. . . .With painful slowness he is now beginning to show signs that it is his right and duty to respond to the kick *in the way he sees fit.*[12]
>
> What of the claim that the blacks are becoming racist? This is a favorite pastime of frustrated liberals who feel their trusteeship ground being washed off from under their feet. These self-appointed trustees of black interests boast of years of experience in their fight for the "rights of the blacks." . . .When the blacks announce that the time has come for them to do things for themselves and all by themselves all white liberals shout blue murder! "Hey, you can't do that. You're being a racist. You're falling into their trap.". . . [But] those who know, define racism as discrimination by a group against another for the purposes of subjugation or maintaining subjugation. In other words one cannot be a racist unless he has the power to subjugate. What blacks are doing is merely to respond to a situation in which they find themselves the objects of white racism. . . . We are collectively segregated against—what can be more logical than for us to respond as a group? When workers come together under the auspices of a trade union to strive for the betterment of their conditions, nobody expresses surprise in the Western world. It is the done thing. Nobody accuses them of separatist tendencies. Teachers fight their battles, garbagemen do the same, nobody

11. Ibid., pp. 19–20.
12. S. Biko, "White Racism and Black Consciousness," in *Student Perspectives on South Africa*, ed. H. W. van der Merwe and D. Welsh (Cape Town, 1972), p. 195.

acts as a trustee for another. Somehow, however, when blacks
want to do their thing the liberal establishment seems to detect an
anomaly. . . . The liberals must understand that the days of the
Noble Savage are gone; that the blacks do not need a go-between
in this struggle for their own emancipation.[13]

The true liberal, according to SASO's analysis, was the white
who directed all his efforts to educating other whites and preparing them to accept a future situation of majority rule.[14] In
the meantime, other cherished liberal principles—academic
freedom, the rule of law, civil liberties—were intermediate
goals meaningful to whites but largely irrelevant to blacks who
were struggling for even more fundamental freedoms.

When SASO was first launched in 1969, reactions among
black students were mixed. Was this a manifestation of
government-inspired "separate development" intruding into
the black world? Were student leaders conforming to apartheid and accepting the National party's long-time contention
that white liberals were an obstruction in the way of African
progress? Among those who accepted SASO for what it
claimed to be, there were still other misgivings. If SASO was
really going to be militant, then its chances of survival appeared slim. Why should students form an allegiance to something which was only going to be a flash-in-the-pan? For students of an ultra-militant bent, on the other hand, SASO
looked too tame. Why waste time on an introverted, elitist,
intellectual movement for "consciousness," when the real
priority was action?

Despite SASO's initial caution in making known its anti-
liberal views, a strong reaction from the NUSAS rank and file
and from white liberals generally was soon forthcoming. In
NUSAS, a minority, including most of the top leadership,
was sympathetic to black initiatives and accepted SASO's
emergence as a healthy development. To the majority, how-

13. Biko, "Black Souls in White Skins?" p. 20.
14. Ibid. Many of these same ideas can be found in Biko's "Black
Consciousness and the Quest for True Humanity," *SASO Newsletter*,
September 1971 (SASO files), reproduced in *Reality*, March 1972, pp.
4–8.

ever, acceptance of black separatism came hard and many of
the attitudes caricatured in SASO attacks were openly exhibited. If whites were not to be allowed to play the role of defenders and saviors of the oppressed, what role was left for
them to play? Excluded from power by the racist white majority,
and excluded from the camp of the underdogs by blacks bent
on going it alone, liberal whites felt a sense of isolation and weakness unknown in the history of South African liberalism. Many
sincere older liberals, firm in their conviction that liberal efforts had worked more to help than to hinder Africans historically, could not help resenting SASO's choice of targets. When
a frontal attack on government policies would probably have
brought rapid retaliation and proscription, SASO had chosen
instead to pick on a "safe" target—the weak liberal fringe—
making it a hapless scapegoat for the real villians of the
situation.[15]

Predictably, accusations that SASO was "racist" came from
all directions, both from genuine liberals with a sincere commitment to nonracialism, and from other opponents of the
government who found it convenient to blame the new SASO
"menace" on the Nationalists. The emergence of SASO, wrote
the East London *Daily Dispatch,* for example,

> is one of the sad manifestations of racist policy at Government
> level. The cornerstone of apartheid is the Bantustan policy,
> through which Blacks are compelled to regard themselves as
> separate people—a people set apart—who can aspire to progress
> only on the basis of exclusivity.
>
> The result is the emergence of a "Blacks only" mentality
> among Blacks. . . . The promoters of SASO are wrong in what
> they are doing. They are promoting apartheid. They are en-
> trenching the idea of racial exclusivity and therefore doing the
> Government's work.
>
> Fortunately they represent only a small minority of Black stu-
> dents.[16]

The pro-government press noted the same apparent con-
gruence of Black Consciousness with apartheid philosophy,

15. For a liberal's reply, see Alan Paton, "Black Consciousness,"
Reality, March 1972, pp. 9–10.
16. "Sad About SASO," *Daily Dispatch*, 10 August 1971.

and drew equally deluded conclusions. A "new spirit . . . has lately taken root among some non-whites in South Africa," observed *Die Burger* in July 1971.

> To a large extent it is the product of disillusionment over the nice-sounding phrases and ideas and programmes preached in the post-war years by the followers of . . . the liberal school of thought. . . . The people with whom this new thinking has taken root reject the condescension with which they have often been regarded by whites who represented themselves as their only friends. And they do not want to be objects of white politics any longer, but desire to determine their future themselves as people in their own right. . . . In South Africa we can be thankful that certain opportunities have been created in advance for the realization of the new ideas. It has been done among other things by the development of Bantu Homelands. . . . [The new spirit thus] fits in well with the objectives of our relations policy.
>
> How much different would the situation have been if such opportunities had not existed?[17]

At the very time *Die Burger* was congratulating the architects of apartheid on the soundness of their policy and the *Dispatch* was taking comfort from the "small" impact of SASO, the organization was sweeping black campuses with its new prescription for the destruction of the apartheid order. As early suspicions and hesitation gave way, and SASO's more positive emphasis on an ideology of Black Consciousness and black pride began to replace the early negative emphasis on destroying liberal "interference," students rallied enthusiastically. Only a relative few had actually personally experienced the racial mixing in NUSAS circles which Biko had attacked; but all black students had experienced the humiliation and thought control imposed by the system of Bantu Education. When SASO spoke of a new need for blacks to define their own goals and values and chart their own course toward a more just society, it stirred a frustrated desire which many black students had long felt but which none had ever been able to articulate with the clarity and persuasiveness which SASO was now exhibiting.

Since SASO at the outset seemed to conform to the government-prescribed formula for racially-segregated or-

17. Quoted in *Cape Times*, 9 July 1971.

ganizations, it encountered little opposition from the authorities in establishing itself on the campuses of Turfloop, Ngoye, and the University of Natal. At Fort Hare, where students had refused since 1960 to elect an SRC, the mechanics of affiliation were more complicated. But by 1971 a Fort Hare SASO branch was in operation, as were branches at the Coloured University of the Western Cape and the Indian University of Durban-Westville, where authorities had prohibited formal affiliation. By 1971 SASO was also well established at the Lutheran Theological College, Federal Theological Seminary next door to Fort Hare in Alice, and the Transvaal College of Education, a teacher-training institution for Indians located in Johannesburg. Correspondence students at the University of South Africa and other Transvaal students were affiliated through a Reef SASO Local Branch (REESO) centered in Johannesburg and directed by Harry Nengwekhulu.

SASO's internal organization and communication with its member campuses proved remarkably strong. Circulation of the *SASO Newsletter* had reached 4,000 by 1972 and issues appeared regularly. Conferences were well-organized and lively. While there were feelings of intense loyalty and even adulation towards the organization's top leadership, deliberate and very successful efforts were also made to identify and indoctrinate promising new cadres at every opportunity. The result, among black university students—a significant percentage of the African intelligentsia and middle-class-to-be of the 1970s and beyond—was thus a level of political education and ideological diffusion never before achieved by any black political organization. To those in South Africa familiar with the course of African politics historically, it was evident that SASO in a remarkably short period had become the most politically significant black organization in the country.

External Influences and the New Definition of "Black"

Although Biko and the other founders of SASO were intent on destroying the influence over black politics of what they called "common society liberalism," they realized that no movement could be based solely on a negative platform. Just as the PAC a decade earlier had turned to the ideological formulations of Nkrumah and the December 1958 All-African Peoples Conference at Accra, SASO too in its efforts to construct a positive ideology of militant self-reliance began actively to shop for ideas in the black world outside South Africa. At SASO's inception in July 1968 this process was already partially underway. By 1970 it had resulted in the identification of SASO with a well-articulated ideology of Black Consciousness.

Like the ideologues of orthodox African nationalism from Lembede onward, Biko and the architects of SASO began from the premise that oppression was most immediately a psychological problem. Seen from this perspective, the liberal approach could never provide a solution because it failed to take into account the spiritual dimension of the African's plight, most importantly his need to cast off his complexes of dependence and deference toward whites. According to SASO's analysis, the greatest check on self-assertion was the African's inferiority complex, instilled over centuries through all the mechanisms of European cultural imperialism. If this check was to be removed, Africans had to create for themselves a convincing new identity and a new pride which could liberate them from their subservient attitudes. Africans had to learn to analyze "white civilization" in a more critical light, and to reevaluate and reject white interpretations of the African past which tended to belittle traditional African values, customs, religion and heroes. New appreciation for the humane and non-materialistic orientations of African tradition had to be fostered and contrasted with the "cold," technocratic, and money-oriented values of European or "Anglo-Boer" culture. Against the individualistic and capitalistic traits of whites, the communalistic and socialistic traditions of African society had to be set in contrast and shown to be equally valid and even superior in the African setting. It would be futile, the SASO founders generally agreed, to try to promote a backward-looking revivalistic movement; rather, the emphasis had to be on the ongoing aspects of culture, and on the anticipation of a future free society in which social, cultural and economic priorities would be rearranged to make South Africa part of Africa once more instead of what it currently was—an extension of Europe into Africa. In most SASO propaganda, however, long-range goals were pointedly left vague and "Black Consciousness" was defined primarily as an orientation toward the present. Black Consciousness, declared the SASO Manifesto adopted in July 1971, was "an attitude of mind, a way of life," in which the blackman saw himself "as self-defined and not as defined by others." It required, above all, "group cohesion and solidarity" so that blacks could be made aware of their collective economic and political power.[18]

Almost point for point, SASO had arrived anew at the diagnosis and cure originally devised by Lembede and Mda in the 1940s under the rubric of "Africanism." But now the diagnosis was more searching and the cure much more likely to be found acceptable by significant sections of the African intelligentsia and even African society at large. When Lembede had talked about Africa as the blackman's continent which would someday make its own unique contribution to the family of nations, he had found few in South Africa who shared his optimistic vision or who felt that a black-run South Africa was a practical political prospect. By 1970, however, the complexion of the world's independent nations had greatly altered; the colonial epoch was drawing to an end, and from holding the overwhelming majority of seats in the United Nations at its founding in 1945, the countries of Europe and their white kindred nations around the world now held less than half. Jets and telecommunications had made the globe much smaller, and with literacy expanding rapidly in the nonwhite world, diffusion of ideas on an international scale could now take place at a pace unthinkable three decades earlier. Black Africa had passed through the transition to political independence with unanticipated speed, and was now wrestling with problems of cultural and political identity. In America, blacks had won

18. *SASO Policy Manifesto*, reproduced in *SASO Newsletter*, August 1971, pp. 10–11, (SASO files). Also see S. Biko, "The Definition of Black Consciousness," unpublished paper, 1971 (SASO files).

their struggle for equal rights under the law, and were now facing even more intractable problems in trying to define their political and cultural goals as a less-than-fully-assimilable minority. Waves generated by African independence lapped at American shores; slogans shouted in American ghettoes echoed in Africa. In South Africa black intellectuals listened and watched, aware of their own unique situation, but also highly sensitive to ideas emanating from elsewhere in the black world.

It is therefore not surprising to find in SASO's formulations on culture and consciousness, all of which are spelled out lengthily in SASO policy papers and articles in the *SASO Newsletter,* that the reinforcing effect of literature and political writings by blacks outside South Africa is very evident and often explicitly acknowledged. To say that SASO's ideology was "imported" would be to assign much too little significance to the life experiences and political intuition of the movement's founders; yet the profound effect of foreign influences on the particular language and slant of Black Consciousness must be recognized if the developments of the early 1970's are to be understood in the total context of the black South African intellectual history. Never had such a deliberate and throughgoing effort been made to borrow and selectively adapt foreign ideas in order to influence mass thinking.[19] And never had an attempt on the part of black intellectuals to affect mass thinking met with such success in so short a period, in part because the same foreign influences at work on the thinking of intellectuals had already independently been at work, through press and radio, on the African urban masses and students in particular, preparing the way for the spread of a new self-image.

19. Historians might point to the repercussions of Booker T. Washington and the "Tuskegee School" on the development of African education in South Africa. While some African educators, including John L. Dube, the first president of the ANC, were influenced by theories of education emanating from the United States, the main impetus behind this cross-national borrowing came from whites and cannot therefore be seen in the same light as the black-initiated borrowings of SASO.

In South Africa, most events and ideological debates in the rest of Africa are filtered through the white press and radio in the process of being reported, with the inevitable distortions; but by the late 1960s some of the writings of African leaders and thinkers had also become available in book form, sold openly in shops or brought into the country in smaller quantities by travelers. The writings of Cheikh Ante Diop and Leopold Senghor on Negritude, Kenneth Kaunda on African humanism, and, most importantly, Julius Nyerere on self-reliance and *ujamaa* or African socialism, while not being widely read by any means, nevertheless began to inspire the interest and admiration of black South African intellectuals. When SASO's founders started their active search for ideological reinforcement, some had already encountered these African writings and turned naturally to them as a source of ideas. Nyerere's 1967 Arusha Declaration on Self-reliance rang true, wrote Pityana in 1971, when it said

> We have been oppressed a great deal; we have been exploited a great deal; and we have been disregarded a great deal. It is our weakness that has led to our being oppressed, exploited and disregarded. Now we want a revolution—a revolution which brings to an end our weakness, so that we are never again exploited, oppressed or humiliated.[20]

"The message," concluded Pityana for his South African readership, "is simple. BLACK MAN YOU ARE ON YOUR OWN. Like Nyerere we must minimize reliance on external aid. No one in a position of power and prosperity can offer such aid as would threaten his own security."[21]

Particularly influential in lending both content and mood to the ideology of Black Consciousness were the writings of Frantz Fanon, some of which had become available in South Africa by 1968. Most widely read was *The Wretched of the Earth*, in which Fanon analyzes settler colonialism and its psychological consequences for rulers and ruled. Among books not

20. Quoted in B. Pityana, "Priorities in Community Development," *SASO Newsletter*, September 1971, p. 14 (SASO files).
21. Ibid., pp. 14–15.

written directly about South Africa, it would have been difficult for SASO's ideologues to find one more pertinent to the South African situation, both in analyzing root causes and in suggesting possible scenarios for future change. Most influential, perhaps, may have been Fanon's cynical views on political morality, which he regarded in the colonial situation as being wholly determined by self-interest. The need to recognize self-serving definitions of good and evil; the desirability of destroying pretense and polarizing racial conflict as a prelude to radical change; the rejection of gradualistic solutions designed by the powerful to perpetuate their control and blunt the anger of the oppressed; a mistrust of bourgeois blacks anxious to step into the shoes of the exploiter—all these features of Fanon's analysis also enter into the writings of SASO leaders on Black Consciousness, though to what extent Fanon's writings were the origin of SASO's analysis or merely a reinforcing supplement to it, it is impossible to say.

Coming to South Africa later in time but affecting black thinking as much or more than writings from Africa were works by black Americans, including Eldridge Cleaver's *Soul on Ice,* the *Autobiography of Malcolm X, Black Power* by Stokely Carmichael and Charles Hamilton, and the writings of James Cone and others on black theology. As a reference group for Africans in South Africa, black Americans—through magazines, movies, and records—had long exerted an influence on tastes in music, dress and slang. The American Supreme Court school desegregation decision of 1954 and the Montgomery bus boycott of 1955 had created ripples of interest in South Africa, and the civil rights struggle of the late 1950s and early 1960s had been covered to some extent in the South African press. But never had social and political ideas originating in black America been subject to as wide and searching scrutiny as the ideas emanating in the "Black Power" aftermath of the civil rights movement.

At first regarded rather uncritically by some Africans as a kind of ideological gospel, the ideas of radical black Americans came eventually to be examined with more insight and appreciation of the contrasting factors in American and South

African society. Rather than detracting from the value of the American example, this emerging appreciation of the uniqueness of South Africa's race conflict seems to have sharpened the analytical thrust of the Black Consciousness movement. Comparisons of the United States and South Africa became popular exercises at SASO leadership training seminars, for example. "The study of the Afro-American approach to their problems offered interesting comparisons between their situation in the States and ours in this country," wrote a member of the SASO executive in 1970, commenting on a training seminar held in September of that year.

> One group was asked to study the significance of the statement "before entering the open society, we must first close our ranks." This statement underlies the "Black Power" philosophy of people like Hamilton and Carmichael. This particular group made the observation that an open society in this country can only be created by blacks, and that for as long as whites are in power they shall seek to make it closed in one way or the other. We then defined what we meant by an open society. . . . The group ended up by stating that the original statement should read "before creating an open society we must first close our ranks." The difference of course is of paramount importance in that in the first one, the Afro-Americans accept that they will never be in a position to change the system in America, and adopt the approach that if you can't beat them, join them—but join them from a position of strength; whereas implicit in the latter statement is a hope to establish a completely new system at some stage. . . . Purely from a consideration of who we are, we realize that it is we who must be allowing others to participate in our system. We must not be the ones to be invited to participate in somebody else's system in our own private yard.[22]

The impact of American ideas in the 1960s on the language

22. "Regional Formation Schools" (by an anonymous member of the SASO executive), *SASO Newsletter*, September 1970, pp. 6–7 (SASO files). Punctuation has been added. A similar exercise at a training seminar in December 1971, this time simulating a meeting between South Africans and black Americans, is described in "Report of Leadership Training Seminars, Edendale Lay Ecumenical Centre, Pietermaritzburg, December 5–8, 1971," p. 2 (SASO files).

of the Black Consciousness movement comes through clearly in the popularity of slogans like "Black Is Beautiful" and the frequent use of such terms as "relevance" and "power structure" in SASO literature. Most significant, however, was the terminological revolution in the use of the word "black" itself. Popularized by younger American militants looking for an alternative to "Negro" and "Coloured," the term "black" by the late 1960s in the United States had become a loose synonym for "nonwhite"—a new catch-all term encompassing all victims of race discrimination. If a man as light-complexioned as Malcolm X could be idolized as a "black" hero, there was no point in pressing too hard for an answer to "how black is 'black'?" "Black" people, in the terminology of American radicalism, were distinguished not by their color per se but by their oppressed condition as the outcasts of affluent white society.

Transferred to South Africa through American writings and news magazines, the term "black" in its new sense of "status-more-than-color" found rapid favor with a few African, Indian and Coloured intellectuals, but gained broader acceptance only gradually over the years from 1968 on. Among radical Africans it was not unusual to hear the term "black" applied to Africans alone, and its use as a synonym for "African" continued to be common, and a source of confusion, long after the wider meaning began to gain ground. Because of the reluctance of many Indians and Coloureds to refer to themselves as "black," SASO's founders, who were anxious to include these groups in their nascent organization, continued until as late as December 1969 to use the term "nonwhite" in identifying SASO's constituency. But as SASO moved toward increasingly sophisticated explanations of its emerging ideology of self-reliance and self-definition, it became clear that use of the term "nonwhite" was totally inconsistent with efforts to promote an aggressively positive self-image among Africans. By mid-1970, therefore, by which time substantial Indian student support had already been won for SASO, the switch to "black" was made. The term "Black Consciousness" was promoted openly, use of "nonwhite" was denounced, and at its July

1970 annual conference, SASO formally amended its own constitution to substitute "black" for "nonwhite."[23]

"There is something to be said about the question 'who is black?'" editorialized the *SASO Newsletter* in September 1970.

> The term . . . must be seen in its right context. No new category is being created but a "re-Christening" is taking place. We are merely refusing to be regarded as non-persons and claim the right to be called positively. . . . Adopting a collective, positive outlook leads to the creation of a broader base which may be useful in time. It helps us to recognize the fact that we have one common enemy. . . . One should grant that the division of races in this country is so entrenched that the blacks will find it difficult to operate as a combined front. The black umbrella we are creating for ourselves at least helps us to make sure that if we are not working as a unit at least the various units should be working in the same direction, being complementary to each other wherever possible. By all means be proud of your Indian heritage or your African culture but make sure that in looking around for somebody to kick at, choose the fellow who is sitting on your neck. He may not be as easily accessible as your black brother but he *is* the source of your discomfort.
>
> Placed in context therefore, the "black consciousness" attitude seeks to define one's enemy more clearly and to broaden the base from which we are operating. It is a deliberate attempt by all of us to counteract the "divide and rule" attitude of the evil-doers.[24]

SASO's new definition of "black" generated a hubbub of controversy among whites and a soul-searching among Indians and Coloureds, especially those of older generations for whom identification with Africans had always been a major unresolved political problem. By January 1971, NUSAS had debated and accepted the new usage, and in July 1972, after reporters from the *Rand Daily Mail* had been expelled from the SASO annual conference because of their paper's continued use of "nonwhite," the *Rand Daily Mail* became the first white newspaper to make the switch to "black."[25] The Institute of

23. "Confidential Report on the 1970 SASO Conference," 1970, p. 4 (SASO files); and "Resolutions Adopted at the 1st General Students' Council July 4th–July 10th," 1970, p. 14 (NUSAS files).
24. "Editorial," *SASO Newsletter*, September 1970, p. 2 (SASO files).
25. *Rand Daily Mail*, 7 July 1972; and *Star*, 17 July 1972. The *Star* declined to switch on the grounds that most Indians and Coloureds had not indicated a preference for the new term.

Race Relations also changed over in July 1972, but the new terminology remained confined to liberal groups and newspapers and did not become a general trend in the white media. Among Indians and Coloureds, with the exception of student converts to SASO and a few avant-garde older intellectuals, the use of "black" as a self-description continued to be regarded with ambivalence. David Curry, a militant leader of the anti-government Coloured Labour party, enthusiastically endorsed SASO's "go it alone" position in 1971, but in his endorsement referred to "Coloured people and Blacks." The Natal Indian Congress, revived by Mewa Ramgobin in October 1971, after endorsing the principle of "black solidarity" at its initial conference, cooled in its attitude to SASO and subsequently voted to dissociate itself from the ideology of Black Consciousness.[26]

The lack of consensus about whether or not to identify themselves as "black" was symptomatic of deeper uncertainties among Indians and Coloureds about whether their best political interests lay in supporting Africans or in maintaining their separate identities as intermediate groups enjoying relatively greater incomes and legal rights. Africans too, as we have seen, had long been of a divided mind on the question of cooperation. Reacting against the attempts to D. D. T. Jabavu, Isaac B. Tabata and others in the 1940s to promote the cause of cooperation, Lembede had declared that while non-European unity might be desirable in theory, in practice it was a "fantastic dream which has no foundation in reality."[27] Following the Durban race riot of 1949, efforts by African and Indian leaders had led to the alliance between the ANC and the South African Indian Congress, a partnership into which some Coloureds were later drawn through the South African Coloured Peoples' Organization. As a model of organizational cooperation and symbolic unity, this alliance of the 1950s marked a significant achievement and probably set back National party plans for total political compartmentalization of the races. At

26. D. M. G. Curry, letter to the Cape *Argus*, 4 February 1971. In another letter to the *Argus* dated 7 February 1972, however, Curry uses "black" in the new sense.
27. See above, p. 76.

the rank-and-file level in the ANC, however, at least in Natal and the Transvaal, cooperation was regarded with mistrust by many, and prejudices, particularly against Indians, persisted. In the PAC, these prejudices had been especially strong, although official PAC policy was to regard Coloureds as Africans and thus as eligible for PAC membership. Sobukwe's personal view, moreover, was that lower class Indians, since they were virtually as oppressed as Africans, also ought to be welcomed into the PAC. This position was strongly opposed by Africanists in Natal and the Transvaal, however, and did not become part of PAC policy.

Thus, between hesitation on the African side, the reluctance of many Indians and Coloureds to see their interests as similar to those of Africans, and the government's continuing efforts to segregate nonwhite groups from one another politically and in every other way, the prospects for African-Indian-Coloured unity might logically have seemed dim at the time SASO set out to forge its new alliance. Why then did SASO's founders choose to pursue their new definition of "black"?

The answer had several sides. First, just as to Lembede, it seemed apparent to the founders of SASO that in theory non-white unity was a desirable thing. As long as the government's aim was to divide and rule, there was always the threat that nonwhites would succumb to the mentality of apartheid and waste their energies attacking one another. By the late 1960s, Nationalist plans to establish separate Indian and Coloured Councils were well underway, and where once the organizations of the Congress Alliance had served as mouthpieces for anti-government Indian and Coloured opinion, a political vacuum had come to exist. The time seemed ripe for a political revival among Indian and Coloured radicals, just as it had among Africans. In the absence of pre-existing separate and rival radical organizations, circumstances seemed favorable for a joint effort. The particular circumstances of SASO's genesis also favored interracial cooperation. As a student at Natal's medical school, the only place in South Africa where African, Indian and Coloured university students were trained and housed together, Biko had been offered a rare opportunity to fashion and test his political ideas in a multiracial environment. He had found that some non-African medical students had ideas very similar to his own, and coming from the eastern Cape where very few Indians live, he had probably arrived in Natal with little or no ingrained anti-Indian biases. Later when he and his African and Indian fellow-radicals from Natal encountered anti-Indian feelings among African students at Turfloop and Ngoye, they were able to argue them around successfully, in part, no doubt, by appealing to the new concept of black as "status-more-than-color" emanating from America. Finally, most compelling of all the arguments for unity was the consensus, articulated so well by Biko and perhaps bolstered by the writings of Fanon, that polarization per se in the race conflict would be a strategy conducive to change. Polarization—the simplification of the conflict from a series of many skirmishes into one battle perceived as a total confrontation between black and white—required not just the initial redefinition of all whites, including liberals, as oppressors, but also required the conceptual regrouping of all non-whites into the single category of "black."

Perspectives on the Struggle

Political veterans in the African community observed the activities and image-building efforts of SASO in its first few years with a mixture of admiration and condescension toward the innocence and exuberance of youth. To politically discerning members of older generations, it sometimes seemed as though the young were again, as in Xuma's time, trying to "march barefoot" against the enemy, not only without a strong organizational base but also without any historical sense of the years of struggle and failure which had preceded their own recent political coming-of-age.

In part, this judgment on SASO's historical perspective was accurate, for until some of the movement's leaders began in 1970–71 to make a deliberate study of black political history, there was little or no awareness among students of events predating their own individual political recollections, which in

Steve Biko speaks at the second General Students' Council of the South African Students' Organisation, held at the University of Natal, July 1971. *John Reader/ Life Magazine © Time, Inc.*

Student demonstrators surge down Soweto street, 4 August 1976. Marchers intended to enter downtown Johannesburg but were turned back by tear gas and police mobile units. *Willie Nkosi/Rand Daily Mail.*

most cases went back only to the late 1950s or early 1960s. Yet within the limits of this most recent time period, it was clear that at least a few historical influences had been at work on SASO's leadership. The ANC and PAC no longer functioned as organizations within South Africa; but as SASO's part of a new generation's historical memory, they were still a force to be reckoned with. The Congress Alliance, for example, had set an important precedent for cooperation between Africans, Indians, and Coloureds. The PAC had foreshadowed the rejection of all assistance from whites and had articulated the same orthodox nationalist goal for which SASO was now calling: the reconstruction of South Africa as an essentially African society into which whites would have to fit as best they could.

These were precedents of which every politicized African was aware, and avoiding any direct identification with older, illegal movements necessarily became an important concern for SASO. When an official of the Natal Indian Congress in December 1971 publicly accused SASO of propagating the policies of the PAC, SASO threatened a libel suit and called the NIC statement "highly defamatory and . . . aimed at prejudicing the survival and effectiveness of SASO."[28] If there was any resemblance between the ideas of SASO and the PAC, Nengwekhulu later remarked, it merely resulted from the similar circumstances which had given rise to the two organizations.[29]

If SASO had absorbed any lessons from the experience of the PAC, these lessons were mainly negative ones. Ideologically, from the SASO perspective, PAC's position had been sound enough; but as an organization PAC had failed woefully, and its failures were not lost on those—the angry youths of 1960—whose lives had been affected by the anticlimax of the post-Sharpeville emergency or, like Biko's, by Leballo's clumsy bravado in the press conference debacle of 1963. The PAC's

28. *SASO Newsletter*, March–April 1972, p. 3. Also see *SASO Newsletter*, January–February 1972, p. 3 and memo by B. Pityana, "Re: SASO v. NIC Controversy," 3 March 1972 (SASO files).
29. Interview.

undoing had not been in its ideology but in its reckless rush to confrontation at a time when circumstances did not favor a black victory. The lessons were clear: patience was more important than heroics; laying a firm psychological foundation for a time of as yet unforeseen circumstances was more important than trying artificially to create a situation of immediate confrontation. "It is very important to rid ourselves of impatience which yields disillusionment in the face of lack of success," editorialized the *SASO Newsletter* in June 1970. "The road will be long and hard, the rewards few and sporadic."[30]

We have seen how between the initial formulation of orthodox African nationalism by Lembede and Mda in the 1940s and the PAC's attempt to launch revolutionary action in 1960, nationalism in the minds of many of its proponents had passed from being seen primarily as a contrived psychological device to being a semi-religious article of faith, interpreted by the literal-minded as an a priori fact of political reality. To the literal-minded nationalist "rebels" of the PAC type, the nationalistic urge was not something to be inculcated in the masses, but rather something which was already latent in the mass mind, ready to explode spontaneously—as in Fanon's apocalyptic vision—when kindled by the spark of heroic leadership. With the emergence of SASO, none of the goals of orthodox nationalism had changed, but at the leadership level there was a clear shift in perception back to the earlier view of nationalism as an intellectual construct and a psychological device rather than a "natural law" of politics. "Black Consciousness seeks to channel the pent-up forces of the angry black masses to meaningful and directional opposition," wrote Biko in 1970; the anger, he suggested, was clearly there, but it lacked any natural channel or direction.[31] The aim of Black Consciousness as an ideology was not to trigger a spontaneous Fanonesque eruption of the masses into violent action, but rather to rebuild and recondition the mind of the oppressed in

30. Editorial, *SASO Newsletter*, June 1970 (SASO files).
31. S. Biko ["Frank Talk"], " 'We Blacks'," *SASO Newsletter*, September 1970, p. 18 (SASO files).

such a way that eventually they would be ready forcefully to demand what was rightfully theirs.

Compared to earlier nationalist thinkers, the formulators of SASO's ideology brought a new sophistication and insight to the analysis of African psychology. This was in part the result of their being much more widely read than most earlier leaders, with the possible exception of Lembede, who by all accounts was an insatiable reader but who did not have available to him in the 1940s the same breadth of analytical literature on race problems available to black university students in the 1960s and 1970s. In addition to the insights gleaned from reading, however, had been the profound lessons of the great silence of the 1960s. The African's problems might always have been dependency, identity-confusion, fear, and a resigned apathy about the future, but at no time had these problems been more starkly apparent than in the 1960s, when all African initiatives and voices of dissent had been forcibly stilled. National party strategy, aimed at conditioning and coercing blacks into an acceptance of apartheid policies, appeared to be at last achieving the desired effects. "Black people under the Smuts government were oppressed but they were still men," wrote Biko in September 1970.

> But the type of black man we have today has lost his manhood. Reduced to an obliging shell, he looks with awe at the white power structure and accepts what he regards as the "inevitable position." . . . In the privacy of his toilet his face twists in silent condemnation of white society but brightens up in sheepish obedience as he comes out hurrying in response to his master's impatient call. . . . His heart yearns for the comfort of white society and makes him blame himself for not having been "educated" enough to warrant such luxury. Celebrated achievements by whites in the field of science—which he understands only hazily—serve to make him rather convinced of the futility of resistance and to throw away any hopes that change may ever come. All in all the black man has become a shell, a shadow of man, completely defeated, drowning in his own misery, a slave and ox bearing the yoke of oppression with sheepish timidity.[32]

32. Ibid., p. 16. Also see S. Biko, "Fear—An Important Determinant in South African Politics," *SASO Newsletter*, September 1971, pp. 10–12 (SASO files).

Older veterans too were aware of the silence which had fallen over black political life, but most tended to regard it as a manifestation of discretion rather than cowardice. To SASO, this attitude in itself was proof that even the most formerly radical people had begun to accept defeat and to accommodate themselves to the system. Looking at the political behavior of their elders, Biko and his colleagues felt that self-censure had become a habit, leading people to accept as legitimate only those political outlets expressly approved by the government. "There is in South Africa an overriding idea to move toward 'comfortable politics' between leaders—'comfortable politics' in the sense that we must move at a pace that doesn't rock the boat," Biko observed in 1972.

> In other words, people are shaped by the system even in their consideration of approaches against the system, . . . shaped in the sense of working out an approach that won't lead them into any confrontation with the system. So they tend . . . to censor themselves, in a much stronger way than the system would probably censor them. For instance, there's no automatic ban on political movements in this country, but you get common talk to that effect amongst people, that any political agitation is banned—which is nonsense. It's not banned.[33]

If allowed to persist over many years as a pattern in black-white political relations, this accommodation, in SASO's view, was bound to lead eventually to an acceptance by blacks of the entire framework of "separate development," in which African aspirations were regarded as legitimate only when channelled into the fragmented thirteen percent of the country set aside as tribal bantustans. In SASO's view, that eventuality had to be forestalled by any means possible, and the attention of the masses focused instead on demands for majority rule and African rights to the "whole loaf"—full citizenship in one hundred percent of South Africa. To keep the masses correctly oriented, continuous agitation was essential.

> Our attitude is that the longer the silence, the more accustomed white society is going to be to that silence, and therefore the more stringent the measures are going to be against anybody who tries

33. Interview.

to undo that situation. Hence there must be some type of agitation. It doesn't matter if the agitation doesn't take a fully directed form immediately, or a fully supported form. But there must be in the minds of the people in existence the idea that somewhere, somehow along the line, we have our own thing going, and our own thing says this. And it must be only a matter of time before they are fully committed to it.[34]

In the days when Lembede and the early Youth League had pressed for a boycott of the Natives' Representative Council and Sobukwe had argued before the delegates to the 1949 Cape provincial ANC conference that boycotts, whether they were fully effective or not, could still "work tremendously on the mental state of the people," Africans had had "their own thing going" in the form of the ANC.[35] Even so, pressures had been strong from within the ranks of politicized Africans—and among personally ambitious would-be leaders—to "try out" the institutions being initiated by the government in the hope that they might prove useful as propaganda forums. The results had been inconclusive, and the Nationalist government had eventually abolished the NRC of its own accord. In the 1950s, urban boycott agitation had been focused for the most part on the relatively insignificant advisory boards, but in Sekhukhuniland, Pondoland, and other rural areas, resistance had gradually mounted to the government's plan to establish tribal "bantu authorities" as a prelude to bantustans. By the 1970s, the dilemma of what to do about "dummy institutions" had grown to a new magnitude and had been thrown back into the cities by the government's ongoing implementation of "separate development" and the emergence of a completely new political phenomenon on the South African scene: the growing national popularity of an outspoken anti-government bantustan leader, Chief Gatsha Buthelezi of the Zulus.

In SASO's response to this revived dilemma of "dummy institutions," all the conflicts of "realist" and "rebel" strategies once more began to come to the fore. Should SASO try to infiltrate bantustans and use Buthelezi, who was open to the

34. Ibid.
35. See above, pp. 80–82, and 186–87.

ideology of Black Consciousness, or should they renounce all aspects of "separate development" and concentrate on promoting their own program outside "the system"? The question remained unresolved throughout 1969–71, though SASO made clear its total rejection of the bantustan principle and busied itself with expansion of its own independent activities both on and off black campuses. Meanwhile, infiltrative politics appeared to hold some promising possibilities, and SASO actively wooed support from such prominent anti-government politicians within "the system" as Curnick Ndamse in the Transkei and David Thebehali in the Soweto UBC.[36] As Buthelezi drew wider and wider publicity by his attacks on government policies and his calls for intertribal unity, his popularity with black students soared, not just at Ngoye among his fellow Zulus, but also among non-Zulus who began to look to him as a national hero in the mold of Mandela, Lutuli and Sobukwe.

Then in mid-1972 it seemed to Biko and others in the inner councils of SASO that the question could no longer be left to settle itself by default. A firm decision on "dummy institutions" had to be taken, particularly as SASO was in the midst of helping launch a national organization—the Black People's Convention—to be an "adult," non-student wing of the Black Consciousness movement. What might otherwise have taken the form of a gradual clarification of policy became instead a dramatic showdown when, without consulting his colleagues in advance, Temba Sono, SASO's outgoing president, delivered a speech at the July 1972 annual conference putting forward the "realist" position on the bantustan question. Mobilizing quickly to bring the issue to a head, Biko and the majority of SASO's executive, who favored the "rebel" position, attacked Sono, called for his resignation, and succeeded in swaying the assem-

36. SASO's debates on "infiltrative politics" are referred to in the *SASO Newsletter*, September 1971, p. 4; "Report of Leadership Training Seminar . . . December 5–8, 1971," pp. 2–3; and "Commissions Presented at 3rd General Students' Council of the South African Students' Organisation, St. Peter's Seminary, Hammanskraall, 2–9 July, 1972" (SASO files).

bled delegates to censure him and demand his departure from the conference site.[37]

The gauntlet had been thrown down, and whatever doubts may have lingered in the minds of some students, SASO thereafter committed itself to a campaign of discrediting and exposing what was seen as the fraudulent notion that blacks could use the institutions of "separate development" to their own advantage. Whereas "realists," including many older African political veterans, argued that politics was the art of the possible and the Africans could not afford to reject even the feeble weapons put into their hands by government policy, SASO's "rebels" argued that the government's policies, whatever their superficial appearance, were masterfully designed eventually to lead blacks into a cul-de-sac at every turn. While "realists" might believe in their own ability to guide the masses in a continuous rejection of apartheid principles, the "rebel" view of mass psychology was more analytical—and more pessimistic. The people as a whole, argued SASO, would quickly become confused and misled by attempts to "use the system against itself"; inevitably, they would be made to accept the government-prescribed rules of the game—just as they, along with the rest of the world, were already being made to accept them when they accorded Buthelezi recognition as a legitimate black leader.[38]

Beyond the University Generation

To assess the impact of Black Consciousness ideology on black society at large, one must of course go beyond the mere articu-

37. See Sono's speech, "In Search of a Free and New Society"; "Minutes of the Proceedings of the 3rd General Students' Council of the South African Students' Organisation, St. Peter's Seminary, Hammanskraal, 2–9 July, 1972," pp. 5, 7; and *SASO Newsletter*, September–October 1972, pp. 13–14 (SASO files).
38. See S. Biko ["Frank Talk"], "Let's Talk About Bantustans," *SASO Newsletter*, September–October 1972, pp. 18–21, for the most complete exposition of SASO's position (SASO files). Also see *Rand Daily Mail*, 11 November 1972.

lation of ideas within student circles, however significant that articulation may in itself have been. University students, as SASO's strategists realized, are an opinionated and often fractious constituency, but of all the groups in black society they were the easiest to reach with organization and the written word, and the readiest to grasp a new ideology based on introspection and a radical reappraisal of entrenched assumptions. The objectives of Black Consciousness were political from the start, but in the interests of their own survival, its propagators chose to mute its political thrust and publicly emphasized its more cultural and intellectual side. Students as a group were attuned to such abstractions as "culture" and "identity"—but was black society as a whole?

SASO's problems in reaching a wider audience were formidable, for to "speak the language of the people" required speaking of more than abstractions like "consciousness" and "value systems." To rural people, such concepts are wholly foreign, and to urban workers they can easily seem an obscure and frivolous luxury when measured against more tangible problems like wages, job security, crowded trains, pass laws, and all life's other daily realities. "To take part in the African revolution, it is not enough to write a revolutionary song," wrote Biko in 1970, quoting Sekou Toure, "you must fashion the revolution with the people. And if you fashion it with the people the songs will come by themselves."[39] But recognizing the problem of student detachment and prescribing the solution of grass roots involvement were not the same as actually achieving that solution in practice. Over and above the problems involved in rephrasing the tenets of Black Consciousness philosophy in everyday language, there were very practical organizational problems arising out of the student situation. Outreach into urban townships and rural reserves required resources like money and automobiles, and also organization of a type that involved not just students acting on their own but coordination with other organizations, even bantustan authorities, willing to cooperate with student projects. Participa-

39. Biko, " 'We Blacks'," p. 19.

tion in voluntary community projects in lieu of vacation-time employment represented a genuine sacrifice for students whose families were already facing the hardship of financing a university education. Time too was a constraint during the academic year. But perhaps most intractable of all was the problem created by the ingrained generation gap in African society: whatever the economic and social changes wrought by city life and formal education, youth was still expected in all situations to defer to age. Students might be regarded as the leaders of the future, but no one—at least until the lessons of 1976 began to come home—ever seriously considered the possibility that they might also be the leaders of the present.

Recognizing the difficulties inherent in trying to initiate a national movement using student leadership, and also recognizing that students after their graduation from university— and from SASO—would have no congenial political arena into which to move, SASO leaders started in early 1971 to explore the possibility of launching an "adult" wing of the Black Consciousness movement. They met in Bloemfontein in April with representatives of six other organizations to discuss the idea of establishing a nationwide "umbrella" organization of black groups. Those six included the Interdenominational African Ministers' Association (IDAMASA), the Association for Educational and Cultural Advancement of African People of South Africa (ASSECA), and the St. Peter's [Seminary] Old Boys Association. A follow-up conference in August addressed by Biko and Buthelezi drew together representatives of twenty-seven organizations and elected an interim committee under the chairmanship of M. T. Moerane, the editor of *The World* and the president of ASSECA, to consider the drawing up of a constitution. When this committee reported at yet a third conference held in December 1971, SASO's efforts to steer the evolving movement in the direction of bold political initiatives met resistance from older delegates, including Moerane and Dr. William Nkomo—founding members of the ANC Youth League who over thirty years had mellowed from "rebels" to "realists"—who favored greater emphasis on cultural and economic causes at least initially. Most present were united on the general principles of black self-assertion as broadly popularized by SASO, and a majority favored defining "black" to include Indians and Coloureds. What older participants seemed to fear was the "gloves off" militance of SASO which appeared likely to lead the organization and anyone involved with it into an early clash with white authority. After fierce debate, a vote showed proponents of the SASO view to be in the majority. Moderate support dwindled, and when the overtly political Black People's Convention was formally launched at Pietermaritzburg in July 1972 under the leadership of Drake Koka, Mthuli Shezi, Saths Cooper and the Reverend A. Mayatula, its constitution and statements of purpose strongly echoed the language of SASO.[40]

It is difficult to say how wide a following the BPC might have attracted had it been able to organize without police intimidation for a longer time. As it turned out, the clash which moderates had feared was not long in coming. In early 1973, simultaneous with the government's first major offensive against SASO, banning orders were issued to the BPC's fledgling leadership. It thereafter became increasingly difficult for the BPC to attract an open following, although, like earlier black movements, it no doubt enjoyed more support than mere formal membership statistics suggested. In late 1973, BPC reported the existence of forty-one branches nationwide, but conceded that bans on officers and the reluctance of printers had effectively prevented the issuing of BPC publications. An earlier organizational setback had occurred when Shezi, the BPC's vice president, died from injuries sustained when he was pushed in front of a train by a white railway official in Germiston in December 1972.

Shezi's death and the banning of Bokwe Mafuna and Drake Koka in March 1973 also set back efforts by SASO and BPC to move into the field of labor organization. Koka, who until his banning was secretary of the Sales and Allied Workers' Associ-

40. Information on the founding of the BPC is drawn in part from an interview of Gwendolen Carter and Benjamin Pogrund with Drake Koka, M. T. Moerane, William Nkomo, and David Thebehali in February 1972.

ation, had been instrumental in the launching in August 1972 of an umbrella Black Allied Workers' Union, while Shezi and Mafuna had been field workers for the SASO-initiated Black Workers' Project, aimed at the establishment of a central council for black unions.

While the Black Consciousness movement faced formidable obstacles in reaching for a mass audience directly or through workers' organizations, it fared somewhat better among black churchmen. Seminary students were among the earliest and most ardent proponents of Black Consciousness and its particular application within the church under the rubric of black theology. Black clergy were instrumental in organizing the widely-publicized Black Renaissance Convention, an important all-in conference which brought together a cross-section of black leaders and intellectuals at St. Peter's Seminary at Hammanskraal, north of Pretoria, in December 1974. Links also grew between SASO, BPC, and the African Independent Churches Association, while new pressures from black clergy within the main white-led churches accelerated a limited redistribution of authority between the races within some denominational hierarchies. Recognizing the threat posed by the new spirit of nationalism among black churchmen generally, the government moved in 1974–75 to destroy one of the most intense centers of Black Consciousness thinking, Federal Theological Seminary in Alice, which was ruthlessly dispossessed of its land and buildings on the pretext that these were needed for the expansion of neighboring Fort Hare.

The political conservatism of white-run churches in South Africa, and their hypocrisy toward black clergy (who have long been paid on differential salary scales and who have only in the rarest of circumstances been appointed to positions of authority over whites), have always made black ministers a potentially politicizable group. As a group and individually, African ministers also have the potential power to influence relatively large numbers of ordinary people in a population having a large percentage of church-goers. That African ministers have in the past more often than not been a conservative influence testifies to the pressure in the churches to avoid

politics. Where individual African clergymen have taken a political stance, that stance has nearly always been a traditional
liberal one, emphasizing the importance of symbolic interracial "bridge building" and the avoidance of hostility toward
whites. Thus the strength of Black Consciousness ideology
among black seminarians and clergy in the 1970s can only be
seen as representing a highly significant shift in opinion,
perhaps auguring a period of reorientation among many black
Christians.

The Black Consciousness movement was clearly more successful in communicating the subtler nuances of its message
inside the walls of academic and religious institutions than
beyond them in black society at large. Nevertheless, even where
the nuances of the message failed to register, a mood was
communicated which could not fail to stir new thinking in the
minds of many ordinary people. Compared to white press
coverage of earlier black political movements, coverage of
SASO was extensive, and while reporting on SASO's statements and actions was not always accurate, no amount of dis-
tortion was able to conceal that the spokesmen of the Black
Consciousness movement were highly courageous individuals
willing to speak their minds without fear. Widespread use
among students of the clenched-fist Black Power salute served
to underline this new fearlessness in a nonverbal language that
even the most politically uneducated or illiterate person could
understand.[41]

By 1972 the defiant new tenor of SASO's stance and its
mocking attitude toward prominent Africans who continued
to behave like so-called "nonwhites" (the new South African
equivalent of the American Uncle Tom) had noticeably altered
the vocabulary and tone of the cautious politics practised
among Africans of the older generation. With SASO to his left,
even Buthelezi could be seen as a moderate, and by the mid-
1970s significant numbers of politicized Zulus had moved into

41. SASO tried in 1972 to popularize T-shirts bearing the clenched
fist emblem, but this failed when the manufacturer was denied clear-
ance by the Publications Control Board. *Rand Daily Mail*, 9 July 1972.

the anti-Buthelezi camp. If Buthelezi was a moderate, anyone to his right in terms of accommodation or non-accommodation to the government's prescriptions for Africans began to look distinctly like a sellout, whether he was operating within "the system" in a bantustan government or a UBC, or outside in anything from a sports club to ASSECA. All black politics, at least at the verbal level, took a pronounced step away from accommodation. For any politician addressing an educated or newspaper-reading African audience, "nonwhite" was out and "black" was in. Coloured opinion swung in an increasingly militant direction. Popular consciousness had unquestionably been raised, whether any of those conscientized were aware of it or not. For politicians seeking a safe niche within the government-created apparatus, "comfortable politics" seemed likely to become more and more uncomfortable.

More important than any effect on blacks of an older generation, however, was the impact of Black Consciousness thinking on the age group next in line behind the 1969–72 SASO generation of university rebels. Almost from the inception of SASO at the university level, efforts were made to recruit support from younger students. By early 1972, city branches of SASO catering to students in high schools and non-university institutions were either in existence or in the process of forming in Pietermaritzburg, Port Elizabeth, Umtata, Kimberley, Bloemfontein, Pretoria, and Springs.[42]

The diffusion of SASO's new mood to the high school generation was given tremendous impetus in mid-1972 by the campus revolts which followed the expulsion of A. O. R. Tiro, a SASO leader, from the University of the North. Tiro's expulsion was prompted by his stinging attack on black education and South African society generally in a graduation address at Turfloop on April 29. When students organized a boycott of classes to protest the expulsion, the authorities closed down the university and announced that all students would have to apply for readmission. Protest boycotts spread to other black cam-

42. "Minutes of the SASO Executive Meeting," 3–5 December 1969, SASO *Newsletter*, September 1970, and *SASO 1972* (SASO files).

puses until by June a nationwide student rebellion was underway. One result was the expulsion or voluntary withdrawal of a
large number of students from black universities, many of
whom then transferred their energies to political activities outside the campuses. In a situation of developing black-white
confrontation in which mere talk hitherto had been the main
activity, younger brothers and sisters were highly impressed by
the action of older students who had put political commitment
above the promotion of their own careers. To the high school
generation, SASO leaders became heroes who had been
bloodied in an actual clash with white authority. One consequence by the end of 1972 was an upsurge in political
consciousness among high school students, leading to the formation of a welter of political youth organizations across the
country. The most notable of these, and the ones which were
to provide the organization impetus behind the township youth
uprisings of 1976, were the South African Students' Movement, formed in Soweto high schools, and the National Youth
Organisation, a federation of youth groups in Natal, the
Transvaal, and the eastern and western Cape.[43]

Once a significant cadre of youthful followers had been imbued with the ideology and mood of SASO, each new political
development simply added fuel to the fire of student
radicalism. In January and February 1973, a wave of spontaneous strikes by black workers swept Durban, prompting
modest concessions from industry and attracting worldwide
publicity. While no black organization could claim credit for
the strikes, they nevertheless demonstrated the potential for
successful industrial action, and set many black radicals thinking seriously for the first time about the problems involved in
forging a worker-student alliance. As if to acknowledge that
blacks had won a round with the Durban strikes, the government chose March 1973 to launch its first major offensive
against the Black Consciousness movement. Banning orders
were issued to Biko, Pityana, and six other SASO and BPC

43. B. Khoapa, ed., *Black Review 1972* (Durban, 1973), pp. 181–84;
and M. P. Gwala, ed., *Black Review 1973* (Durban, 1974), pp. 62–68.

leaders, and when new individuals came forward to take leadership positions, they too were banned. It was clear by this time, however, that the government had greatly underestimated SASO's appeal and momentum, for this counterthrust came far too late to stop the spread of the Black Consciousness movement; instead, it created martyrs for the black cause, as did the assassination of Tiro, who died in February 1974 in Botswana from the explosion of a parcel bomb.

In early 1974 came the fall of the Portuguese government, followed by Mozambique's rapid advance to independence. Police bans on rallies organized by BPC and SASO to celebrate the installation of Frelimo's transitional government on 25 September 1974 touched off new campus disorders, with Turfloop once more taking the lead. High school students were again caught up in the mood of defiance, with that mood now being reinforced gradually year by year with the influx of new university graduates into the teaching profession. The performance of black drama and music by mushrooming township cultural groups had also by this time become a significant factor in the diffusion of Black Consciousness ideology.

Weighed against the forward surge of political consciousness among black youth, government efforts to suppress SASO and its allied organizations by means of bans and detentions proved conspicuously inadequate. Court action also failed to achieve its objectives. The seventeen-month-long trial of the "SASO Nine"—nine national leaders of SASO and the BPC charged under the Terrorism Act for fomenting disorder at the time of the 1974 Frelimo support rallies—far from helping the government to intimidate actual and potential activists, appears to have had the opposite effect. Aware that the eyes of the country were on them, the accused used the trial to restate the nationalist viewpoint, and took every opportunity to symbolize their defiance of the state by singing freedom songs and raising clenched fists in the courtroom. Thus, instead of contributing to the suppression of Black Consciousness ideology, the trial, by giving the accused a continuous public platform through the press, merely disseminated that ideology even more widely, and held up to youth once again a model of "rebel" courage. Convicted in December 1976 and sentenced to terms on Robben Island, the defendants could depart from the political stage confident that the freedom movement had never been stronger.[44]

44. The SASO Nine, who were given sentences of from five to ten years for contraventions of the Terrorism Act, were: Saths Cooper, Zithulele Cindi, Mosioua Lekota, Aubrey Mokoape, Strini Moodley, Muntu Myeza, Pandelani Nefolovhodwe, Nkwenkwe Nkomo, and Kaborane Sedibe.

9

From Black Consciousness to Black Power? The 1980s and Beyond

WHEN LEMBEDE AND HIS NATIONALIST COLLEAGUES of the 1940s preached that a process of mental reorientation would open the way for African liberation, they were saying what many students of colonialism were later to observe: that the colonial relationship becomes unstable not necessarily when conditions among the oppressed are at their worst, but rather at the point when the colonized masses begin to perceive their condition as fundamentally unacceptable. To Lembede and to his disciples in the Africanist movement and the PAC, the observation was essentially a theoretical one, resting more on emotional and intellectual conviction than on any direct verification by experience. Today, however, it appears from the widespread outbreaks of urban violence and the ever-escalating level of coercion required by the regime, that the South African order is becoming increasingly unstable—and that one of the prime causes of this instability is the ideological reorientation taking place among the younger generation of urban blacks. Lembede's hypothesis is gradually being verified in the crucible of events.

But to confirm the central importance of the psychological factor in the South African conflict does not necessarily bring the resolution of the conflict any nearer. For African nationalists, the road from Black Consciousness to Black Power is still a long and uncharted one, just how long and difficult neither Lembede nor most of his ideological heirs were ever able fully to imagine. Lembede foresaw that the awakening of national consciousness would ultimately result in the explosion of the black man's latent "atomic energy," but whether that explosion would occur spontaneously and move the masses toward victory by some natural law of history, or whether victory would depend on careful planning and organization, Lembede does not seem to have been concerned to speculate. Sobukwe too, although he appreciated the formidable odds against a rapid African victory, nevertheless underestimated the importance of organization and overvalued the spontaneous ability of the masses to somehow "find a way" once heroic leaders had "shown the light" by preaching African nationalism. In the minds of "rebels" reacting against overcautious "realist" leadership, the idea died hard that the people were ready to act if the leaders would only be prepared to lead.

In SASO, this exaggerated faith in the spontaneous revolutionary disposition of the masses was largely abandoned in favor of a more hardheaded emphasis on patient organization. Patience and hard work among students brought advances in a relatively short time. But when the youthful activists of 1976 attempted to translate their power over the student generation into a mobilization of older workers to stage work stoppages, they soon revealed the limits of their organizational strength. Two brief sympathy strikes in late August and mid-September 1976 were well supported, but when called upon to launch a five-day stoppage in November, workers declined to pit themselves against white authority again. The strike effort collapsed and the students were forced to settle for a much more limited show of strength, and one involving far greater sacrifice for themselves than for whites—the widespread temporary closure of Bantu Education schools. Throughout the 1976 events, just as at the time of earlier historical watersheds, African political consciousness rose with tremendous momentum, but Black Power remained elusive.

What of the future? In an article published in *Africa South* almost twenty years ago, Julius Lewin presented one of the first

serious commentaries on the potential for revolution in South
Africa, and drew the conclusion that given the tremendous
imbalance of power and resources between the races, the country faced "no revolution round the corner."[1] Many analysts
since Lewin have tackled the same challenging question, and
some have marshaled impressive evidence in support of their
arguments that South Africa is or is not moving inexorably
toward violent revolution.

Among those who continue to see the prospects for revolution as remote, some rest their case primarily on the argument
that South Africa's coercive controls are efficient enough to
contain all threats to the security of the state indefinitely.
Others argue that the ruling whites are sufficiently secure and
flexible to pursue a tightly controlled course of political reform
which, if correctly conceived and combined with effective suppression of opposition, could succeed in keeping black discontent within manageable limits for many years to come. Among
economic analysts, the trend is away from the optimistic predictions of the 1960s, which assumed that economic growth
would somehow erode apartheid by bringing to light its supposed economic irrationalities; instead the tendency of current
analysis is to emphasize the remarkable ability of South Africa's
economy to adjust itself to changing pressures without dismantling its essential feature, which remains the exploitation
of cheap labor. Given white leadership which is flexible and
which suffers no crisis of political will, many observers conclude that the South African system, however inherently unstable, is capable of maintaining itself indefinitely.

Because the prosperity and status of whites under the present system rests to such an extent on the exploitation of blacks,
only the most sanguine optimist could foresee an evolutionary
process of voluntary white capitulation leading to a just redistribution of resources between the races. The present political
system precludes such a possibility, as the Spro-cas Political

1. "No Revolution Round the Corner," *Africa South*, 1958, reproduced in J. Lewin, *Politics and Law in South Africa, Essays on Race Relations* (London, 1963), pp. 107–115.

Commission noted in 1973: "Insofar as the present government is responsive to the claims, interests and wishes of its Nationalist supporters, and insofar as any white government would be beholden to an exclusively white electorate, these must serve as serious obstacles to their enacting any significant measures for sharing power and wealth."[2] The only actual alternatives therefore, at this vantage point in time, appear to be indefinite survival of the present structure of power through a successful combination of force and adaptation (which might deserve the term "reform" if its effects were genuinely ameliorative), or, eventually the more likely, revolutionary change, presumably following an unsuccessful combination of force and adaptation on the part of whites.

It is no more possible in concluding this study than it was at the outset to predict the future course of events in South Africa with any certainty. Much will depend on how the leadership of the National party reacts to increasing pressure, both from within the country's borders and beyond. Foreign powers will also play a crucial part in bolstering or undermining the ability of the South African regime to survive. In this study, the emphasis on African nationalism had precluded any direct consideration of either of these areas—Afrikaner politics or the realm of international relations—vital as they are to South Africa's future. The focus has been solely on the dynamics of black politics, and it is to this area that observations about the future must therefore be confined.

In looking to the future, Paul Kruger's exhortation to remember the past is as apt as ever. Just as any shrewd appraisal of the National party's future must draw on a knowledge of Afrikaner history, so too must any estimate of the future of black nationalism rest on an appreciation of the African's long struggle against racial domination. In spite of the cogency of many of the arguments put forward for or against the durability of the South African regime, one looks in vain in much of the contemporary commentary for any recognition of the his-

2. Patrick Laurence and F. Van Zyl Slabbert, *Towards An Open Plural Society* (Johannesburg, 1973), p. 45.

torical factor of black political initiatives as a variable in the total array of competing forces. Yet one cannot look back at past black political efforts without appreciating the scope for African maneuver and countermaneuver which has existed in every period, regardless of severe constraints. Too often discussions of South Africa's future appear to proceed on the assumption that whites alone are the instigators of action, while blacks essentially are and will remain the objects of white political, administrative or economic manipulation, swayed by forces and factors wholly beyond their own control. Taken in historical perspective, this is an unrealistic approach to the politics of South Africa, and one which could give rise to significant miscalculation regarding the future. No one, of course, denies that African mass attitudes are crucial, whether measured in terms of amorphous apathy or anger, or more precisely according to some sliding scale of feelings of relative deprivation. But what appears to be too frequently underrated is the ability of politically astute African leaders to anticipate and manipulate these mass attitudes to serve African group ends. It is their gradually increasing capacity to do exactly this which has been a central theme of this study.

Government-initiated reforms, to cite one highly manipulable area, have already created political opportunities as well as obstacles for African leadership. Just as Bantu Education has backfired politically by inspiring deep African mistrust of government retribalization strategies, so also may the entire bantustan exercise succeed in the end in reinforcing African aspirations for a unitary state and an interethnic nationalism, provided that black leaders can turn popular suspicion of government measures to ideological advantage. The National party, however defensive its motives, regards the bantustan program as a genuine reform because it foresees that Africans within the bantustan context will have opportunities for dignity and personal advancement which can never be opened to them in "white" South Africa. The counterimage of the bantustans, however—which nationalists will continue to propagate through every available channel—stresses the indignity of narrow tribal identity, especially to the urban African, and the emptiness of promises of advancement, which bantustans will be able to fulfill only for a handful of overpaid "good boy" politicians and bureaucrats. So heavy has been the barrage of scorn directed at bantustan "collaborators" from the nationalist side that it seems doubtful that the weight of African political opinion could be shifted in favor of bantustans in the foreseeable future.

Thus, although the ultimate success of "separate development" depends on remolding the aspirations of politically ambitious Africans through a carefully engineered system of rewards and punishments, it is by no means certain that the government can achieve this goal in the face of persistent counterpropaganda from the African side. In the politically critical township of Soweto, where members of the government-sponsored Urban Bantu Council became the target of repeated attacks during the 1976 uprising, the government's efforts to remold African political life are already a palpable failure. "Comfortable" politics-within-the-system may still be less hazardous than the "rebel" politics of confrontation, but—at least in Soweto—it is by no means a safe road to public esteem. It is possible that future adjustments in tactics on the part of the government might eventually succeed in winning increased legitimacy for the political structures of "separate development." Looking back in time, however, one thing seems certain, and that is that Verwoerd and the planners who conceived the idea of bantustans in the late 1950s seriously underestimated the rate at which African political consciousness, subject to the manipulation of African nationalist leaders, would grow and become a powerful counterforce to the strategy of the apartheid engineers.

The greater the general popular suspicion of the regime, the easier it becomes, relatively speaking, to arouse black opinion against specific apartheid policies. Antigovernment agitation is not likely to contribute to effective mass action, however, unless plausible and appealing ideological alternatives to "separate development" are at the same time being kept before the eyes of the black public. When the mass media mention independent African states, the ends of nationalist ideology are served without any action on the part of nationalists themselves being required. We saw in the evolution of the PAC what potent emotions were generated by the events and hopes surrounding the independence of Ghana in the late 1950s. Now, two decades later, the demonstration effect of independent Africa is still a powerful impetus toward nationalist thinking, as are the ongoing struggles for black rule in Rhodesia and Namibia. In Mozambique and Angola, the victory of African guerrilla forces has brought the lesson of white vulnerability very close to home, particularly since the triumph of Angola's MPLA was achieved in the face of military intervention by South Africa itself.

Other signals passing across the screen of popular perceptions also help to direct mass aspirations toward the goal of black rule in a united South Africa. Foreign governments declare themselves in favor of majority rule. Exiled nationalist leaders appear before international organizations and gather declarations of support. Even in the unlikely event that the South African government could coerce all its internal critics into silence, these external influences would still be at work, as would the influence of "separate development" rhetoric itself, which, as many people have pointed out, works indirectly to lend legitimacy to the basic concept of African self-determination.

Added to these factors reinforcing nationalist ideas in the popular mind is the very important direct influence of nationalist propaganda, overt and covert, within South Africa itself. Occasionally one hears the assertion that the South African regime "will not allow political dissent or opposition to exist outside the channels that it has created,"[3] and one writer has labeled as mere wishful thinking the claim that new political activists will always come forward to replace those suppressed.[4] But these negative assessments of the scope for black

3. M. Savage, "Major Patterns of Group Interaction in South African Society," in *Change in Contemporary South Africa*, ed. L. Thompson and J. Butler (Berkeley and Los Angeles, 1975), p. 301.
4. H. Adam, *Modernizing Racial Domination* (Berkeley and Los Angeles, 1971), p. 67.

agitation are ahistorical. Whether or not the government has "allowed" African nationalist opposition to exist since the banning of the ANC and PAC over seventeen years ago, that opposition has continued to surface again and again, and black spokesmen have continued to articulate nationalist goals publicly in spite of the extreme and ever-increasing hazards of so doing.

It is quite possible that as the risks of extra-parliamentary opposition intensify, a shift may occur away from efforts to organize aboveboard political bodies like SASO and BPC and toward indirect forms of organization instead, through cultural and religious groups, or through civic organizations like the Black Parents' Association formed at the height of the Soweto disturbances. Even more probable is that the future will see increasing nationalist agitation emanating from within government-sponsored "dummy institutions," in spite of the obvious image ambiguities involved for those committed nationalists who decide to take shelter in the protected "collaborator" role. Already it is apparent that Gatsha Buthelezi—in spite of continuing bitter attacks from the Black Consciousness movement, and perhaps in part because of them—has over the past few years become one of the most important disseminators of African nationalist ideology. Moreover, Buthelezi has now moved beyond the stage of merely articulating nationalist aspirations, and is actively creating organizational bases for nationalism through the formation of the Inkatha movement and the Black Unity Front between in-system and anti-system nationalists. To argue that Buthelezi is a net asset to the regime because he lends credibility or legitimacy to bantustans is seriously to undervalue his role as a propagandist for nationalism. Buthelezi is, in fact, the strongest evidence that black initiatives can lead to the backfiring of the best-laid plans of the apartheid strategists.

Thus, notwithstanding the tremendous power of the South African security apparatus to intimidate opponents through imprisonment, brutality, bans, and censorship, it is nevertheless clear that the government lacks the ability to close all doors to African nationalist consciousness. One of the essential prerequisites to mass mobilization would therefore appear to be present in the contemporary South African situation, assuming that Africans themselves do not become embroiled in internecine ideological battles which might undermine their future unity. For a major psychological precondition for popular action to be present, however, is no guarantee that people will indeed *act*, contrary to the assumption of Lembede and many of his "rebel" disciples. A belligerent ideology, as the PAC discovered in 1960, may be important, but it is by no means the only force at work shaping popular predispositions toward action. Before the ripeness or unripeness of a revolutionary situation can be judged, answers must also be sought to further questions regarding the popular state of mind. We can do no more than suggest some of these major questions here.

In assessing the durability of the present order one needs to ask, for example, whether economic grievances among blacks have reached a threshold level where feelings of relative deprivation—the gap between expectations and capacities to achieve their fulfillment—are both widespread and intense.[5] In the past, some observers have concluded that although African expectations are continually rising, the capacity of the economic system to satisfy those expectations has generally been sufficient to keep African discontent from reaching unmanageable extremes. Since the late 1960s, the upward mobility of blacks into skilled and semiskilled jobs as a result of white manpower shortages has often been cited as a factor assuaging the discontent of those at the higher levels of the black income scale; whether or not this advance has created new unfulfilled expectations among lower-income blacks is a matter for speculation. Another critical unknown is what the cumulative consequences may be of the prolonged period of inflation, recession and unemployment through which South Africa is currently passing. Even if survey data were available to confirm impressionistic observations about rising discontent, it would still be

5. These conclusions draw on the analysis of the concept of relative deprivation and of other factors related to political instability as developed in Ted Gurr's *Why Men Rebel* (Princeton, 1970).

difficult to foresee at what threshold of dissatisfaction black inclinations toward action might no longer be bottled up by fear, insecurity, and other countervailing attitudes.

Specific African attitudes toward political activism are another important area of unknown variables. Whether or not discontented groups in any society tend to translate their grievances into political action can depend on a wide variety of traditions, perceptions, and regime responses. We have seen how the adherence of the ANC to a policy of nonviolence over half a century was in part the result of the Christian and liberal traditions of the African middle class, and in part a reflection of the view that violence would always fail, given the government's overwhelming monopoly on the instruments of force. Under this gloss of middle class values and assessments of political reality dominant at the leadership level, other groups within African society, both rural and in varying stages of urbanization, have tended to display an unpredictable mixture of passivity and aggression, cautious acquiescence broken by occasional isolated cases of rebel boldness. It is certain that in the years since Sharpeville the attitudes of Africans of all classes toward both the moral legitimacy and the ultimate probability of political violence have hardened. What is still unclear in the wake of the events of 1976 is whether violence is now regarded by an increasing number of blacks as more likely to be successful than in the past. In this regard the regime faces a difficult dilemma in calculating its response to urban uprisings. If it eventually responds with reforms that are genuinely ameliorative, many Africans are likely to conclude that violence is the best way to achieve progress. If the government continues to reject genuine reforms and tries to stonewall its way forward on the basis of pre-1976 policies, many Africans—and especially the young—will no doubt come to regard even more destructive levels of violence as legitimate.

This observation brings back a recurrent theme in the history of black struggle in South Africa, namely the important socializing effect of watershed events in African political life. The Cape franchise crisis of 1936, the period of World War II, and the emergency of 1960 were such watersheds, and the urban revolt of 1976 will take its place alongside these earlier times of crisis in its deep impact on the developing political perceptions of black youth. One major result is likely to be the inuring of the upcoming generation to the realization that the struggle may claim many lives—an effect which Kuper would call part of the socialization of courage.[6] Only time can tell what effect such new perceptions, growing out of the experience of sharp black-white confrontation, will have on the character of future black leadership. If history is any guide, one would predict that the rebel inclinations of today's student generation will develop over time into attitudes with a higher ratio of realism to emotionalism. At the same time, it appears that the older stereotypes of "rebel" and "realist" may be moving toward convergence as the actual prospects for rebellion become increasingly real. Where the "realist" of thirty years ago put little faith in the capacity of the African masses to take collective action and looked instead for other ways to prick the consciousness of whites, today there is a widespread recognition that white attitudes move in the direction of accommodating black demands only after those demands are first put forward with a show of strength, as they were, for example, in the Durban strikes of 1973. "Rebels" on their part, having now experienced the confrontation toward which rebel temperament has inclined them for so long, may now move even farther away from the old romantic faith in mass spontaneity which tended in the past to work against a commitment to patient organization.

Where all these adjustments in black thinking are leading, individually and cumulatively, only time will tell. Also unresolved, if orthodox African nationalism continues to dominate black political thinking, is the vital question: after Black Power—what? The ideology of Black Consciousness, for all its success in helping to arouse Africans to a new sensitivity to oppression, is in the end primarily a transitional philosophy, aimed at overcoming the psychological handicaps which have

6. L. Kuper, *Race, Class and Power* (London, 1974), p. 109.

crippled Africans politically for so long. Its constructive potential, and that of African nationalist ideology generally, will almost certainly prove too limited once a more searching analysis of political and economic problems becomes an urgent requirement in the struggle. As the ideology of Black Consciousness outlives its usefulness, the onus will be on black leadership to keep black ideology closely attuned to popular needs and to the exigencies of a changing situation. If black leaders fail to do this, as many have failed in the past, the prospects for successful revolution will be remote indeed. If they rise to the intellectual task of ideological innovation, however, not only may they hasten the launching of a successful revolution, but they will also move South Africa nearer to the ultimate goal: a new social order worthy of everything sacrificed and suffered for its attainment.

Epilogue

        SINCE LATE 1976 WHEN THE CONCLUSION OF THIS book was written, events in South Africa have brought to a close a distinct phase in the politics of black liberation.

On 12 September 1977, Steve Biko died in detention in Pretoria after being tortured and beaten by security police. Five weeks later, on 19 October, police jailed dozens of government opponents not previously detained, and the minister of justice, James Kruger, announced that bans had been imposed on all the constituent organizations of the Black Consciousness movement. Proscribed along with SASO and the Black People's Convention were sixteen other organizations including the South African Students' Movement (SASM), the National Youth Organisation, the Soweto Students Representative Council (an offshoot of SASM), Black Community Programmes, and the Zimele Trust (a prisoners' fund)—the last two being organizations in which Biko had involved himself during his period of restriction in Kingwilliamstown.[1] On the same day, Kruger also ordered *The World* to cease publication, citing the alleged inflammatory tenor of its reporting in connection with Biko's death. *The World's* editor, Percy Qoboza, was among those detained, and banning orders were issued to

1. The other organizations banned were ASSECA, the Black Parents Association, the Black Women's Federation, the Border Youth Organisation, the Christian Institute of Southern Africa (a multiracial organization of anti-apartheid churchmen), the Eastern Province Youth Organisation, the Medupe Writers' Association, the Natal Youth Organisation, the Transvaal Youth Organisation, the Union of Black Journalists, and the Western Cape Youth Organisation.

Beyers Naude and Donald Woods, two prominent whites who had publicly supported Biko and the Black Consciousness movement.

On the face of it, the crackdown of 19 October appeared to be aimed at quelling the continuing urban disorder which had thrown South Africa into an undeclared state of emergency since June 1976. Had this been the government's sole objective, however, the organizations banned might have been suppressed months earlier, before student pressure through the Soweto Students Representative Council had successfully effected in June 1977 the en masse resignation of the Soweto Urban Bantu Council and before a boycott of Soweto secondary schools had resulted by August in the virtual collapse of Bantu Education in Johannesburg. A more complete explanation of the crackdown and its timing must take into account the exigencies of white politics, in particular Vorster's desire to win political advantage at a time of tension within his own party and uncertainty in the ranks of the white opposition. With a national election called for 30 November, the crackdown was designed to please the National party *verkramptes* while at the same time helping to pull in the wavering remnants of the dissolved United party around a useful political bogey: foreign "meddling" in South Africa's internal affairs. Coming soon after a wave of foreign rebukes over Biko's death, the bans of 19 October raised a howl of international protest and even prompted the United Nations Security Council to vote a mandatory ban on arms sales to South Africa. The outcry served Vorster's purposes well. Only the National party, he reminded his electorate, could tell the rest of the world in no uncertain terms to leave South Africa alone to resolve its own problems. On 30 November Vorster received the mandate he desired, emerging with the widest Nationalist majority in Parliament since 1948.

On the African side, it is still too soon to tell whether the ban on the organizations of the Black Consciousness movement will be a genuine blow to nationalist aspirations or a blessing in disguise. The field will be temporarily open for bantustan politicians to monopolize the headlines, and the anti-collaboration campaign so successfully waged by Soweto high school students against the UBC and ethnically organized schoolboards will no doubt lose momentum. Gatsha Buthelezi, whose stock was low among black militants at the time of the bans, may be able to use the eclipse of some of his "outside-the-system" rivals to make a new bid for mass support, challenging the government to suppress Inkatha, his KwaZulu-based political party which now claims a national membership of 120,000. Any rise in Inkatha's status, on the other hand, may in turn stir non-Zulus to react in fear at the prospect of "Zulu domination," a reaction which plays neatly into the government's strategy of ethnic divide-and-rule.

Arguing the case that the Black Consciousness bans will set back the progress of mass mobilization, some might point to how much the initial rapid spread of the Black Consciousness movement depended on the freedom to propagate nationalist ideology in organizational conferences and meetings with relative openness. Now lacking access to such opinion-making forums, activists will face the problem of how to maintain popular support and understanding of radical aims. To those who predict that the crackdown of 1977 will result in a period of organizational dormancy, however, the early history of SASO is again instructive. The hostile attitude of the government to banned organizations, as Biko pointed out to his colleagues in the late 1960s, did not mean that all political activity was ipso facto banned. The task of blacks was to take the offensive and organize themselves, regardless of government reactions. It is too soon to tell to what extent new militant black organizations may spring up to fill the vacuum left on 19 October. It would be wrong, however, to assume that the pattern of the early 1960s will be repeated. Kuper's socialization of courage has already proceeded too far.

It seems certain—and this would be argued by revolutionaries who see the October bans as a disguised blessing—that the proscription of SASO, BPC, and their sister bodies will produce a greatly increased commitment to underground activity, especially among students but to some extent also among members of older generations. If the political fortunes of the National party were served by the crackdown, so too were the fortunes of the exile ANC, which has been trying hard since the strong emergence of the Black Consciousness movement to make itself relevant to the rising generation. Trials of ANC activists apprehended inside South Africa during the 1970s provide some clue to the ANC's continuing effort to set up cells and recruiting networks. To what extent the fierce sentences being passed on convicted ANC members may offset the new post-1977 attraction of the younger generation to the ANC underground is uncertain. But it seems likely that among the teenagers who willingly faced police bullets after hundreds of their fellows had already been shot in the uprising of 1976 there will be many willing to face the hazards of an illegal underground. It would be inaccurate to say that October 1977 marks the start of an underground phase in black politics, since underground organization was well under way by the mid-1970s and to a lesser degree existed even after the crushing of Umkonto we Sizwe and Poqo in the 1960s. Nevertheless, it is safe to predict a shift in black resistance from primarily legal to primarily illegal organization.

If the bans of October 1977 mark the end of an era in black South African politics, it is not solely because the organizational structure of the freedom struggle has changed, however. An ideological crossroads has also been reached. The revolution in popular attitudes for which orthodox African nationalists hoped and worked for more than three decades has become a reality. The generation coming of age today in South Africa is the embodiment of the Africanist vision of Lembede: proud, self-reliant, determined. The founders and stalwarts of the Black Consciousness movement, however heavy the price they have paid in death, imprisonment, bans and exile, have handed intact to their as-yet-undetermined successors their movement's major achievement: an urban African population psychologically prepared for confrontation with white South Africa.

This is a time for stocktaking in the ranks of African leadership. As in past watershed periods, the challenge facing leaders is to bring themselves into step with the needs of the times: to mold an ideology which can capture the popular imagination and combine it with a strategy that maximizes African strength. For leaders and would-be leaders now in exile—removed from the immediate conflict but temporarily in a position of strength relative to leaders inside—this challenge is a formidable one. As exiles they live in the past as well as the present. In their ongoing search for a formula of liberation, their own history unavoidably itself becomes a factor: either as a constraint for those who are too small-minded to forget yesterday's dogmas and quarrels, or as a positive resource for those who approach the past with the desire to draw constructively from its many lessons. How wisely they deal with that choice historians of the future must assess.

December 1977
Nairobi

Appendix

Composition of ANC and PAC Leadership by Age and Class, 1957–1960

GENERALIZATION DRAWN FROM INADEQUATE STATIS-
TICS can be hazardous, but the conclusions reached on pp.
221–23 may receive some tentative support from the following tables. These are based on samples of ANC and PAC
leadership which are small and not necessarily representative
of the organizations' wider followings. The samples include
a small assortment of ordinary members, plus lower, middle,
and top-rank leaders—men and women who spoke publicly
from political platforms and were in many cases arrested and
tried for their political activities.

The ANC group is comprised of 97 members of the ANC
arrested in the 1956–61 Treason Trial. Four Treason Trial-
ists known to be Africanists have been omitted. The PAC
group is comprised of these four, the 23 Africans tried in
Johannesburg in connection with the pass campaign of March
1960, plus 51 PAC leaders and followers in Cape Town, most
of whose names appear in police notes as speakers at PAC
rallies. The occupations and approximate ages of these 51 have
been set down by Elliot Magwentshu, a PAC activist whose

memory of the Cape Town situation is very good. The absence of high school students and underrepresentation of *tsotsis* in the PAC sample (the Cape Town group includes only a few) explain the failure of this data to reflect what has been hypothesized to be the more middle-class makeup of the PAC. Ages given are for 1959–60 in the case of PAC, and for 1957–58 in the case of ANC.

Top ranking leaders (members of the National Executive Committees) of ANC and PAC have been listed separately for purposes of comparison, and this has meant adding several individuals who are not included elsewhere in the samples.

AGE

	AGE	ANC		PAC	
		Percent	*Number*	*Percent*	*Number*
Top Rank	20–29	—	—	33.3	5
Leaders	30–39	30.8	4	40.0	6
(National Executives)	40–49	30.8	4	26.7	4
	over 50	38.4	5	—	—
		100.0	13	100.0	15
	20–29	14.3	12	46.4	32
Middle and Lower	30–39	47.7	40	36.2	25
Rank Leaders	40–49	26.0	22	11.6	8
	over 50	12.0	10	5.8	4
		100.0	84	100.0	69

CLASS

CLASS	ANC		PAC	
	Percent	*Number*	*Percent*	*Number*
Top Rank Leaders (National Executives)				
Professional elite	70.0	9	20.0	3
Other middle class	22.8	3	53.3	8
Working class	—	—	—	—
Trade unionists	7.2	1	6.7	1
University students	—	—	20.0	3
	100.0	13	100.0	15
Middle and Lower Rank Leaders				
Professional elite	3.6	3	—	—
Other middle class	45.2	38	40.6	28
Working class and trade unionists	51.2	43	59.4	41
	100.0	84	100.0	69

Sources: A. Sampson, *The Treason Cage,* pp. 225–34; *South Africa's Treason Trial,* Johannesburg, n.d., (Carter-Karis collection); Trial transcript of *Reg. vs. Robert Sobukwe and twenty-two others,* 1960; and private communication from Elliot Magwentshu.

Bibliography

Manuscript and Documentary Sources

Only collections are included. Individual documents are cited in footnote references. Documentary sources for which no collection is cited in footnote references are in the author's collection.

Cape Town. Archives of the National Union of South African Students. Footnote references are to "NUSAS files."

Chicago. CAMP collection. Documentary collection of Gwendolen M. Carter and Thomas G. Karis, Microfilm. Footnote references are to "Carter-Karis collection."

Chicago. CAMP collection. Documents presented in evidence at the South African Treason Trial of 1956–61. Microfilm. (See Trial Materials, below.)

Chicago. CAMP collection. Papers of Silas Molema. Microfilm.

Chicago. CAMP collection. South African Congress of Democrats: Papers, 1956–61. Microfilm.

Collins, Colin. Draft dissertation chapter on "Black Consciousness."

Durban. Papers of the South African Students' Organisation. Footnote references are to "SASO files."

Documents presented in evidence at the Cape Town trial of Philip Kgosana, *Reg. vs. Synod Madlebe and Others*, 1960. Loaned by B. Khaketla. (See Trial Materials, below.)

Johannesburg. Gubbins Library, University of the Witwatersrand. Holdings include the papers of Edward Roux.

Johannesburg. South African Institute of Race Relations. Holdings include the papers of Alfred B. Xuma.

Lakaje, Charles. Untitled autobiographical MS, loaned by himself.

Maseru. Files of the Pan Africanist Congress, including the scrapbooks of J. N. Pokela.

Maseru. Police files.
Miscellaneous papers of Benjamin Pogrund, loaned by himself.
Stanford. Hoover Institution. South Africa: A Collection of Political
   Documents. Microfilm. Documents collected by Benjamin Pog-
   rund. Footnote references are to "Hoover microfilms."

Ephemeral Periodicals

Printed or mimeographed periodicals of short duration or
irregular publication, now found mainly in documentary
collections rather than among ordinary library periodicals
collections. Footnote references to articles in these periodicals include a reference to the collection in which the periodical can be found.

The African Advocate (Gubbins Library)
The Africanist (Carter-Karis collection, Hoover microfilms, Gubbins
   Library and files of the PAC, Maseru)
African Lodestar, later *The Lodestar* (Carter-Karis collection)
Afrika (Carter-Karis collection)
Analysis (Gubbins Library)
ANC Bulletin (Hoover microfilms)
ANC Voice (Hoover microfilms)
Azania News (Author's collection)
Black Star (Carter-Karis collection)
Bulletin of the South African Peace Council (Hoover microfilms)
Congress Voice (Hoover microfilms)
Counter Attack (Carter-Karis collection, Hoover microfilms, COD pa-
   pers, CAMP)
Freedom (Carter-Karis collection, Gubbins Library)
Ikhwezi Lomso (Hoover microfilms)
Inyaniso (Carter-Karis collection)
Isizwe (Carter-Karis collection)
Izwe-Lethu (Author's collection)
NUSAS Newsletter (NUSAS files)
PAC Newsletter (Carter-Karis collection)
Pan Africanist News and Views, later *PAC News and Views* (Carter-Karis
   collection)
Pioneer (Carter-Karis collection)
SASO Newsletter (SASO files)
South Africa Freedom News (Carter-Karis collection)
The SOYAN (Hoover microfilms)
Spark (Hoover microfilms)

Spotlight on South Africa (Author's collection)
University Christian Movement Newsletter (NUSAS files)
Vanguard (Carter-Karis collection, Hoover microfilms)

Non-Ephemeral Periodicals

Printed periodicals published regularly and found among library periodicals collections.

Advance
Africa and the World
Africa Confidential
The African Communist
Africa South, later *Africa South in Exile*
Africa Today
Africa X-Ray Report
Anti-Apartheid News
The Bantu World, later *The World*
Cape Argus
Cape Times
Christian Science Monitor
Clarion
The Classic
The Commentator
Contact
Crisis and Change
Die Beeld
Die Burger
Drum
Fighting Talk
Financial Times (London)
The Forum
The Friend
Golden City Post

Ikwezi
Ilanga lase Natal
Imvo Zabantsundu
Indian Opinion, later *Opinion*
Inkululeko
Inkundla ya Bantu
Journal of Racial Affairs
Liberation
Natal Mercury
The New African
New Age
New York Times
The Observer (London)
Peoples World
Pro Veritate
Race Relations Journal
Rand Daily Mail
Reality
Sechaba
South African Labour Bulletin
South African Outlook
Southern Africa
The Star
Sunday Express (Johannesburg)
Sunday Times (Johannesburg)
The Times (London)

Trial Materials

Crown vs. F. Adams and Twenty-nine Others (the Treason Trial, 1956–61), Supreme Court of South Africa. Trial Transcript. Microfilm. Boston University Library.

Regina vs. Robert Sobukwe and Twenty-two Others, 1960, Magistrate's Court, Regional Division of Johannesburg. Trial transcript. Microfilm. CAMP collection.

Regina vs. Synod Madlebe and Others, 1960, Regional Court for the
Regional Division of Cape Peninsula. Documents presented in evidence. Loaned by B.Khaketla.

South African Trials. Microfilm. CAMP collection.

The State vs. Johannes Monyake and Others, 1960–61, Magistrate's Court,
Regional Division of South Transvaal. Trial transcript. Microfilm.
CAMP collection.

Official Publications

Cape of Good Hope, *South African Native Affairs Commission: Report,
1903–1905,* Cape Town, 1905.

Republic of South Africa, House of Assembly, *Debates.*

———, Senate, *Debates.*

———, Department of Justice, List of persons who have been office-
bearers, officers, members or active supporters of the Communist
Party of South Africa, *Government Gazette,* November 16, 1962.

———, *Commission of Enquiry into the Events at Paarl, on the 20th to 22nd
of November 1962,* (Snyman Commission), Minutes of Evidence,
Cape Town, 1963.

———, *Report of the Paarl Commission of Enquiry: Report of the Commission
Appointed to Enquire into the Events on the 20th to 22nd November, 1962,
at Paarl, and the Causes Which Gave Rise Thereto,* (Snyman Commission), Pretoria, 1963.

———, *Report of the Commissioner of the South African Police for the Half-
Year Ended 30th June, 1963,* Pretoria, 1964.

———, Buro of Statistics, *South African Statistics, 1968,* Pretoria, 1968.

Union of South Africa, House of Assembly, *Debates.*

———, Senate, *Debates.*

———, *Report of the Native Churches Commission,* Cape Town, 1925
(U.G. 39/1925).

Union of South Africa, *Report of the Native Laws Commission, 1946–48*
(Fagan Commission), Pretoria, 1948 (U.G. 28/1948).

———, *Report of the Select Committee on Suppression of Communism Act
Enquiry,* Pretoria, 1952 (S.C. 6/1952) and 1953 (S.C. 10/1953).

———, *Report of the Langa Commission of Enquiry* (Diemont Commission), Cape Town, 1960.

———, *Commission of Enquiry to Enquire Into the Events in the Districts of
Vereeniging (Namely the Sharpeville Location and Evaton) and Vanderbijlpark, Transvaal Province, on 21st March, 1960,* Minutes of evidence
and exhibits, Pretoria, 1960.

———, *Annual Report of the Commissioner of the South African Police for
the Year 1960,* Pretoria, 1961.

Books, Articles and Pamphlets

Pamphlets issued by the ANC, PAC, CPSA, COD, AAC and NEUM are not listed because they appear in documentary collections. Articles appearing in listed periodicals are also not included.

Adam, Heribert. *Modernizing Racial Domination: South Africa's Political Dynamics.* Berkeley and Los Angeles: University of California Press, 1971.

―――. "The Rise of Black Consciousness in South Africa." *Race* 15, no. 2 (October 1973): 149–65.

―――, and Adam, Kogila, eds. *South Africa: Sociological Perspectives.* London: Oxford University Press, 1971.

Andrews, William H. *Class Struggles in South Africa.* Cape Town: no publisher, 1941.

Asheron, Andrew. "Race and Politics in South Africa." *New Left Review,* No. 53 (January–February 1969): 55–67.

"Banned Leader of the South African Students' Organisation." "A Black South African's View of the Present Urban, Rural and Industrial Situation in the Republic." Paper no. 24 in *The Conditions of the Black Worker,* Study Project on External Investment in South Africa and Namibia. Uppsala, 1975. Pp. 244–76.

Benson, Mary. *The African Patriots.* London: Faber and Faber, 1963; republished as *South Africa: The Struggle for a Birthright.* Harmondsworth, Middlesex: Penguin Books, 1966.

―――. *Chief Albert Lutuli of South Africa.* London: Oxford University Press, 1963.

―――, ed. *The Sun Will Rise: Statements From the Dock by Southern African Political Prisoners.* London: International Defence and Aid Fund, 1974.

Bernstein, Hilda. *The World That Was Ours.* London: Heinemann, 1967.

―――. *For Their Triumphs and For Their Tears: Conditions and Resistance of Women in Apartheid South Africa.* London: International Defence and Aid Fund, 1975.

Biesheuvel, S. "The Influence of Social Circumstances on the Attitudes of Educated Africans." *South African Journal of Science* 53, no. 12 (July 1957): 309–14.

Biko, B. S., ed. *Black Viewpoint.* Durban: Black Community Programmes, 1972.

Black Religion in South Africa. Special number of *African Studies* 33, no. 2 (1974).

Black Sash. *Memorandum on the Application of the Pass Laws and Influx Control.* No place of publication. 1971.

Blaxall, Arthur. *Suspended Sentence*. London: Hodder and Stoughton, 1965.

Bloom, Harry. *Transvaal Episode*. Berlin: Seven Seas, 1959.

Bloom, Leonard. "Self Concepts and Social Status in South Africa: A Preliminary Cross-Cultural Analysis." *Journal of Social Psychology* 51 (1960): 103–12.

————, de Crespigny, A. R. C., and Spence, J. E. "An Interdisciplinary Study of Social, Moral, and Political Attitudes of White and Non-White South African University Students." *Journal of Social Psychology* 54 (1961): 3–12.

Blumberg, Myrna. *White Madam*. London: Victor Gollancz, 1962.

Boetie, Dugmore. *Familiarity Is The Kingdom of the Lost*. Greenwich, Connecticut: Fawcett, 1970.

Boulanger, M. "Black Workers and Strikes in South Africa." *Race* 15, no. 3 (January 1974): 351–59.

Brandel-Syrier, Mia. *Reeftown Elite: A Study of Social Mobility in a Modern African Community on the Reef*. London: Routledge and Kegan Paul, 1971.

Brett, E. A. *African Attitudes: A Study of the Social, Racial and Political Attitudes of Some Middle Class Africans*. Johannesburg: SAIRR, 1963.

Brokensha, Miles, and Knowles, Robert. *The Fourth of July Raids*. Cape Town: Simondium, 1965.

Brookes, Edgar H., ed. *Apartheid: A Documentary Study of Modern South Africa*. London: Routledge and Kegan Paul, 1968.

————, and Macaulay, J. B. *Civil Liberty in South Africa*. Cape Town: Oxford University Press, 1958.

————, and Webb, Colin. *A History of Natal*. Pietermaritzburg: University of Natal Press, 1965.

————. *Power, Law, Right and Love: A Study in Political Values*. Durham: Duke University Press, 1963.

Brookfield, H. C., and Tatham, M. A. "The Distribution of Racial Groups in Durban." *Geographical Review* 47, no. 1 (January 1957): 44–65.

Brown, Douglas. *Against the World: Attitudes of White South Africa*. Garden City: Doubleday, 1968.

Brown, William O. "The Nature of Race Consciousness." *Social Forces* 10, no. 1 (1931): 90–97.

————. "Race Consciousness Among South African Natives." *American Journal of Sociology* 40, no. 5 (March 1935): 569–81.

————. *Race Relations in the American South and in South Africa*. Boston: Boston University Press, 1959.

Bundy, Colin. "The Emergence and Decline of a South African Peasantry." *African Affairs* 71, no. 285 (October 1972): 369–88.

Bunting, Brian. *The Rise of the South African Reich*. Harmondsworth, Middlesex: Penguin Books, 1964.

———. *The Story Behind the Non-White Press*. No place of publication: New Age, 1960 (?).

Burger, J. (pseud. of Leo Marquard). *The Black Man's Burden*. London: Victor Gollancz, 1943.

Burrows, R. *Indian Life and Labour in Natal*. Johannesburg: SAIRR, 1952 (?).

Buthelezi, M. Gatsha. *White and Black Nationalism, Ethnicity and the Future of the Homelands*. Johannesburg: SAIRR, 1974.

Callan, Edward. *Albert John Luthuli and the South African Race Conflict*. Kalamazoo: Western Michigan University Press, 1962.

Calpin, George H. *Indians in South Africa*. Pietermaritzburg: Shuter and Shooter, 1949.

Calvocoressi, Peter. *South Africa and World Opinion*. London: Oxford University Press, 1961.

Carmichael, Stokely, and Hamilton, Charles V. *Black Power: The Politics of Liberation in America*. New York: Vintage Books, 1967.

Carter, David. "The Defiance Campaign—A Comparative Analysis of the Organization; Leadership, and Participation in the Eastern Cape and the Transvaal." In *Institute of Commonwealth Studies, Collected Seminar Papers on the Societies of Southern Africa in the 19th and 20th Centuries*. London, October 1970–June 1971. Pp. 76–97.

Carter, Gwendolen M. "African Nationalist Movements in South Africa." *Massachusetts Review*, Autumn 1963, pp. 147–64.

———. *Black Initiatives for Change in Southern Africa*. Eleventh Melville J. Herskovits Memorial Lecture, Edinburgh, 1973.

———. *The Politics of Inequality*. Revised edition. New York: Praeger, 1959.

———. *Separate Development: The Challenge of the Transkei*. Johannesburg: SAIRR, 1966.

———, Karis, Thomas G., and Stultz, Newell. *South Africa's Transkei: The Politics of Domestic Colonialism*. Evanston: Northwestern University Press, 1967.

Christian Action. *Bram Fischer Q. C.* London: Christian Action, 1966.

———. *The Purge of the Eastern Cape*. London: Christian Action, 1966 (?).

Churchill, Rhona. *White Man's God*. New York: Hodder and Stoughton, 1962.

Cilliers, S. P. *A Sociological Perspective on the South African Situation*. Johannesburg: SAIRR, 1971.

Clare, John. "The Liberal Dilemma of Alan Paton." *The Times* (London), 22 July 1971, p. 14.

"The Communist Party in South Africa." *Africa Report* 6, no. 3 (March 1961): 5–6 ff.

Cope, John. *South Africa*. London: Ernest Benn, 1965.

Cope, R. K. *Comrade Bill: The Life and Times of William Andrews, Work-*

ers' Leader. Cape Town: Stewart Printing Co., 1944 (?).

Cowen, Denis V. *The Foundations of Freedom, with Special Reference to Southern Africa.* London: Oxford University Press, 1961.

Crijns, Arthur G. J. *Race Relations and Race Attitudes in South Africa.* Nijmegen: Janssen, 1960.

Danziger, Kurt. "Ideology and Utopia in South Africa: A Methodological Contribution to the Sociology of Knowledge." *British Journal of Sociology* 14 (1963): 59–76.

———. "The Psychological Future of an Oppressed Group." *Social Forces* 42, no. 1 (October 1963): 31–40.

———. "Self-Interpretations of Group Differences in Values (Natal, South Africa)." *Journal of Social Psychology* 47 (1958): 317–25.

———. "Value Differences Among South African Students." *Journal of Abnormal and Social Psychology* 57, no. 3 (November 1958): 339–46.

Davenport, T. R. H. *The Beginnings of Urban Segregation in South Africa: The Natives (Urban Areas) Act of 1923 and Its Background.* Grahamstown: Institute of Social and Economic Research, Rhodes University, 1971.

———, and Hunt, K. S. *The Right to the Land.* Cape Town: David Philip, 1974.

Davidson, Basil, Slovo, Joe, and Wilkinson, A. R. *Southern Africa: The New Politics of Revolution.* Harmondsworth, Middlesex: Penguin Books, 1976.

Davis, John A., and Baker, James K., eds. *Southern Africa in Transition.* New York: Praeger, 1966.

Davis, R. Hunt. *Bantu Education and the Education of Africans in South Africa.* Athens, Ohio: Center for International Studies, 1972.

de Gruchy, Joy. *The Cost of Living for Urban Africans.* Johannesburg: SAIRR, 1959.

de Kiewiet, Cornelius W. *A History of South Africa: Social and Economic.* London: Oxford University Press, 1941, 1966.

———. *The Anatomy of South African Misery.* London: Oxford University Press, 1956.

———. "Fears and Pressures in the Union of South Africa." *Virginia Quarterly Review,* Winter 1954, pp. 27–45.

de Ridder, J. C. *The Personality of the Urban African in South Africa: A Thematic Apperception Test Study.* London: Routledge and Kegan Paul, 1961.

Desmond, Cosmas. *The Discarded People: An Account of African Resettlement in South Africa.* Harmondsworth, Middlesex: Penguin Books, 1971.

De Villiers, H. H. W. *Rivonia: Operation Mayibuye.* Johannesburg: Afrikaanse Pers-Boekhandel, 1964.

Doxey, G. V. *The Industrial Colour Bar in South Africa.* Cape Town: Oxford University Press, 1961.

Draper, Theodore. *The Rediscovery of Black Nationalism.* New York: Viking Press, 1970.

Dube, John L. "Are Negroes Better Off in Africa?" *The Missionary Review* 17 (August 1904): 583–86.

Duncan, Patrick. "Is Apartheid an Insoluble Problem?" *Race* 6, no. 4 (April 1965): 263–66.

———. *South Africa's Rule of Violence.* London: Methuen, 1964.

———. "Questions and Answers on South Africa." *Peace News,* 14 June 1963, p. 5.

Duncan, Patrick, Sr. *Suggestions for a Native Policy.* Johannesburg: Central News Agency, 1912.

Duncan, Sheena. *The Plight of the Urban African.* Johannesburg: SAIRR, 1970.

DuPreez, A. B. *Inside the South African Crucible.* Cape Town: H.A.U.M., 1959.

Edelstein, Melville L. *What do Young Africans Think? An Attitude Survey of Urban African Matric Pupils in Soweto with Special Reference to Stereotyping and Social Distance: A Sociological Study.* Johannesburg: SAIRR, 1972.

"The End of the Road for Poqo." *Peace News,* 27 December 1963, pp. 1–2.

Fagan, H. A. *Our Responsibility: A Discussion of South Africa's Racial Problems.* Stellenbosch: Die Universiteits-Uitgewers en Boekhandelaars, 1960.

Fanon, Frantz. *Black Skin, White Masks.* New York: Grove Press, 1967.

———. *The Wretched of the Earth.* New York: Grove Press, 1968.

Feit, Edward. *African Opposition in South Africa.* Stanford: Hoover Institution Press, 1967.

———. "Community in a Quandary: The South African Jewish Community and 'Apartheid'." *Race* 8, no. 4 (April 1967): 395–408.

———. "Conflict and Cohesion in South Africa: A Theoretical Analysis of the Policy of 'Separate Development' and its Implications." *Economic Development and Cultural Change* 14, no. 4 (July 1966): 484–96.

———. "Generational Conflict and African Nationalism in South Africa: The African National Congress 1949–1959." A paper presented at the annual meeting of the African Studies Association, October 1968.

———. *South Africa: The Dynamics of the African National Congress.* London: Oxford University Press for the Institute of Race Relations, 1962.

———. *Urban Revolt in South Africa 1960–1964: A Case Study.* Evanston: Northwestern University Press, 1971.

First, Ruth. *117 Days.* Harmondsworth, Middlesex: Penguin Books, 1965.

————, ed. *South Africans in the Soviet Union.* Johannesburg: 1955(?).

Fischer, Abram. *What I Did Was Right.* London: Mayibuye Publications, 1966 (?).

Fisher, John. *The Afrikaners.* London: Cassell, 1969.

Forman, Lionel. *Black and White in S.A. History.* No place of publication: New Age, n.d.

————, and Sachs, E. S. *The South African Treason Trial.* London: John Calder, 1957.

Frankel, Philip. "Black Power in South Africa." *New Nation* (Pretoria) 6, no. 3 (October 1972): 3–7.

Freed, Louis Franklin. *Crime in South Africa.* Cape Town: Juta and Co., 1963.

Friedmann, Marion, ed. *I Will Still be Moved: Reports from South Africa.* Chicago: Quadrangle Books, 1963.

The Future of South Africa: A Study by British Christians. London: SCM Press, 1965.

Ghandi, Mohandas K. *Satyagraha in South Africa.* Madras: S. Ganesan, 1928.

Geiss, Imanuel. *The Pan-African Movement.* London: Methuen, 1974.

Gibson, Richard. *African Liberation Movements: Contemporary Struggles Against White Minority Rule.* London: Oxford University Press, 1972.

Gluckman, Max. *Order and Rebellion in Tribal Africa.* New York: Free Press of Glencoe, 1963.

Gordimer, Nadine. "Some Monday for Sure." *Transition* 18 (1965): 9–15.

————. "Where Do Whites Fit In?" *Twentieth Century* 165, no. 986 (April 1959): 326–31.

————. "Why Did Bram Fischer Choose Jail?" *New York Times Magazine,* 14 August 1966, pp. 40–41 ff.

Gurr, Ted. *Why Men Rebel.* Princeton: Princeton University Press, 1970.

Gwala, Mafika Pascal, ed. *Black Review 1973.* Durban: Black Community Programmes, 1974.

Hammond-Tooke, David. "Chieftainship in Transkeian Political Development." *Journal of Modern African Studies* 2, no. 4 (1964): 513–29.

Handbook of Black Organizations. Durban: Black Community Programmes, 1973.

Hellmann, Ellen. *Problems of Urban Bantu Youth.* Johannesburg: SAIRR, 1940.

————. "The Development of Social Groupings Among Urban Africans in the Union of South Africa." In *Social Implications of Industrialization and Urbanization in Africa South of the Sahara.* London: UNESCO, 1956.

———, ed. *Handbook on Race Relations in South Africa.* Cape Town: Oxford University Press, 1949.

———. "The Native in the Towns." In *The Bantu-Speaking Tribes of South Africa,* edited by I. Schapera. Cape Town: Maskew Miller, 1937.

———. *Soweto, Johannesburg's African City.* Johannesburg: SAIRR, 1971.

———. "The Twilight Existence of Urban Africans." *New Nation* (Pretoria) 6, no. 3 (October 1972): 10–13.

Hepple, Alexander. *South Africa: A Political and Economic History.* London: Pall Mall Press, 1966.

———. *South Africa: Workers Under Apartheid.* Second edition. London: International Defence and Aid Fund, 1971.

———. *Verwoerd.* Baltimore: Penguin Books, 1967.

Herd, Norman. *1922: Revolt on the Rand.* Johannesburg: Blue Crane Books, 1966.

Hey, P. D. *The Rise of The Natal Indian Elite.* Pietermaritzburg: Shuter and Shooter, 1961.

Hill, Christopher R. *Bantustans: The Fragmentation of South Africa.* London: Oxford University Press for the Institute of Race Relations, 1964.

Hirsch, M. I. *For Whom the Land? An Historical Study and Practical Assessment of Multiracial Southern Africa—The Factors and Trends, Ways and Means.* Salisbury: A. W. Bardwell and Co., 1967.

Hodgkin, Thomas. "A Note on the Language of African Nationalism." In *African Affairs,* no. 1, edited by Kenneth Kirkwood. St. Anthony's Papers, no. 10 (1961): 22–40.

Hooper, Charles. *Brief Authority.* London: Collins, 1960.

Hopkinson, Tom. *In the Fiery Continent.* London: Victor Gollancz, 1962.

Horner, D. B., ed. *Labour Organisation and the African.* Johannesburg: SAIRR, 1975.

Horrell, Muriel. *Action, Reaction and Counter-Action: A Brief Review of Non-White Political Movements in South Africa.* Johannesburg: SAIRR, 1971.

———, comp. *African Education: Some Origins, and Development until 1953.* Johannesburg: SAIRR, 1963.

———. *Bantu Education to 1968.* Johannesburg: SAIRR, 1968.

———, comp. *Days of Crisis in South Africa: (Events Up to 15th May 1960).* Johannesburg: SAIRR, 1960.

———. *A Decade of Bantu Education.* Johannesburg: SAIRR, 1964.

———. *Legislation and Race Relations.* Revised edition. Johannesburg: SAIRR, 1966.

———. *Non-European Policies in the Union and the Measure of Their*

Success: A Survey of the Conflicts Between Economic Trends and Ideological Planning. Johannesburg: SAIRR, 1954.

————. *The "Pass Laws."* Johannesburg: SAIRR, 1960.

————. *South African Trade Unionism.* Johannesburg: SAIRR, 1961.

————. *South Africa's Non-white Workers.* Johannesburg: SAIRR, 1956.

————. *South Africa's Workers: Their Organisations and the Patterns of Employment.* Johannesburg: SAIRR, 1969.

————, comp. *A Survey of Race Relations in South Africa.* Issued annually by the South African Institute of Race Relations. Johannesburg: 1948–1976.

————. *The Urban Population of the Transvaal (1969).* Johannesburg: SAIRR, 1969.

Houghton, D. Hobart. *The Tomlinson Report: A Summary of the Findings and Recommendations in the Tomlinson Commission Report.* Johannesburg: SAIRR, 1969.

————, and Walton, Edith M. *The Economy of a Native Reserve.* Pietermaritzburg: Shuter and Shooter, 1952.

Houser, George. *Non-Violent Revolution in South Africa.* New York: Fellowship Publications, 1953.

Hubbard, Michael. *African Poverty in Cape Town, 1960–1970.* Johannesburg: SAIRR, n.d.

Huddleston, Trevor. *Naught For Your Comfort.* London: Collins, 1956.

Hudson, William; Jacobs, G. F; and Biesheuvel, Simon. *Anatomy of South Africa: A Scientific Study of Present Day Attitudes.* Cape Town: Purnell, 1966.

Human, J. J. *South Africa 1960: A Chronicle.* Cape Town: Tafelberg-Uitgewers, 1961.

Hunter, Guy, ed. *Industrialisation and Race Relations.* London: Oxford University Press, 1965.

Hunter, Monica. *Reaction to Conquest: Effects of Contact with Europeans on the Pondo of South Africa.* Second edition. London: Oxford University Press, 1961.

Hutchinson, Alfred. *The Road to Ghana.* London: Victor Gollancz, 1960.

Hutt, W. H. *The Economics of the Colour Bar.* London: André Deutsch for the Institute of Economic Affairs, 1964.

The Indian South African. Johannesburg: SAIRR, 1967.

Innes, Duncan. *Our Country, Our Responsibility.* London: The Africa Bureau, n.d.

Institute for Industrial Education. *The Durban Strikes 1973.* Durban and Johannesburg: Ravan Press and the Institute for Industrial Education, 1974.

International Defence and Aid Fund. *BOSS: The First Five Years.* London: International Defence and Aid Fund, 1975.

International University Exchange Fund. *Who Are The Real Terrorists?*

A Document on the SASO/BPC Trial. Geneva: International University Exchange Fund, 1977.

Jabavu, D. D. T. *The Black Problem: Papers and Addresses on Various Native Problems*. Second edition. Alice: Lovedale Press, 1921 (?).

————. *"Native Disabilities" in South Africa*. Alice: Lovedale Press, 1932.

————. *The Segregation Fallacy and Other Papers*. Alice: Lovedale Press, 1928.

Jabavu, Noni. *The Ochre People: Scenes from a South African Life*. London: Murray, 1963.

Jaspan, M. A. "South Africa 1960–1961: The Transition from Passive Resistance to Rebellion." *Science and Society* 25, no. 2 (Spring 1961): 97–106.

Johns, Sheridan W. "The Birth of Non-White Trade Unionism in South Africa." *Race* 9, no. 2 (1967): 173–92.

————. "Marxism-Leninism in a Multi-Racial Environment: The Origins and Early History of the Communist Party of South Africa, 1914–1932." Ph.D. thesis, Harvard University, 1965.

————. "Obstacles to Guerrilla Warfare—A South African Case Study." *Journal of Modern African Studies* 11, no. 2 (1973): 267–303.

Jordaan, K. A. "The Communist Party of South Africa—Its Counter-Revolutionary Role." *World Revolution* 1, no. 2 (Spring 1968): 12–20.

Joseph, Helen. *If This Be Treason*. London: André Deutsch, 1963.

————. *Tomorrow's Sun: A Smuggled Journal From South Africa*. London: Hutchinson, 1966.

July, Robert W. *The Origins of Modern African Thought: Its Development in West Africa During the Nineteenth and Twentieth Centuries*. London: Faber and Faber, 1968.

Kadalie, Clements. *My Life and the ICU*. London: Frank Cass and Co., 1970.

Kalb, Madeleine G. "The Soviet View of the Union of South Africa." Essay for the certificate of the Russian Institute, Columbia University, 1959.

Kantor, James. *A Healthy Grave*. London: Hamilton Hamish, 1967.

Karis, Thomas G. "South Africa." In *Five African States*, edited by Gwendolen M. Carter, pp. 471–616. Ithaca: Cornell University Press, 1963.

————, and Carter, Gwendolen M., eds. *From Protest To Challenge: A Documentary History of African Politics in South Africa 1882–1964*. 4 volumes. Stanford: Hoover Institution Press, 1972, 1973 and 1977.

————. *The Treason Trial in South Africa: A Guide to the Microfilm Record of the Trial*. Palo Alto: Hoover Institution Press, 1965.

Kentridge, F., and Coaker, N. *Some Aspects of the Rights in Respect of Fixed Property of Persons Living in the South-Western Complex of Native Townships, Johannesburg*. Johannesburg: SAIRR, n.d.

Keppel-Jones, Arthur. *South Africa: A Short History*. London: Hutchinson, 1949, 1966.

———. *When Smuts Goes: A History of South Africa From 1952 to 2010, First Published in 2015*. Pietermaritzburg: Shuter and Shooter, 1950.

Kerr, Alexander. *Fort Hare 1915–1948: The Evolution of an African College*. New York: Humanities Press, 1968.

Keto, Clement T. "Black American Involvement in South Africa's Race Issue." *Issue* 3, no. 1 (Spring 1973): 6–11.

Khoapa, Ben A., ed. *Black Review 1972*. Durban: Black Community Programmes, 1973.

King, Kenneth. *Pan-Africanism and Education*. London: Oxford University Press, 1971.

Kirkwood, Kenneth, and Webb, Maurice. *The Durban Riots and After*. Johannesburg: SAIRR, 1949 (?).

Kleinschmidt, Horst, ed. *White Liberation*. Johannesburg: Spro-cas, 1972.

Kotze, D. A. *African Politics in South Africa 1964–1974, Parties and Issues*. Pretoria: J. L. Van Schaik, 1975.

Kuper, Leo. *An African Bourgeoisie: Race, Class, and Politics in South Africa*. New Haven: Yale University Press, 1965.

———. "The Control of Social Change: A South African Experiment." *Social Forces* 33, no. 1 (October 1954): 19–29.

———. *Passive Resistance in South Africa*. New Haven: Yale University Press, 1957.

———, and Smith, M. G., eds. *Pluralism in Africa*. Berkeley and Los Angeles: University of California Press, 1969.

———. *Race, Class and Power: Ideology and Revolutionary Change in Plural Societies*. London: Duckworth, 1974.

———. "Racialism and Integration in South African Society." *Race* 4, no. 2 (May 1963): 26–31.

———. "Theories of Revolution and Race Relations." *Comparative Studies in Society and History* 13, no. 1 (January 1971): 87–107.

Landis, Elizabeth. *Repressive Legislation of the Republic of South Africa*. New York: United Nations, 1969.

Laurence, John. *The Seeds of Disaster: A Guide to the Realities, Race Policies and World-Wide Propaganda Campaigns of the Republic of South Africa*. London: Victor Gollancz, 1968.

Leftwich, Adrian, ed. *South Africa: Economic Growth and Political Change*. London: Allison and Busby, 1974.

Legassick, Martin. *Class and Nationalism in South African Protest: The South African Communist Party and the "Native Republic," 1928–1934*. Syracuse: Syracuse University, 1973.

———. "Legislation, Ideology and Economy in Post-1948 South Africa." *Journal of Southern African Studies* 1, no. 1 (October 1974): 5–35.

——— "South Africa: Forced Labor, Industrialization, and Racial Differentiation." In *The Political Economy of Africa*, edited by Richard Harris, pp. 227–70. New York: John Wiley and Sons, 1975.

———, and Shingler, J. "South Africa." In *Students and Politics in Developing Countries*, edited by Donald K. Emmerson, pp. 103–45. New York: Praeger, 1968.

Legum, Colin. *Pan-Africanism: A Short Political Guide*. Revised edition. New York: Praeger, 1965.

———, and Legum, Margaret. *The Bitter Choice: Eight South Africans' Resistance to Tyranny*. Cleveland: World Publishing, 1968.

———, and Legum, Margaret. *South Africa: Crisis For The West*. London: Pall Mall, 1964.

Leiss, Amelia C., ed. *Apartheid and United Nations Collective Measures: An Analysis*. New York: Carnegie Foundation, 1965.

Le May, G. H. L. *Black and White in South Africa: The Politics of Survival*. New York: American Heritage Press, 1971.

Lembede, Anton M. "The Conception of God as Expounded By or As It Emerges From the Writings of Great Philosophers—From Des Cartes to the Present Day." MA thesis, University of South Africa, 1945.

Lerumo, A. (pseud. of Michael Harmel). *Fifty Fighting Years: The Communist Party of South Africa 1921–1971*. London: Inkululeko Publications, 1971.

Lewin, Julius. *Politics and Law in South Africa: Essays on Race Relations*. London: Merlin Press, 1963.

———. *The Struggle for Racial Equality*. New York: Humanities Press, 1967.

Lincoln, C. Eric. *The Black Muslims in America*. Boston: Beacon Press, 1961.

Louw, Anna M. *20 Days That Autumn: 21st March–9th April 1960,A Novel*. Cape Town: Tafelberg-Uitgewers, 1963.

Luthuli, Albert. *Let My People Go: An Autobiography*. London: Collins, 1962.

McClellan, Grant S., ed. *South Africa*. New York: H. W. Wilson, 1962.

MacCrone, I. D. *Race Attitudes in South Africa*. Johannesburg: Witwatersrand University Press, 1965.

Macmillan, W. M. *Africa Beyond the Union*. Johannesburg: SAIRR, 1949.

———. *Bantu, Boer and Briton: The Making of the South African Native Problem*. Oxford: Clarendon Press, 1963.

Mahabane, Zaccheus R. *The Good Fight: Selected Speeches of Rev. Zaccheus R. Mahabane*. Evanston: Program of African Studies, Northwestern University, 1966.

Mahomo, Nelson. "The Rise of the Pan Africanist Congress of South Africa." MA thesis, Massachusetts Institute of Technology, 1968.

Maimane, Arthur. "The Day After." *Transition* 27 (1966): 8–12.

Malherbe, Paul N. *Multistan: A Way Out of the South African Dilemma.* Cape Town: David Philip, 1974.

Mandela, Nelson. *No Easy Walk To Freedom: Articles, Speeches, and Trial Addresses of Nelson Mandela.* London: Heinemann, 1965.

Manganyi, N. C. *Being-Black-In-The-World.* Johannesburg: Spro-cas and Ravan Press, 1973.

Mann, J. W. "Race-Linked Values in South Africa." *Journal of Social Psychology* 58 (1962): 31–41.

Mannheim, Karl. *Essays on the Sociology of Knowledge.* New York: Oxford University Press, 1952. Especially "The Problem of Generations," pp. 276–320.

Marais, J. S. *The Cape Coloured People 1652–1937.* London: Longmans, Green, 1939.

Marks, Shula. *Reluctant Rebellion: The 1906–8 Disturbances in Natal.* Oxford: Clarendon Press, 1970.

Marquard, Leo. *Liberalism in South Africa.* Johannesburg: SAIRR, 1965.

———. *The Native in South Africa.* Second edition. Johannesburg: Witwatersrand University Press, 1948.

———. *The People and Policies of South Africa.* Third edition. London: Oxford University Press, 1969.

———. See also under pseudonym, J. Burger.

Marx, Gary T., and Useem, M. "Majority Involvement in Minority Movements: Civil Rights, Abolition, Untouchability." *Journal of Social Issues* 27, no. 1 (1971): 81–104.

Matthews, Z. K. "The Black Man's Outlook." *Saturday Review*, 2 May 1953.

———. "Social Relations in a Common South African Society." Supplement to *Optima*, March 1961.

———. "South Africa: A Land Divided Against Itself." *Yale Review* 42 (June 1953): 513–28.

———. "The Tribal Spirit Among Educated South Africans." *Man* 35 (February 1935): 26–27.

May, Henry John. *The South African Constitution.* Third edition. Cape Town and Johannesburg: Juta and Co., 1955.

Mayer, Philip. *Townsmen or Tribesmen.* Cape Town: Oxford University Press, 1961.

Mbanjwa, Thoko, ed. *Apartheid, Hope or Despair for Blacks?* Black Viewpoint No. 3. Durban: Black Community Programmes, 1976.

———, ed. *Black Review 1974/5.* Durban: Black Community Programmes, 1975.

———, ed. *Detente.* Black Viewpoint No. 2. Durban: Black Community Programmes, 1976 (?).

Mbeki, Govan. *South Africa: The Peasants' Revolt*. Harmondsworth, Middlesex: Penguin Books, 1964.

Mdhluli, S. V. H. *The Development of the African*. Mariannhill: Mariannhill Mission Press, 1933.

Meer, Fatima. "Black Nationalism—Homeland Nationalism." In *Church and Nationalism in South Africa*, edited by Theo Sundermeier, pp. 129–40. Johannesburg: Ravan Press, 1975.

Memmi, Albert. *The Colonizer and the Colonized*. Boston: Beacon Press, 1967.

Mitchell, J. C. "Urbanization, Detribalization and Stabilization in Southern Africa: A Problem of Definition and Membership." In *Social Implications of Industrialization and Urbanization in Africa South of the Sahara*, pp. 693–711. London: UNESCO, 1956.

Mitchison, Naomi. *A Life For Africa: The Story of Bram Fischer*. London: Merlin Press, 1973.

Modisane, Bloke. *Blame Me On History*. London: Thames and Hudson, 1963.

Mokgatle, Naboth. *Autobiography of an Unknown South African*. Berkeley and Los Angeles: University of California Press, 1971.

Molema, Silas M. *The Bantu—Past and Present*. Edinburgh: W. Green and Son, 1920.

Molteno, Donald B. *Betrayal of "Natives Representation."* Johannesburg: SAIRR, 1959.

Moore, Basil, ed. *Black Theology: The South African Voice*. London: C. Hurst and Co., 1973.

Motlhabi, Mokgethi, ed. *Essays on Black Theology*. Johannesburg: University Christian Movement, 1972.

Mphahlele, Ezekiel. *The African Image*. New York: Praeger, 1962.

———. "The African Intellectual." In *Africa in Transition: Some BBC Talks on Changing Conditions in the Union and the Rhodesias*, edited by Prudence Smith. London: Max Reinhardt, 1958.

———. "The Dilemma of the African Elite." *Twentieth Century* 165, no. 986 (April 1959): 319–25.

———. *Down Second Avenue*. London: Faber and Faber, 1965.

Msimang, H. Selby. *H. Selby Msimang Looks Back*. Johannesburg: SAIRR, 1971.

Mtolo, Bruno. *Umkonto We Sizwe: The Road to the Left*. Durban: Drakensberg Press, 1966.

Muller, A. L. *Minority Interests: The Political Economy of the Coloured and Indian Communities in South Africa*. Johannesburg: SAIRR, 1968.

Munger, Edwin S. *Afrikaner and African Nationalism: South African Parallels and Parameters*. London: Oxford University Press for the Institute of Race Relations, 1967.

Neame, L. E. "The African National Congress." *Contemporary Review*, no. 1114 (October 1958): 206–10.

Nengwekhulu, Ranwedzi (Harry). "Education for Blacks in South Africa: A Radical Alternative." *Free Southern Africa*, no. 1 (May 1973): 42–50.

Ngcobo, Selby Bangani. "African Elite in South Africa." *International Social Science Bulletin* 8, no. 3 (1956): 431–40.

Ngubane, Jordan K. *An African Explains Apartheid*. London: Pall Mall, 1963.

———. *Should the Natives Representative Council Be Abolished?* Cape Town: The African Bookman, 1946.

Niebuhr, Reinhold. *Moral Man and Immoral Society: A Study in Ethics and Politics*. New York: Charles Scribner's Sons, 1932.

Nixon, Charles. "The Conflict of Nationalism in South Africa." *World Politics* 11, no. 1 (October 1958): 44–68.

Nkondo, Gessler, ed. *Turfloop Testimony: The Dilemma of a Black University in South Africa*. Johannesburg: Ravan Press, 1976.

Nkosi, Lewis. *Home and Exile*. London: Longmans, 1965.

———. "On South Africa [The Fire Some Time]." *Transition* 38 (1971): 30–34.

———. "Robert Sobukwe: An Assessment." *Africa Report* 7, no. 4 (April 1962): 7–9.

Nkrumah, Kwame. *Africa Must Unite*. New York: Praeger, 1963.

Nyquist, Thomas E. *Toward a Theory of the African Upper Stratum in South Africa*. Athens, Ohio: Center for International Studies, 1972.

Omer-Cooper, J. D. *The Zulu Aftermath: A Nineteenth Century Revolution in Bantu Africa*. London: Longman, 1966.

Pachai, B. *Mahatma Gandhi in South Africa*. Johannesburg: SAIRR, 1969 (?).

Padmore, George. *Pan-Africanism or Communism? The Coming Struggle For Africa*. London: Dennis Dobson, 1956.

Paton, Alan. *Civil Rights and Present Wrongs*. Johannesburg: SAIRR, 1968.

———. *Hope for South Africa*. London: Pall Mall, 1958.

———. *The Long View*. New York: Praeger, 1968.

———. *South African Tragedy: The Life and Times of Jan Hofmeyr*. New York: Charles Scribner's Sons, 1965.

Paton, David M. *Church and Race in South Africa*. London: SCM Press, 1958.

Patterson, Sheila. *Colour and Culture in South Africa: A Study of the Status of the Cape Coloured People Within the Social Structure of the Union of South Africa*. London: Routledge and Kegan Paul, 1953.

———. *The Last Trek: A Study of the Boer People and the Afrikaner Nation*. London: Routledge and Kegan Paul, 1957.

Pauw, B. A. *The Second Generation: A Study of the Family Among Urbanised Bantu in East London*. London: Oxford University Press, 1963.

Peart-Binns, John S. *Ambrose Reeves*. London: Victor Gollancz, 1973.

Pelzer, A. N., ed. *Verwoerd Speaks: Speeches 1948–1966*. Johannesburg: APB Publishers, 1966.

Perry, Ann. *African Secondary School Leavers: Employment Experiences and Attitudes to Employment*. Johannesburg: SAIRR, n.d.

Pettigrew, Thomas F. "Social Distance Attitudes of South African Students." *Social Forces* 38, no. 3 (March 1960): 246–53.

Phillips, Norman. *The Tragedy of Apartheid: A Journalist's Experiences in the South African Riots*. New York: McKay, 1960.

Phillips, Ray E. *The Bantu in the City: A Study of Cultural Adjustment on the Witwatersrand*. Alice: Lovedale Press, 1938.

———. *The Crux of the Race Problem: Are Black People Human Beings?* Stellenbosch: Student's Christian Association of South Africa, 1947.

Pienaar, S. W., and Sampson, Anthony. *South Africa: Two Views of Separate Development*. London: Oxford University Press for the Institute of Race Relations, 1960.

Plaatje, Solomon T. *Native Life in South Africa: Before and Since the European War and the Boer Rebellion*. Fourth edition. New York: The Crisis, 1920 (?).

"Planner of Revolt." *West Africa* 46, no. 2370 (3 November 1962): 1209.

Political Representation of Africans in the Union. Johannesburg: SAIRR, 1942.

"The Poqo Affair." *Africa, Latin America, Asia Revolution* 1, no. 3 (July 1963): 77–81.

Potekhin, I. I. *The Formation of a National Community Among the South African Bantu*. Moscow: 1956.

Potter, Elaine. *The Press as Opposition: The Political Role of South African Newspapers*. London: Chatto and Windus, 1975.

Ralston, Richard D. "American Episodes in the Making of an African Leader: A Case Study of Alfred B. Xuma (1893–1962." *International Journal of African Historical Studies* 6, no. 1 (1973): 72–93.

Randall, Peter, ed. *Anatomy of Apartheid*. Johannesburg: Spro-cas, 1970.

———, ed. *Apartheid and the Church: Report of the Church Commission of the Study Project on Christianity in Apartheid Society*. Johannesburg: Spro-cas, 1972.

———, ed. *Directions of Change in South African Politics*. Johannesburg: Spro-cas, 1971.

———, ed. *Education Beyond Apartheid: Report of the Education Commis-*

sion of the Study Project on Christianity in Apartheid Society. Johannesburg: Spro-cas, 1971.

————, ed. *Law, Justice and Society: Report of the Legal Commission of the Study Project on Christianity in Apartheid Society*. Johannesburg: Spro-cas, 1972.

————, ed. *Power, Privilege and Poverty: Report of the Economics Commission of the Study Project on Christianity in Apartheid Society*. Johannesburg: Spro-cas, 1972.

————, ed. *Some Implications of Inequality*. Johannesburg: Spro-cas, 1971.

————, ed. *South Africa's Minorities*. Johannesburg: Spro-cas, 1971.

————, ed. *South Africa's Political Alternatives: Report of the Political Commission of the Study Project on Christianity in Apartheid Society*. Johannesburg: Spro-cas, 1973.

————. *A Taste of Power*. Johannesburg: Spro-cas, 1973.

————, ed. *Towards Social Change: Report of the Social Commission of the Study Project on Christianity in Apartheid Society*. Johannesburg: Spro-cas, 1971.

————, and Desai, Yunus. *From "Coolie Location" to Group Area, Johannesburg's Indian Community*. Johannesburg: SAIRR, 1967.

Reader, D. H. *The Black Man's Portion*. Cape Town. Oxford University Press, 1961.

Reeves, Ambrose. *Justice in South Africa*. London: The Africa Bureau, 1955.

————. *Shooting at Sharpeville: The Agony of South Africa*. London: Victor Gollancz, 1960.

———— *South Africa—Yesterday and Tomorrow*. London: Victor Gollancz, 1962.

Reyburn, Lawrence. *African Traders: Their Position and Problems in Johannesburg's South-Western Townships*. Johannesburg: SAIRR, 1960.

Ringrose, H. G. *Trade Unions in Natal*. Cape Town: Oxford University Press, 1951.

Rive, Richard. *Emergency*. New York: Macmillan, 1970.

Roberts, Michael, and Trollip, A. *The South African Opposition* 1939/45. London: Longmans, Green, 1947.

Robertson, Janet. *Liberalism in South Africa* 1948–1963. Oxford: Clarendon Press, 1971.

Robeson, Eslanda. *African Journey*. New York: John Day, 1945.

Routh, Guy. *Industrial Relations and Race Relations*. Johannesburg: SAIRR, n.d.

Roux, Edward. *S. P. Bunting: A Political Biography*. Johannesburg: published by the author, 1944.

————. *Time Longer Than Rope: A History of the Black Man's Struggle for*

Freedom in South Africa. Madison: University of Wisconsin Press, 1966.

————, and Roux, Win. *Rebel Pity: The Life of Eddie Roux*. London: Rex Collings, 1970.

Russell, D. E. H. *Rebellion, Revolution and Armed Force: A Comparative Study of Fifteen Countries With Special Emphasis on Cuba and South Africa*. New York: Academic Press, 1974.

Sachs, Bernard. *The Road From Sharpeville*. New York: Marzani and Munsell, 1961.

Sachs, E. S. *The Choice Before South Africa*. New York: Philosophical Library, 1952.

Sampson, Anthony. *Common Sense About Africa*. London: Victor Gollancz, 1960.

————. *Drum: A Venture into the New Africa*. London: Collins, 1956.

————. *The Treason Cage: The Opposition on Trial in South Africa*. London: Heinemann, 1958.

Samuels, L. H., Houghton, D. H., and Fourie, F. *South Africa's Changing Economy*. Johannesburg: SAIRR, 1955.

"Sandor." *The Coming Struggle for South Africa*. London: Fabian Society, 1963.

Schlemmer, Lawrence. *Employment Opportunity and Race in South Africa*. Denver: University of Denver, 1973.

————. *The Negro Ghetto Riots and South African Cities*. Johannesburg: SAIRR, 1968.

————. "Political Adaptation and Reaction Among Urban Africans in South Africa." *Social Dynamics* 2, no. 1 (1976): 3–18.

————. *Social Change and Political Policy in South Africa: An Assessment of the Future of Separate Development and of Possible Alternatives*. Johannesburg: SAIRR, 1970.

Scott, Michael. *A Time to Speak*. London: Faber and Faber, 1958.

Segal, Ronald. *African Profiles*. Baltimore: Penguin Books, 1962.

————. *Into Exile*. London: Jonathan Cape, 1963.

————. *Political Africa: A Who's Who of Personalities and Parties*. London: Stevens and Sons, 1961.

Sharp, Gene. "No Co-Existence with Oppression: The Story—as Told to Gene Sharp—of the Pan-Africanist Non-Violent Struggle in South Africa." *Peace News*, 13 May 1960.

A Short Pictorial History of the University College of Fort Hare, 1916–1959. Alice: Lovedale Press, 1961.

Simons, H. J., and Simons, R. E. *Class and Colour in South Africa 1850–1950*. Harmondsworth, Middlesex: Penguin Books, 1969.

Skota, T. D. Mweli. *The African Who's Who*. Johannesburg: Central News Agency, 1965.

————. *The African Yearly Register*. Johannesburg: R. L. Esson and Co., 1932.

Stanton, Hannah. *Go Well, Stay Well: South Africa, August 1956 to May 1960*. London: Hodder and Stoughton, 1961.

Strong, John A. "Political Socialization: A Study of Southern African Elites." D.S.S. thesis, Syracuse University, 1968.

Sundkler, Bengt. *Bantu Prophets in South Africa*. Second edition. London: Oxford University Press, 1961.

Suttner, Sheila. *Cost of Living in Soweto 1966*. Johannesburg: SAIRR, 1966.

Tambo, Oliver. "Umkonto We Sizwe!" *African Revolution* 1, no. 1 (May 1963): 6–8.

Tatz, C. M. *Shadow and Substance in South Africa: A Study in Land and Franchise Policies Affecting Africans, 1910–1960*. Pietermaritzburg: University of Natal Press, 1962.

Temkin, Ben. *Gatsha Buthelezi: Zulu Statesman*. Cape Town: Purnell, 1976.

Thema, R. V. Selope. "Non-European Political Moves in South Africa: Moderate African Opinion Opposed to Civil Disobedience Campaign." *African World*, May 1952, pp. 11–12.

Thoahlane, Thoahlane, ed. *Black Renaissance. Papers From the Black Renaissance Convention*. Johannesburg: Ravan Press, 1975.

Thomas, Wolfgang, ed. *Labour Perspectives on South Africa*. Cape Town: David Philip, 1974.

Troup, Freda. *Forbidden Pastures: Education Under Apartheid*. London: International Defence and Aid Fund, 1976.

————. *South Africa: An Historical Introduction*. London: Eyre Methuen, 1972.

Turner, Richard. *The Eye of the Needle*. Johannesburg: Spro-cas, 1972.

Turok, Ben. "Class Structure and National Ideology in South Africa." A paper prepared for the 8th World Congress of Sociology of the International Sociology Association, Toronto, August 1974.

————. "South Africa: The Search for a Strategy." In *The Socialist Register*, edited by R. Milliband and J. Saville. London: Merlin Press, 1973.

————. *Strategic Problems in South Africa's Liberation Struggle: A Critical Analysis*. Richmond, B.C., Canada: LSM Information Center, 1974.

United Nations Unit on Apartheid. *Chief Albert J. Lutuli: Statements and Addresses*. New York: United Nations, 1969.

Van den Berghe, Pierre. *Caneville: The Social Structure of a South African Town*. Middletown, Connecticut: Wesleyan University Press, 1964.

————. "Language and Nationalism in South Africa." *Race* 9, no. 1 (July 1967): 37–46.

————. "Race Attitudes in Durban, South Africa." *Journal of Social Psychology* 57 (1962): 55–72.

————. *South Africa: A Study in Conflict*. Berkeley and Los Angeles: University of California Press, 1967.

Van der Horst, Sheila. "The Effects of Industrialisation on Race Relations in South Africa." In *Industrialisation and Race Relations*, edited by Guy Hunter, pp. 97–140. London: Oxford University Press, 1965.

Van der Merwe, H. W., and Welsh, David, eds. *Student Perspectives on South Africa*. Cape Town: David Philip, 1972.

Van Eck, H. J. *Some Aspects of the South African Industrial Revolution*. Johannesburg: SAIRR, 1953.

Van Jaarsveld, F. A. *The Awakening of Afrikaner Nationalism* 1868–1881. Cape Town: Human and Rousseau, 1961.

Van Rensburg, Patrick. *Guilty Land*. Harmondsworth, Middlesex: Penguin Books, 1962.

Vatcher, W. H. *White Laager*. London: Pall Mall, 1965.

Vilakazi, Absolom. "Race Relations in South Africa." In *Race Relations in World Perspective*, edited by A. Lind, pp. 313–38. Honolulu: University of Hawaii Press, 1955.

————. *Zulu Transformations: A Study of the Dynamics of Social Change*. Pietermaritzburg: University of Natal Press, 1962.

Walker, Oliver. *Kaffirs Are Lively: Being Some Backstage Impressions of the South African Democracy*. London: Victor Gollancz, 1948.

Walshe, Peter. "Black American Thought and African Political Attitudes in South Africa." *Review of Politics* 32, no. 1 (January 1970): 51–77.

————. "The Origins of African Political Consciousness in Southern Africa." *Journal of Modern African Studies* 7, no. 4 (December 1969): 583–610.

————. *The Rise of African Nationalism in South Africa: The African National Congress* 1912–1952. Berkeley and Los Angeles: University of California Press, 1971.

"Walter Sisulu, South Africa's Underground Leader." *African Revolution* 1, no. 2 (June 1963): 126–30.

Webb, Peter R. "South Africa's Black Mood." *Newsweek*, 10 May 1971, p. 11ff.

Welsh, David. *The Roots of Segregation: Native Policy in Colonial Natal, 1845–1910*. Cape Town: Oxford University Press, 1971.

"What is Poqo?" *Venture*, May 1963, pp. 8–10.

Wilson, Francis. *Labour in the South African Gold Mines 1911–1969*. Cambridge: Cambridge University Press, 1972.

————. *Migrant Labour*. Johannesburg: Spro-cas, 1972.

————, and Perrot, D., eds. *Outlook On a Century: South Africa 1870–1970*. Braamfontein: Lovedale Press and Spro-cas, 1972.

Wilson, Monica, and Mafeje, Archie. *Langa: A Study of Social Groups in an African Township*. Cape Town: Oxford University Press, 1965.

———, and Thompson, Leonard, eds. *The Oxford History of South Africa*. 2 volumes. Oxford: Clarendon Press, 1969 and 1971.

Wolton, Douglas G. *Whither South Africa?* London: Lawrence and Wishart, 1947.

Worrall, Denis. *Separate Development: 1970, the Politics of Decolonisation*. Cape Town: SAIRR, 1970.

———. "South Africa's 'Partition Election'." *Africa Report* 11, no. 5 (May 1966): 25–26.

Index

345